Question&Answer

CRIMINAL LAW

Develop your legal skills

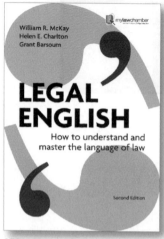

William R. McKay
Helen E. Charlton
Grant Barsoum

LEGAL ENGLISH
How to understand and master the language of law

Second Edition

9781408226100

Steve Foster
HOW TO WRITE BETTER LAW ESSAYS
Tools and techniques for success in exams and assignments

new edition

9781447905141

THE LONGMAN DICTIONARY OF LAW
Eighth Edition

P. H. Richards · L. B. Curzon

9781408261538

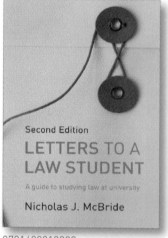

Second Edition
LETTERS TO A LAW STUDENT
A guide to studying law at university

Nicholas J. McBride

9781408218808

Written to help you develop the essential skills needed to succeed on your course and prepare for practice.

Available from all good bookshops or order online at:
www.pearsoned.co.uk/law

Question&Answer

CRIMINAL LAW

2nd edition

Nicola Monaghan
Senior Tutor in Law, Barrister, FHEA
Coventry University London Campus

Harlow, England • London • New York • Boston • San Francisco • Toronto • Sydney • Auckland • Singapore • Hong Kong
Tokyo • Seoul • Taipei • New Delhi • Cape Town • São Paulo • Mexico City • Madrid • Amsterdam • Munich • Paris • Milan

Pearson Education Limited
Edinburgh Gate
Harlow CM20 2JE
United Kingdom
Tel: +44 (0)1279 623623
Web: www.pearson.com/uk

First published 2012 (print)
Second edition published 2014 (print and electronic)

ISBN: 978-0-273-78375-6 (print)
       978-0-273-78377-0 (PDF)
       978-0-273-78376-3 (eText)

British Library Cataloguing-in-Publication Data
A catalogue record for the print edition is available from the British Library

10 9 8 7 6 5 4 3 2 1
17 16 15 14 13

Print edition typeset in 10/13pt Helvetica Neue LT Pro by 35
Print edition printed in Malaysia (CTP-VVP)

NOTE THAT ANY PAGE CROSS REFERENCES REFER TO THE PRINT EDITION

Contents

Supporting resources

Visit the Law Express Question & Answer series companion website at **www.pearson.co.uk/lawexpressqa** to find valuable learning material including:

- **Additional essay and problem questions** arranged by topic for each chapter give you more opportunity to practise and hone your exam skills.
- **Diagram plans** for all additional questions assist you in structuring and writing your answers.
- **You be the marker** questions allow you to see through the eyes of the examiner by marking essay and problem questions on every topic covered in the book.
- Download and print all **Attack the question** diagrams and **Diagram plans** from the book.

Also: The companion website provides the following features:

- Search tool to help locate specific terms of content.
- Online help and support to assist with website usage and troubleshooting.

For more information please contact your local Pearson sales representative or visit **www.pearsoned.co.uk/lawexpressqa**

Acknowledgements

I would like to thank the anonymous reviewers, both academics and students, who have provided feedback on the book during the writing process. I would also like to thank Gabriella Playford at Pearson for her support and encouragement throughout this project. This book is dedicated to my students at Coventry University London Campus.

Nicola Monaghan

Publisher's acknowledgements

Our thanks go to all reviewers who contributed to the development of this text, including students who participated in research and focus groups which helped to shape the series format.

What you need to do for every question in Criminal Law

This book is intended to serve as a companion guide to supplement your study of Criminal Law. In addition to reading your main textbook, you should refer to this book for guidance on how to answer exam questions on Criminal Law. Both essay-style questions and problem scenarios on all the commonly assessed topics are covered in the book. As you read through the book, you should remember that each 'answer' given here is only one of a possible range of answers which could be given. These are by no means the 'right answer' but merely serve to demonstrate one possible approach to a question.

There are certain issues which should usually be addressed in every answer to a problem question on Criminal Law. First, you will need to identify the relevant offences which may have been committed in the scenario. Secondly, you will need to break down the offence into its actus reus and mens rea elements, and finally, you should apply the legal principles relating to these elements to the question. If a question involves identifying a defence, you should, similarly, break down and apply the elements of that defence to the question. You should adopt this logical structure for most answers to problem questions, and you will notice that this is the structure adopted throughout the book. Different skills are involved in answering essay questions on Criminal Law. You will need to identify the relevant issue that the question is addressing and provide a critical evaluation of the issue.

You will notice that the citations of cases have been included in the answers the first time the case is mentioned. In most institutions, you will not be expected to remember the citations of cases for the exam. However, you should check with your Criminal Law tutor to find out whether you are expected to know the dates of the cases.

Guided tour

What you need to do for every question in Criminal Law

What to do for every question – Identify the key things you should look for and do in any question and answer on the subject, ensuring you give every one of your answers a great chance from the start.

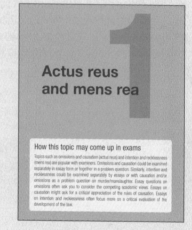

Actus reus and mens rea

How this topic may come up in exams – Understand how to tackle any question on this topic by using the handy tips and advice relevant to both essay and problem questions. In-text symbols clearly identify each question type as they occur.

How this topic may come up in exams

Topics such as omissions and causation (actual reus) and intention and recklessness (mens rea) are popular with examiners. Omissions and causation could be examined separately in essay form or together in a problem question. Similarly, intention and recklessness could be examined separately by essays or with causation and/or omissions as a problem question on murder/manslaughter. Essay questions on omissions often ask you to consider the competing academic views. Essays on causation might ask for a critical appreciation of the rules of causation. Essays on intention and recklessness often focus more on a critical evaluation of the development of the law.

 Essay question   **Problem question**

Attack the question – Use these diagrams as a step-by-step guide to help you confidently identify the main points covered in any question asked. Download these from the companion website to use as a useful revision aid.

■ Attack the question

Answer plans and Diagram plans – A clear and concise plan is the key to a good answer and these answer and diagram plans support the structuring of your answers, whatever your preferred learning style.

Diagram plan

Answer plan

→ Define theft and state where it comes from.

→ Discuss whether Samantha is liable for theft of the overpayment. In particular, you should consider section 5(4) of the Theft Act 1968.

→ Consider the theft arising from Samantha's conduct in placing a 50% off label on the outfit. This requires consideration of appropriation.

→ Discuss whether Samantha has stolen the catalogue. Section 2(1) of the Theft Act 1968 will be important here.

→ Consider whether there was a theft of the £10 note. Who does this belong to? Is Samantha dishonest?

Answer with accompanying guidance – Make the most out of every question by using the guidance to recognise what makes a good answer and why. Answers are the length you could realistically hope to produce in an exam to show you how to gain marks quickly when under pressure.

Answer

This question requires a critical evaluation of the assertion that the actus reus elements of theft are so widely construed that the actus reus has now reached 'vanishing point'. It is true that the actus reus elements of theft have been very widely interpreted by the courts. Ormerod and Williams make their assertion in respect of the meaning given to 'appropriation'.[1] Such a wide interpretation of the actus reus means that liability for theft will generally be determined by the mens rea elements. This in turn requires attention to be given to the law relating to the mens rea elements; in particular, the *Ghosh* [1982] 2 All ER 689 test applied in respect of dishonesty must be scrutinised.[2]

Theft is defined in section 1(1), Theft Act 1968 as the dishonest appropriation of property belonging to another with the intention to permanently deprive the other of it.[3] The prosecution must prove all five elements in order to secure a conviction: *Lawrence v MPC* [1971] 2 All ER 1253. The actus reus elements of 'appropriation',

consent was obtained by fraud. However, this narrow interpretation of *Gomez* meant that there could be no appropriation where a valid gift was given *inter vivos*. In *Hopkins and Kendrick* [1997] 2 Cr App R 524, the Court of Appeal criticised *Mazo*. The position was finally considered by the House of Lords in *Hinks* [2001] 2 AC 241. The House extended the approach taken in *Gomez* and held that a valid gift could be appropriated. This decision has been criticised for extending the scope of appropriation too far and creating a conflict between criminal and civil law.

It is clear that a very wide interpretation is applied to 'appropriation'. A broad approach is also taken in respect of the remaining actus reus elements of theft: 'property' and 'belonging to another'.[10]

[2 These two sentences draw further on the consequences of the observation made by Ormerod and Williams. The explanation put forward here demonstrates a very good degree of knowledge and appreciation of the subject and gains you higher marks.]

Case names clearly highlighted – Easy-to-spot bold text makes those all important case names stand out from the rest of the answer, ensuring they are much easier to remember in revision and an exam.

[10 Do not forget to address the other actus reus elements of theft. Property and belonging to another have also been widely construed, despite not receiving quite as much judicial and academic]

✓ Make your answer stand out

- You could critically evaluate the Law Commission's recommendation that duress may amount to a partial defence to first degree murder.
- You could consider the practical implications on plea bargaining and the argument that the proposed structure would provide defendants with more incentive to maintain a not guilty plea to first degree murder and prosecutors with more incentive to accept a guilty plea to second degree murder.
- You should refer to further academic writing on the recommendations, such as Wilson, W., The structure of criminal homicide [2006] Crim LR 471 and Ashworth, A., Principles, pragmatism and the Law Commission's recommendations on homicide law reform [2007] Crim LR 333.
- You might offer a comparative view of the structure of homicide offences in other common law countries such as the US, Australia, Canada, New Zealand.

Make your answer stand out – Really impress your examiners by going the extra mile and including these additional points and further reading to illustrate your deeper knowledge of the subject, fully maximising your marks.

! Don't be tempted to . . .

- Simply set out the current law on murder and manslaughter – you are being asked specifically about the framework of homicide offences and reform.
- Use this question as an excuse to just 'rant' about the law of homicide. Instead, you must provide a structured critique of the structure of homicide offences and the proposed reforms.
- Focus on just one element of murder or manslaughter. This question is looking for a much wider appreciation of the scope of murder and manslaughter and their relationship.

Don't be tempted to – Points out common mistakes ensuring you avoid losing easy marks by understanding where students most often trip up in exams.

Bibliography – Use this list of further reading to really delve in and explore areas in more depth, enabling you to excel in exams.

Bibliography

Allen, M. J. (2009) *Textbook on Criminal Law*, 10th edn. Oxford: Oxford University Press.
Allgrove, B. and Sellers, S. (2009) The Fraud Act 2006: is breach of confidence now a crime? 4 JIPLP 278.
Ashworth, A. (1989) The scope of criminal liability for omissions. LQR 424.
Ashworth, A. (1993) Taking the consequences. In S. Shute (ed.), *Action and Value in Criminal Law*. Oxford: Clarendon Press.

Guided tour of the companion website

 Book resources are available to download. Print your own **Attack the question** and **Diagram plans** to pin to your wall or add to your own revision notes.

 Additional Essay and Problem questions with **Diagram plans** arranged by topic for each chapter give you more opportunity to practise and hone your exam skills. Print and email your answers.

 You be the marker gives you a chance to evaluate sample exam answers for different question types for each topic and understand how and why an examiner awards marks. Use the accompanying guidance to get the most out of every question and recognise what makes a good answer.

All of this and more can be found when you visit **www.pearsoned.co.uk/lawexpressqa**

Table of cases and statutes

■ Cases

A (a juvenile) v R [1978] Crim LR 689 153, 162
Adomako [1995] 1 AC 171 8, 9, 10, 11, 43, 68, 69, 73, 74, 79, 83
Ahluwalia [1992] 4 All ER 889 59
Airedale NHS Trust v Bland [1993] AC 89 3
Aitken [1992] 1 WLR 1006 91, 102
Allan and others [1965] 1 QB 130 236
Anderson [1986] AC 27 264
Anderson v Morris [1966] 2 QB 110 240, 244
Attorney General for Jersey v Holley [2005] UKPC 23 52, 59
Attorney General for Northern Ireland v Gallagher [1963] AC 349 190, 210
Attorney General's Reference (No. 1 of 1975) [1975] QB 773 234
Attorney General's Reference (No. 4 of 1980) [1981] 1 WLR 705 32
Attorney General's Reference (No. 6 of 1980) [1981] 2 All ER 1057 94, 102

B (a minor) v DPP [2000] 1 AC 428 27
Bailey [1983] 1 WLR 760 182
Bainbridge [1960] 1 QB 129 235
Baker and Wilkins [1997] Crim LR 497 209
Barnes [2004] EWCA Crim 3246 103
Becerra and Cooper (1976) 62 Cr App R 212 241, 266
Beckford v R [1988] AC 130 200, 204
Belfon [1976] 1 WLR 714 99
Bingham [1991] Crim LR 433 182, 186

Bird [1985] 2 All ER 513 200, 204
Blaue [1975] 1 WLR 1411 14, 68
Bowen [1996] 2 Cr App R 157 208, 209, 256
Bratty v Attorney General for Northern Ireland and Sullivan [1984] AC 156 181, 182, 185
Bree [2008] QB 131 111, 259
Brown [1985] Crim LR 212 153, 157
Brown [1994] 1 AC 212 95, 103, 104, 111
Bryce [2004] EWCA Crim 1231 234, 264
Burgess [1991] 2 QB 92 185

Campbell (1991) 93 Cr App R 350 217, 224, 264
Caparo Industries plc v Dickman [1990] 2 AC 605 68
Cato [1976] 1 WLR 110 9, 11, 13, 68, 69, 74, 260
Chan-Fook [1994] 1 WLR 689 89
Charlson (1955) 39 Cr App R 37 185
Cheshire [1991] 1 WLR 844 10, 14, 15, 40, 68, 69, 251
Church [1966] 1 QB 59 32, 43, 67, 68, 74, 77, 260
Clarke [1972] 1 All ER 219 181, 185
Clegg [1995] 1 AC 482 200, 203
Clinton [2012] EWCA Crim 2 52, 61, 252
Codere (1917) 12 Cr App R 21 181
Cole [1994] Crim LR 582 210, 256
Cole v Turner (1705) 6 Mod Rep 149 89, 93
Collins [1973] QB 100 153, 157, 265
Collins v Wilcock [1984] 1 WLR 1172 89, 90, 93, 102, 180
Comer v Bloomfield (1971) 55 Cr App R 305 223
Constanza [1997] 2 Cr App R 492 89
Cunningham [1957] 2 QB 396 21, 89, 94, 95, 250

Statutes

Actus reus and mens rea

How this topic may come up in exams

Topics such as omissions and causation (actus reus) and intention and recklessness (mens rea) are popular with examiners. Omissions and causation could be examined separately in essay form or together in a problem question. Similarly, intention and recklessness could be examined separately by essays or with causation and/or omissions as a problem question on murder/manslaughter. Essay questions on omissions often ask you to consider the competing academic views. Essays on causation might ask for a critical appreciation of the rules of causation. Essays on intention and recklessness often focus more on a critical evaluation of the development of the law.

■ Attack the question

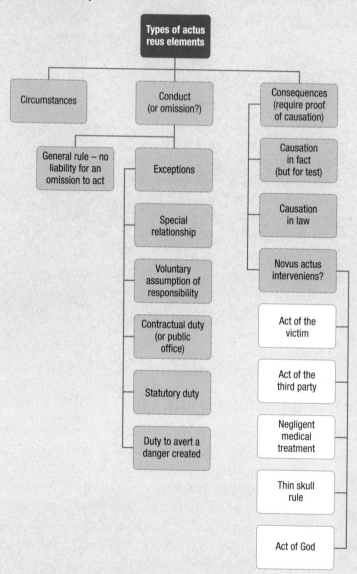

A printable version of this diagram is available from www.pearsoned.co.uk/lawexpressqa

 Question 1

'Since imposing liability for omissions as well as acts would be too restrictive of human freedom it should be allowed only in the most morally uncontroversial circumstances.'
(William Wilson (2011), *Criminal Law: Doctrine and Theory*, 4th edn, Longman)

To what extent does the law impose liability on a person for an omission to act? Is the law too restrictive of human freedom?

Answer plan

➡ Set out the general rule and exceptions.

➡ Consider the two opposing academic views.

➡ Discuss the arguments put forward by Williams and Ashworth.

➡ Conclude by addressing the point made by Wilson in the quote.

Diagram plan

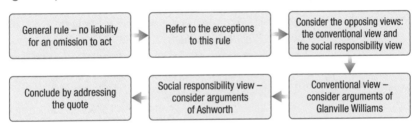

A printable version of this diagram plan is available from www.pearsoned.co.uk/lawexpressqa

Answer

[1] Begin by setting out the general rule and explaining it in your own words.

There is generally no liability for an omission to act. This means that a person can only usually be held criminally liable where he has performed a positive act.[1] However, there are six exceptions where the law imposes a duty to act upon a person and failure to so act can lead to criminal liability.

The first exception applies where there is a special relationship between the parties, such as a parent–child relationship (***Gibbins and Proctor*** (1918) 13 Cr App R 134), a doctor–patient relationship (***Airedale NHS Trust v Bland*** [1993] AC 89). A special relationship

3

will result in a duty being imposed upon the defendant to act to assist the other. However, there is uncertainty over how far this category extends to other relationships, such as siblings and spouses.[2] **Smith** [1979] Crim LR 251 suggests that a married couple owe a duty to one another. However, this case was not relied upon in **Hood** [2004] 1 Cr App R (S) 73. A husband was deemed to owe a duty to his wife, but this decision appears to have been made on the basis of a voluntary assumption of responsibility (he was her carer).[3] It is also unclear whether the duty extends to civil partnerships, cohabiting couples or former spouses.

Voluntarily assuming responsibility for someone is another exception to the general rule. Where a defendant voluntarily assumes responsibility for someone (e.g., by acting as carer), the law imposes a duty upon them to continue to do so (**Stone and Dobinson** [1977] 2 All ER 341, **Instan** [1893] 1 QB 450 and **Gibbins and Proctor**). A defendant may be under a contractual duty to act. Any failure to act in accordance with the terms of the contract may result in criminal liability (**Pittwood** (1902) 19 TLR 37). Similarly, a person in public office, such as a police officer, will have a duty to act in accordance with their position (**Dytham** [1979] QB 722). A statutory provision may impose a duty on a person to act, such as s. 1, Children and Young Persons Act 1933, which makes it an offence for a person with responsibility for a child to wilfully neglect the child, and s. 170, Road Traffic Act 1988, which makes it an offence for a person to fail to provide his details after an accident or to report it to the police.

There is a duty on a defendant to act in order to avert a danger which he has created. In **Miller** [1983] 2 AC 161, the defendant fell asleep smoking a cigarette and woke to find the mattress on fire. He then fell asleep in another room. He was convicted of arson. When the defendant noticed the fire, he was under a duty to take steps to avert the danger. He was convicted due to his failure to so act. The obligation imposed by the law upon the defendant here was not restrictive of his freedom, as only a minimal contribution from him was required (e.g., phoning the fire brigade).[4] This principle was applied in **DPP v Santana-Bermudez** [2003] EWHC 2908 to impose a duty upon the defendant to warn a police officer that he had a hypodermic needle in his pocket. The duty arose after the defendant created a dangerous situation by telling the officer that he had no needles in his pockets prior to a search.

[2] Point out the uncertainty within the law as well as setting out the matters upon which the law is clear. This demonstrates that you have a fuller understanding of the topic.

[3] This sentence provides your interpretation of the case and shows that you have understood it fully.

[4] Relate your answer back to the quote in the question. This sentence adds some commentary to your answer and avoids a wholly descriptive narrative.

There are two academic arguments relating to whether or not criminal liability should be imposed for an omission to act. Professor Williams advocates the conventional view, while Professor Ashworth prefers the social responsibility view. Ashworth states that these two views are not polar opposites.

The conventional view is that A should not be compelled to serve B. Williams argues that there is a clear moral distinction between an act and an omission. He states that we have 'stronger inhibitions against active wrongdoing than against wrongfully omitting'[5] ('Criminal omissions: the conventional view' [1991] LQR 86).[6]

[5] If you can remember key quotes from academic articles, these will increase your chances of earning a higher grade.

[6] Cite key academic articles and do not rely solely upon textbooks when revising.

According to this view, the law aims to maximise each individual's autonomy and liberty. Citizens should not be encouraged to interfere in the lives of strangers, nor should they be forced to help strangers; imposing such a duty upon citizens would be too onerous. The conventional view holds that the criminal law should acknowledge an individual's choice, rather than compel an individual to act to protect a stranger. By compelling an individual to act, the law is 'allowing liability to be governed by chance' by thrusting the obligation to assist a person in peril upon 'a chance passer-by, who may well prefer not to become involved at all' (Ashworth [1989]) 'The scope of criminal liability for omissions' LQR 424). Ashworth states that 'stopping to help is part of the morality of aspiration, not the morality of duty'.

Imposing a duty on individuals to act to help another in peril would also increase the possibility of mass liability and would be impractical. Imagine a situation where a swimmer is drowning in the sea and is watched by a crowd on a beach. Who does the law compel to help the swimmer? Should everybody be liable for failing to assist? The conventional view holds that the criminal law should only impose liability for omissions in 'clear and serious cases' and should be confined to situations where the defendant has voluntarily assumed responsibility towards another or there exists a special relationship.

By contrast, the social responsibility view is that A should be under a legal duty to assist B, because society recognises that he have a duty to support and help each other. Ashworth (1989) argues that this view '. . . grows out of a communitarian social philosophy which stresses the necessary interrelationship between individual behaviour and collective goods'. This approach relies on the argument that all of society will benefit from the duty to be helped when in extreme peril. However, it safeguards liability by insisting that the peril far outweighs cost or inconvenience to the person required to assist. Ashworth argues that liability should be limited to those who had particular opportunity to assist.

It must be acknowledged that there is a comparative argument for extending the scope of the duty. European countries, such as France and Germany, impose a duty on citizens to assist in an 'easy rescue'.[7] However, in England, no matter how easy the rescue, no duty will be imposed upon a person to assist a person, unless an exception applies.

[7] This sentence demonstrates your knowledge of the comparative view.

In conclusion, Wilson's acknowledgement that liability for omissions should only be imposed in morally uncontroversial cases reflects the current law.[8] The restriction on human freedom referred to by Wilson can be reconciled with the social responsibility view: '. . . the value of one citizen's life is generally greater than the value of another citizen's temporary freedom' (Ashworth 1989). It can also be justified on a conventional approach as it only applies in morally uncontroversial cases.

[8] Once again, tie the academic argument made back to the quote in the title.

✓ Make your answer stand out

- Use the famous example of A, who is able to save B from drowning by holding out his hand, but abstains from doing so in order that B might be drowned (see J. Fitzjames Stephen (1887), *A Digest of the Criminal Law*).
- Refer to judicial comment, such as the judgments of Lord Coleridge CJ in *Instan* and Lord Lane CJ in *Stone and Dobinson*.
- Consider also more recent applications of the *Miller* principle, such as *DPP* v *Santana-Bermudez* [2003] EWHC 2908 (Admin) and *Evans* [2009] EWCA Crim 650.
- Refer to Professor Hogan's view that the law should not punish defendants like Dytham for the consequences which he might have prevented. He should only be punished for neglecting to perform the obligation of his office, and not for the harm he did not prevent but did not cause (see Hogan (1987) Omissions and the duty myth, in P. Smith (ed.), *Criminal Law Essays in Honour of JC Smith*, London: Butterworths).

? Question 2

Rachel has been in a relationship with her boyfriend, Marcel, for two years. They decide that Rachel should move in with Marcel and Marcel's children from a former relationship, his four-year-old son, Franklin, and his six-year-old daughter, Jacqui.

One day, Jacqui falls and strikes her head in a playground. An hour after the accident, Jacqui begins to experience headaches and vomiting. However, Marcel refuses to take her to see a doctor, saying that she is just 'faking it to get attention'. When Jacqui becomes delirious 12 hours later, Rachel takes her to the Accident and Emergency department of the local hospital. She is examined by Dr Collins, who gives Jacqui a paracetamol and sends her home. In fact, Jacqui was displaying symptoms of internal bleeding. She dies at home from a brain haemorrhage. Medical evidence suggests that if she had received the appropriate treatment an hour after the accident Jacqui would not have died.

Rachel looks after Franklin during the week while Marcel is at work. Rachel is not used to being around children and she finds it difficult to cope with living with Franklin. Three months after moving in, Rachel is left to look after Franklin while Marcel goes away on a month-long business trip. Rachel begins to get very frustrated with Franklin's behaviour. One day, when Franklin refuses to tidy up his toys, Rachel decides to punish him by making him go without dinner. She then decides not to feed him any more. Franklin becomes weak and dies from malnutrition.

Discuss the liability of Marcel and Rachel for the deaths of Jacqui and Franklin.

Answer plan

→ Consider whether Marcel could be guilty of gross negligence manslaughter by his failure to seek medical assistance for Jacqui.

→ Explore whether Marcel's omission was the cause of Jacqui's death.

→ Discuss whether Rachel might be guilty of gross negligence manslaughter in respect of Franklin's death.

→ Consider also whether Rachel is the cause of Franklin's death.

Diagram plan

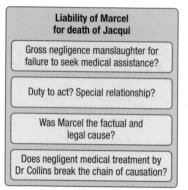

Liability of Marcel for death of Jacqui

Gross negligence manslaughter for failure to seek medical assistance?

Duty to act? Special relationship?

Was Marcel the factual and legal cause?

Does negligent medical treatment by Dr Collins break the chain of causation?

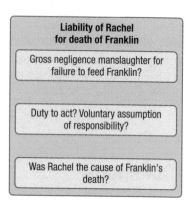

Liability of Rachel for death of Franklin

Gross negligence manslaughter for failure to feed Franklin?

Duty to act? Voluntary assumption of responsibility?

Was Rachel the cause of Franklin's death?

A printable version of this diagram plan is available from www.pearsoned.co.uk/lawexpressqa

Answer

[1] Identify the potential offences and the key issues at the very start to demonstrate that you have read and understood the question.

[2] The most logical structure for this question is to deal with the liability of each defendant in turn. Use headings to ensure that you maintain your structure and focus.

[3] Set out the four elements of gross negligence manslaughter at the start and then apply the law relating to each one in turn.

[4] Set out the general rule but explain that an exception might apply here.

[5] Select the specific exception which applies in this particular problem scenario.

This question requires consideration of the criminal liability of Marcel and Rachel for the deaths of Jacqui and Franklin respectively. Marcel and Rachel may be guilty of gross negligence manslaughter. This question requires consideration of liability by omission and the issue of causation.[1] The criminal liability of Marcel and that of Rachel will be examined in turn.

Liability of Marcel[2]

In determining whether Marcel is guilty of gross negligence manslaughter in respect of the death of Jacqui, it is necessary to examine the four elements of gross negligence manslaughter. The prosecution must prove that Marcel owed Jacqui a duty of care, that he breached that duty of care, that his breach caused Jacqui's death, and that his conduct (or omission) was grossly negligent (see **Adomako** [1995] 1 AC 171).[3]

There is generally no liability for an omission to act. However, there are a number of exceptions to this general rule.[4] If it can be shown that Marcel owed Jacqui a duty of care, then he may be liable for any omission to act in accordance with that duty. As Jacqui was his daughter, the special relationship[5] between parent and child means that the common law imposes a duty on Marcel to act and seek medical assistance for his daughter (*Gibbins and Proctor* (1918) 13 Cr App R 134). Marcel breaches that duty by failing to seek medical assistance for his daughter despite her head injury. He has not met the standard of care to be expected of a reasonable man, but he has fallen far below that standard (*Adomako*), thus breaching his duty.

The next question requires consideration of the rules of causation. It must be proved that Marcel was both the factual and legal cause of Jacqui's death. Causation in fact is relatively simply established. The test for causation in fact is the 'but for' test (*White* [1910] 2 KB 124). Applying this test, we must ask: but for Marcel's failure to seek medical assistance for Jacqui an hour after the accident, would she have died? Jacqui would not have died had she received appropriate medical treatment an hour after the accident. So, but for Marcel's failure to seek medical assistance for Jacqui, she might not have died.[6]

^6 Ensure that you apply the test for factual causation.

Legal causation is less straightforward. The prosecution must prove that the omission by Marcel was a more than minimal cause of Jacqui's death (*Cato* [1976] 1 WLR 110). This is the *de minimis* principle. In *Smith* [1959] 2 QB 35, it was held that a defendant would be the legal cause of the result if he was an 'operating and substantial' cause of the result. There is clearly more than one cause of death here: both Marcel's failure to seek medical assistance for Jacqui and Dr Collins' negligent medical treatment are causes of her death. However, we are only concerned with the liability of Marcel.[7] It is clear that Dr Collins' involvement does not preclude Marcel's liability for her death because 'the accused's act need not be the sole cause, or even the main cause, of the victim's death, it being enough that his act contributed significantly to that result'[8] (per Goff LJ in *Pagett* (1983) 75 Cr App R 279). It can be said that Marcel's failure to seek medical assistance an hour after the accident certainly contributed significantly towards her death because medical evidence showed that she would have survived had she received the appropriate treatment an hour after the accident.

^7 This sentence shows the examiner that you can distinguish between Dr Collins' potential liability and his treatment as a potential intervening event in respect of Marcel's liability.

^8 If you can remember short key quotes from judgments, use them to support your argument.

The next issue to consider is whether there is a *novus actus interveniens* (an intervening act) that breaks the chain of causation. The only potential intervening act here is the negligent medical treatment

[9] State the general rule at the start.

provided by Dr Collins. However, for policy reasons, negligent medical treatment does not automatically break the chain of causation.[9] In order for Marcel to escape liability, Dr Collins' conduct would have to be 'so independent' of Marcel's omission and 'so potent in causing death' that it renders Marcel's omission insignificant (per Beldam LJ in **Cheshire** [1991] 1 WLR 844). Dr Collins' treatment here is clearly negligent but it does not render Marcel's omission insignificant. The negligent medical treatment is very unlikely to break the chain of causation.

The final element the prosecution must prove is gross negligence. The jury must consider 'whether having regard to the risk of death involved, the conduct of the defendant was so bad in all the circumstances as to amount . . . to a criminal act or omission' (**Adomako**). The jury will consider the risk of death involved with head injuries, and if they determine that Marcel's conduct was grossly negligent, he will be convicted of gross negligence manslaughter.

Liability of Rachel

In order to establish that Rachel is guilty of gross negligence manslaughter in respect of the death of Franklin, the prosecution must prove that she owed Franklin a duty of care, that she breached that duty, that her breach caused Franklin's death, and that her conduct (or omission) was grossly negligent (**Adomako**).

The first issue to consider is whether Rachel owed Franklin a duty of care. As she is not his parent, there is no special relationship. However, it might be argued that Rachel has voluntarily assumed responsibility for Franklin. She has now moved in with Marcel and the children and she is tasked with looking after Franklin for a month while Marcel is away on business.[10] Thus, she can be said to have voluntarily assumed responsibility for him (**Stone and Dobinson** [1977] QB 354). However, she breaches that duty by falling below the standard to be expected of a reasonable person when she stops feeding him.

[10] Use the facts provided in the problem question to support your argument.

Turning next to the rules of causation, Rachel is clearly the factual cause of Franklin's death. Applying **White**, but for Rachel refusing to feed Franklin, he would not have died from malnutrition. Rachel is also clearly a legal cause of Franklin's death because she was a more than minimal cause of death (**Cato**), and she was an 'operating and substantial' cause of his death (**Smith**).

Finally, the prosecution must prove that Rachel was grossly negligent. The jury must again consider 'whether having regard to the risk of death involved, the conduct of the defendant was so bad in all the circumstances as to amount . . . to a criminal act or omission' (**Adomako**). There is a high risk of death involved in failing to feed a four-year-old child. It is likely that the jury would consider Rachel's conduct to be so bad in all the circumstances as to amount to a criminal omission and, thus, to be grossly negligent. Consequently, she is likely to be convicted of gross negligence manslaughter.

✓ **Make your answer stand out**

- Adopt a clear and logical structure, dealing with the liability of each defendant in turn.
- Use any short key quotes from judgments that you can remember. For instance, you could refer to the judgments of the courts in *Pagett, Smith, Cheshire* in this question.
- Ensure that you state the general approach of the courts to negligent medical treatment as an intervening event.
- You should correctly cite and apply the test in *Cheshire*.

❗ Don't be tempted to . . .

- You are not asked to consider the liability of Dr Collins, so do not discuss whether or not he might be liable for gross negligence manslaughter. This is a different issue from the one you are required to explore in respect of Marcel's potential liability, which is whether or not Dr Collins' negligent treatment could break the chain of causation and absolve Marcel of liability.
- There is no need to list all of the possible exemptions to the general rule that there is no liability for an omission. Just focus on those that are relevant to the particular question.
- Similarly, there is no need to list all of the possible intervening events in respect of legal causation. Instead, you should apply the law which is directly relevant to the question.

 Question 3

'The reason for requiring that the defendant should be shown to have causal responsibility for the conduct, consequence or state of affairs lies in the principle of individual autonomy . . . Thus the approach of the criminal law is to affix causal responsibility to the last individual whose voluntary behaviour impinged on the situation.' (Ashworth (2009) *Principles of Criminal Law*, 6th edn, Oxford: Oxford University Press.)

Critically evaluate the above statement in relation to causation.

Answer plan

→ Distinguish between factual and legal causation.

→ Discuss case law on intervening events.

→ Critically evaluate the law on causation.

→ Conclude by addressing the quote.

Diagram plan

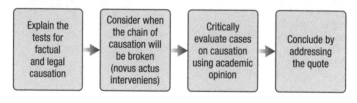

Explain the tests for factual and legal causation ➡ Consider when the chain of causation will be broken (novus actus interveniens) ➡ Critically evaluate cases on causation using academic opinion ➡ Conclude by addressing the quote

A printable version of this diagram plan is available from www.pearsoned.co.uk/lawexpressqa

Answer

This question requires a critical evaluation of the rules of causation and in particular, the approach taken by the courts to *novus actus interveniens* (new intervening acts) which break the chain of causation. Ashworth states that the rules of causation are underpinned by the principle of individual autonomy which 'respects individuals as capable of choosing their acts and omissions' who can be regarded as responsible for the normal consequences of their conduct.[1] However, some events/acts will intervene to break the chain of causation and absolve a defendant of responsibility. The rules of causation are largely based upon voluntariness. A voluntary or

[1] This sentence makes reference to the quote in the title and explains it a little further, demonstrating your understanding of the question.

[2] Begin by setting out the general approach of the law.

[3] Point out at the very start the problematic areas of the topic to demonstrate your wider understanding of the area.

foreseeable act of the victim or a third party will not break the chain of causation, whereas an involuntary (unforeseeable) act may.[2] However, causation is a complex area which lacks clarity, particularly in relation to the independence/potency test in respect of medical negligent treatment.[3]

The prosecution must prove that the defendant's act is both a factual and legal cause of the prohibited consequence. Factual causation is satisfied by the application of the 'but for' test (*White*). Legal causation is used to describe the requirement that the defendant's act must be sufficiently proximate to the consequence. It is often stated that the defendant's act must be a more than minimal cause of the consequence; this is the *de minimis test* (*Cato*). In *Pagett*, the 'significant contribution' test was applied in respect of legal causation and in *Smith* (1959) this was expressed as the 'operating and substantial cause' test. Even where factual causation has been established and the defendant is a more than minimal cause of the result, the defendant may be absolved of liability where there is an intervening event which breaks the chain of causation. However, the chain of causation will only be broken in certain circumstances.

Acts of a third party will only break the chain of causation if they are voluntary. This means they must be 'free, deliberate and informed': Goff LJ in *Pagett*. The defendant in *Pagett* was held responsible for the death of his girlfriend. He held her hostage and shot at a police officer who shot back, killing her. The defendant was convicted on the basis that the police officer was acting instinctively in self-defence and out of a public duty to arrest the defendant, thus his actions were not 'free, deliberate and informed'. The rationalisation of this decision can be criticised. Ashworth suggests that a better rationale would have been along the lines of a 'doctrine of alternative danger' (*Principles of Criminal Law*, 6th edn (2009), Oxford: Oxford University Press).[4]

[4] Use academic critique to demonstrate your wider reading.

Acts of the victim will break the chain of causation where they are 'daft' or so unexpected that 'no reasonable man could be expected to foresee it': *Roberts* (1971) 56 Cr App R 95. This approach was also adopted in *Williams and Davies* (1992) 95 Cr App R 1. In *Marjoram* [2000] Crim LR 372, the Court of Appeal confirmed that the subjective characteristics of the accused may be taken into account here.

However, a pre-existing condition of the defendant which renders the defendant particularly vulnerable to the injury inflicted or death will not serve to absolve the defendant of liability. This is known as the 'thin skull rule'. In **Blaue** [1975] 1 WLR 1411, the thin skull rule was extended to encompass religious beliefs. Lawton LJ stated that defendants 'must take their victims as they find them. This . . . means the whole man, not just the physical man'. Thus, a refusal of treatment based on religious beliefs will not break the chain of causation. How far this principle extends to other beliefs, however, is unclear.[5]

[5] This sentence demonstrates that you are thinking around the subject rather than simply stating everything you know about causation.

In respect of negligent medical treatment, the courts have been reluctant to allow the negligence of a doctor to absolve the defendant of liability for policy reasons. In **Smith**, it was held that only if medical negligence was 'so overwhelming as to make the original wound merely part of the history' would the chain of causation be broken (per Parker LJ).[6] Similarly, in **Cheshire**, the Court of Appeal held that medical negligence will not break the chain of causation unless the medical treatment was so independent of the defendant's acts and so potent in causing death that it renders the defendant's acts insignificant. This is the 'independence/potency' test and this test was also applied in **Gowans and Hillman** [2003] EWCA Crim 3935.

[6] Use quotes from judgments to show your wider knowledge of the subject.

However, a very different approach was taken in the earlier case of **Jordan** (1956) 40 Cr App R 152. In this case, it was held that medical negligence could break the chain of causation if it was 'palpably wrong'. However, this is an extreme authority, and although it has not been overruled, it has been limited to its own facts by Lawton LJ in **Blaue**.[7]

[7] This paragraph shows that you are able to compare and contrast conflicting authorities and that you have understood the area well.

The independence/potency test may be criticised. As Ormerod states, 'It is difficult to know what "so independent" and "so potent" mean' (*Smith and Hogan Criminal Law*, 13th edn (2011), Oxford: Oxford University Press). If one considers first the words 'so independent': in all of the cases on negligent medical treatment, the defendant's act causes the victim to undergo the treatment. Ormerod argues that if this in itself renders the act 'dependent', then the defendant has caused the death, irrespective of how 'outlandish' the treatment. Ormerod submits that is not the intended meaning of 'so independent'. Similarly, the words 'so potent' are problematic. In criticising this term, Ormerod provides an example of a victim who is wounded by the defendant and hospitalised for that wound. If he then contracts MRSA in an unclean hospital as the wound has healed, and dies, did the court in *Cheshire* intend that the defendant is not a legal cause of death? Ormerod submits that this is unlikely. These criticisms demonstrate that the test in *Cheshire* is confusing and inaccessible and, as such, is of limited use.[8]

[8] Demonstrate that you have read widely and understood academic commentary on the area.

In criticising the 'independence/potency' test, Ormerod suggests that a better test would be one in which the chain of causation could be broken where the treatment was 'so extraordinary as to be unforeseeable'. Such a test based upon foreseeability would certainly bring negligent medical treatment into line with many of the other authorities relating to *novus actus interveniens.*[9]

[9] This sentence provides your opinion on the case law and the academic critique.

In conclusion, it is clear that causation is generally based upon the principle of individual autonomy. A defendant will be absolved of liability where an unforeseeable or involuntary act of the victim or a third party intervenes to break the chain of causation. However, the approach taken in cases of negligent medical treatment seems somewhat out of line with the rest of the law relating to causation and this area of law could benefit from further clarification.

✓ Make your answer stand out

- Refer to further academic critique on causation, such as Hart, H. and Honoré, A., *Causation in the Law*, 2nd edn (1985), Oxford: Oxford University Press.

- You should refer to further cases on causation, such as *Hayward* (1908) 21 Cox CC 692 on the thin skull rule and *Holland* (1841) 2 Mood & R 351 and *Dear* [1996] Crim LR 595 on self-neglect by the victim.

- Consider the argument that the Court of Appeal in *Blaue* should have adopted the 'reasonable foresight' approach adopted in *Roberts*. You should also refer to the fact that this is the approach taken in the law of tort and the distinction drawn by Lawton LJ in *Blaue* between the functions of criminal law and that of tort. Consider whether this approach is justifiable and any academic commentary on this point (see Williams, case commentary (1976) CJL 15 and Allen, M.J., *Textbook on Criminal Law*, 10th edn (2009) Oxford: Oxford University Press).

- You should refer to other academic commentary, such as Wilson, W., *Criminal Law Doctrine and Theory*, 4th edn (2011), London: Pearson Longman.

! Don't be tempted to . . .

- Simply set out everything you know about causation. A descriptive account will not provide you with the opportunity to attain the highest marks. You must address the question directly and include academic critique.

- Provide detailed accounts of the facts of every case. You should not really cite the facts of a case in an answer to an essay question unless they are particularly relevant to the point you are making. For an example, see the reference to *Pagett* in the essay above.

❓ Question 4

'It might . . . be expected that the meaning of such a fundamental term [as intention] would have been settled long ago, but this is not so. The cases are inconsistent, judicial opinion has recently changed and there is still some measure of uncertainty.' (Ormerod, D., *Smith and Hogan Criminal Law*, 13th edn (2011)).

Critically evaluate the meaning of intention in criminal law. To what extent do you agree with the above statement?

Answer plan

➜ Define intention.

➜ Consider case law relating to the meaning of intention.

➜ Explore academic opinion.

➜ Conclude by addressing the quote.

Diagram plan

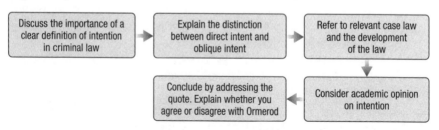

A printable version of this diagram plan is available from www.pearsoned.co.uk/lawexpressqa

Answer

This question requires consideration of the meaning of 'intention' in criminal law. Ormerod suggests that, despite the judicial attention given to intention, its meaning remains uncertain.[1] It is true that the decisions of the courts have been inconsistent and unclear over the years and Parliament has not intervened to clarify the law. However, the law has appeared more settled since the House of Lords decision in **Woollin** [1999] AC 82.[2] The importance of a clear definition of intention should not be underestimated. Intention is the mens rea requirement for some of the most serious offences in criminal law, including murder. Murder carries mandatory life imprisonment; such a serious threat to an individual's liberty upon conviction requires that the elements of the offence be precisely and clearly defined. As Lord Bingham states, '. . . the law must be accessible and so far as possible intelligible, clear and predictable' ('The Rule of Law' (2007) CLJ 67). The law must be adequately clear and accessible, so that an individual can find out what it is and be aware if his or her conduct will fall foul of it. The law must also be certain so that a trial judge is able to explain its meaning confidently to a jury. Nevertheless, the meaning of intention has been the subject of much uncertainty over the years.[3]

Although intention is now recognised as a subjective concept, it was given an objective meaning by the House of Lords in **DPP v Smith** [1961] AC 290. It was to be conclusively presumed that a person intends the natural and probable consequences of his acts. Such a presumption is not justifiable. Where the offence is of a serious nature, the mens rea required in order to establish criminal liability should depend upon the subjective state of mind of the actual defendant, rather than on any objective assessment. This case was criticised and it no longer represents the current law. Section 8 of the Criminal Justice Act 1967 confirms that intention is subjectively assessed.

In the majority of cases in which the issue of whether the defendant's intention is in issue, the jury are not given judicial direction as to the meaning of intention. This is because intention is an ordinary word used in everyday language, and the jury should use their common sense in determining its meaning. There are two types of

---

[1] Address the quote in the question from the very start.

[2] Provide your opinion at the start to show that you have considered the question carefully.

[3] This paragraph shows the examiner that you recognise the importance of the question and this area of law and demonstrates wider thinking.

intention: direct intent and oblique intent. Direct intent involves a defendant's aim or purpose. This form of intention is relatively straightforward; so the jury are not given any direction by the judge. Oblique intent may be present if, although the defendant did not desire the consequences, he did foresee that they were virtually certain to occur (*Woollin*). In the rare cases in which oblique intention arises, a judge should give the jury a direction as to the meaning of intention. Although one might have thought that intention should be easy to define, case law demonstrates that it has proved difficult to define the degree of foresight necessary for oblique intent.[4]

[4] This sentence indirectly refers to the quote and demonstrates that you are focused on the question.

According to the House of Lords in *Hyam* [1975] AC 55, intention could be established if the defendant foresaw death or GBH as a highly probable result. This test was criticised for being too close to recklessness. It is important to maintain a clear distinction between the meanings of intention and recklessness in order to adequately distinguish between the offences of murder and manslaughter. There is also a significant moral difference between wanting a result to occur and merely foreseeing it as highly probable.

[5] Compare the effect of the cases against one another.

In *Moloney* [1985] AC 905, the House of Lords retreated from *Hyam*.[5] Lord Bridge stated that the golden rule is that the judge should avoid any elaboration and leave it to the jury's good sense to decide whether the accused acted with the necessary intent, unless the judge is convinced that further explanation is necessary. His Lordship stated that a jury should consider two questions: 'First, was death or really serious injury in a murder case . . . a natural consequence of the defendant's voluntary act? Secondly, did the defendant foresee that consequence as being a natural consequence of his act?'[6] If the answer is yes to both, the jury may infer that the defendant intended the consequence.

[6] It is worth learning the key quotes from leading judgments for the exam, along with the name of the judge.

In *Hancock & Shankland* [1986] AC 455, Lord Scarman held that '. . . the *Moloney* guidelines . . . are unsafe and misleading. They require a reference to probability. They also require an explanation that the greater the probability of a consequence the more likely it is that the consequence was foreseen and that if that consequence was foreseen the greater the probability is that that consequence was also intended'. The repeated references to 'probabilities' did little to clarify the position and to provide a certain distinction between intention and recklessness.

In *Nedrick* [1986] 1 WLR 1025, the Court of Appeal laid down a narrower test, which forms the basis of the current law. The court held that where a direction was necessary '. . . the jury should be directed that they are not entitled to infer the necessary intention, unless they feel sure that death or serious bodily harm was a virtual certainty . . . as a result of the defendant's actions and that the defendant appreciated [this]'. This is a much narrower test than that in *Hyam*, and it means that the distinction between recklessness and intention is clearer. This was approved by the House of Lords in *Woollin* (the word 'infer' was changed to 'find'). It was also held that foresight by the defendant that a result is a virtually certain consequence of his actions is merely evidence of intention. The trial judge in *Woollin* was criticised for directing the jury on intention using the phrase 'substantial risk'. The House held that the judge should not have departed from *Nedrick* and that 'substantial risk' was wider than 'virtual certainty'. Lord Steyn stated that: 'By using the phrase "substantial risk" the judge blurred the line between intention and recklessness, and hence between murder and manslaughter. The misdirection enlarged the scope of the mental element required for murder.'

[7] Address the question in your conclusion.

[8] This sentence demonstrates wider thinking and that you have read the *Nedrick/Woollin* direction properly.

[9] Include some academic opinion to demonstrate your wider reading.

In conclusion, although the meaning of intention has proved difficult to define, the law appears more settled now.[7] However, it should be acknowledged that most of the cases defining intention are murder cases. *Woollin* is limited specifically to murder, thus it remains unclear what approach the courts should take in respect of other offences.[8] Allen states 'it would be highly undesirable if courts were to adopt a different approach to the meaning of intention in other offences' (*Textbook on Criminal Law*, 10th edn (2009), Oxford: Oxford University Press).[9] Thus, it is true that some degree of uncertainty as to the meaning of intention remains.

Make your answer stand out

- As this area is very case law based, you should try to remember some of the key quotes from the main cases, along with the name of the relevant judge. This demonstrates to the examiner that you have a detailed understanding of the area.

- You could discuss the effect of the decision that foresight is evidence of intention, rather than intention as a matter of law and the case of *Matthews and Alleyne* [2003] 2 Cr App R 30.

- You could also discuss further the trend towards subjectivity in criminal law and the reasons why an objective approach to intention would not be appropriate. You should include discussion of the theoretical rationale behind different approaches to liability.

- Refer to academic opinion, such as Professor Smith's commentary on *Woollin* at [1998] Crim LR 890. Professor Smith welcomed the decision in *Woollin* because 'it draws a firm line between intention and recklessness' at p. 891.

- You might also refer to articles such as Norrie, A., After *Woollin* [1999] Crim LR 532; and Williams, G., Oblique intention [1987] CLJ 417 and The mens rea for murder: leave it alone (1989) 105 LQR 387.

 Don't be tempted to . . .

- Misstate the direction from *Nedrick/Woollin*. There are two limbs to the direction, one objective one and one subjective one. It is not enough to simply refer to 'foresight of virtual certainty', you must set out the test in full.

- Recite the facts of *Hyam, Moloney, Woollin*, etc. Other than the fact that these cases all involved murder, the precise facts are not directly relevant to the question. You will waste time if you set out the facts when the question is asking for a critical appreciation of the judgments/opinions.

- Confuse the different tests from *Hyam, Moloney, Hancock and Shankland* and *Nedrick*.

❖ Question 5

'[W]e are still some way from reaching a fair and coherent doctrine of recklessness in the English criminal law.' (Andrew Halpin, *Definition in the Criminal Law* (2004) at p. 120.)

To what extent do you agree with the above statement?

Answer plan

➡ Refer to the current law on recklessness under *Cunningham* [1957] 2 QB 396 and *G* [2003] UKHL 50.

➡ Discuss the problems associated with the old law under *MPC* v *Caldwell* [1982] AC 341.

➡ Any criticisms of the current law?

➡ Judicial and academic opinion on recklessness.

Diagram plan

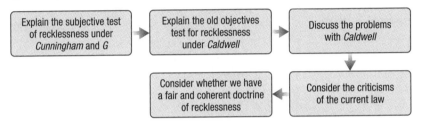

A printable version of this diagram plan is available from www.pearsoned.co.uk/lawexpressqa

Answer

The law on recklessness has been subject to academic scrutiny for years. Prior to 2003, there were two legal tests of recklessness: one was a subjective meaning of recklessness from ***Cunningham*** [1957] 2 QB 396 and the other was an objective definition adopted by the House of Lords in ***MPC v Caldwell*** [1982] AC 341, which applied to criminal damage. In ***G*** [2003] UKHL 50, the House of Lords overruled ***Caldwell***, confirming that a subjective test should apply in respect of criminal damage. Thus, since 2003 it would appear that the subjective approach to recklessness has prevailed and that the law is settled. However, academics have argued that the law is in fact still not settled following ***G***.[1] Whether there is indeed a clear and settled definition of recklessness will be considered below.

[1] Address the question in your introduction to ensure that you engage with the question asked.

The subjective test of recklessness from ***Cunningham*** requires that 'the accused has foreseen that the particular kind of harm might be done, and yet has gone on to take the risk of it' (per Byrne J). This test was further developed in later cases including ***Stephenson*** [1979] 1 QB 695, in which Lane LJ stated that recklessness involved

[2] Set out the subjective test of recklessness to demonstrate your knowledge of the law.

[3] This sentence shows that you have fully understood the test.

[4] Set out the objective test of recklessness from *Caldwell*.

[5] If you do wish to mention the facts of a case in order to make a particular point, you should do so briefly.

[6] This sentence develops your argument further by explaining why having two tests is confusing.

conscious risk taking where the risk is an unreasonable one to take.[2] Thus, there is also an objective element to this test – a defendant will only be reckless where the risk is objectively unjustifiable.[3] This subjective (or advertent) test of recklessness was applied to offences until the decision in *Caldwell* in 1981, in which the House of Lords held that a second test of recklessness should apply in cases of criminal damage. This second test was expressed in more objective terms, Lord Diplock stating that recklessness requires the defendant to: (i) do an act which creates an obvious risk of damage; and (ii) give no thought to the possibility of there being any such risk, or recognising some risk he goes on to do the act anyway.[4] This was labelled as the objective test of recklessness due to the fact that a defendant who inadvertently took a risk which was obvious to the reasonable person would be deemed to be reckless. The *Caldwell* test was also applied to the offence of causing by reckless driving in *Lawrence* [1982] 1 AC 510. Thus, two tests of recklessness existed.

However, the *Caldwell* test was heavily criticised throughout its existence. One of the major problems with Caldwell was that this objective test could lead to harsh results when applied in respect of children or those with a lower capacity to appreciate risk: for example see *Elliott* v *C* [1983] 1 WLR 939, in which the defendant was a child of low intelligence who did not appreciate the risk of criminal damage involved in her act due to her age, lack of understanding and exhausted state.[5] Such considerations were irrelevant under *Caldwell* and the High Court ordered the justices to convict the defendant. It was precisely this issue which eventually led to *Caldwell* being overruled in *G*. Lord Bingham stated that the decision in *Caldwell* led to 'obvious unfairness'.

Having two separate tests of recklessness was problematic as it over-complicated the law and was confusing for juries. Where a defendant was charged with both criminal damage and a non-fatal offence against the person, the jury would be directed to apply both tests of recklessness, a different test for each offence.[6] It was also illogical to have two separate tests and meanings of recklessness.

A further criticism was that the objective test of recklessness from *Caldwell* blurred the distinction between the concept of recklessness and that of negligence which is traditionally objectively assessed. It also contradicted the subjective trend within criminal law – intention is subjectively assessed. Lord Bingham stated that the mens rea of an offence should depend upon proof of a culpable state of mind and thus should be assessed subjectively. His Lordship took the view that mere stupidity should not expose a defendant to conviction of serious crime.[7]

[7] Referring to what a particular judge has said demonstrates that you have read and understood the judgment.

These criticisms led to the House of Lords overruling **Caldwell** in **G** and restoring a subjective test of recklessness in relation to criminal damage. Lord Bingham stated that the House of Lords in Caldwell has misinterpreted the meaning of 'recklessness' within section 1 of the Criminal Damage Act 1971. The House adopted the definition proposed by the Law Commission (1989): 'a person acts "recklessly" . . . with respect to: (i) circumstances when he is aware of a risk that it exists or will exist; (ii) a result when he is aware of a risk that it will occur; and it is, in the circumstances known to him, unreasonable to take the risk.'

However, despite this decision, academics argue that the law on recklessness is still not clear. One criticism of **G** is that the House restricted the decision to criminal damage. As **Caldwell** recklessness also applied to other offences, e.g., causing death by reckless driving and other statutory offences requiring proof of recklessness, the question which must now be asked is why these offences were not also dealt with or indeed whether **Caldwell** recklessness still applies to these.

Halpin (2004) expresses concern about Lord Bingham's understanding of mens rea. He criticises Lord Bingham for taking a 'strict subjectivist' approach, according to which culpability is associated with intention to bring about a result or awareness of a risk of that result. Halpin highlights serious offences which have required proof of objective recklessness or negligence; he comments: 'if we took Bingham's support of the strict subjectivist position seriously, it would follow that liability for the serious offences of causing death by reckless driving, manslaughter and rape has been established under English law without any requirement of mens rea, and without any need to find fault on the part of the defendant.' (Halpin 2004, p. 104)

[8] You should refer to any alternative approaches suggested by academics who have criticised the approach of the courts.

The question raised is to what degree inadvertence should be culpable. Some commentators support a test which provides a compromise between subjective and objective approaches[8] (Tadros, V., 'Recklessness and the duty to take care', in S. Shute and A. Simester (eds.), *Criminal Law Theory* (2002)). Crosby recognises that 'a definition of recklessness that is too subjective can allow those who are blameworthy to avoid criminal liability. Alternatively, a test that is too objective can lead to injustice without being capacity based. It is submitted that a synthesis of the two approaches is required' (Crosby, C., 'Recklessness – the continuing search for a definition' (2008) 72 JCL 313). This is an issue requiring further consideration by the courts. Thus, although *G* appears to have simplified the law in certain respects, the decision of the House is open to academic criticism and there is a need for further judicial guidance.

✓ Make your answer stand out

- There is a wealth of academic literature on recklessness which you could refer to in your answer.
- You might wish to refer to some of the theory surrounding recklessness and culpability. A good starting point is Tadros, V., Recklessness and the duty to take care, in S. Shute and A. Simester (eds.), *Criminal Law Theory* (2002).
- You could also explore the judicial reasoning in cases such as *Caldwell, Lawrence, Elliott* v *C* in more detail and explore the case of *Reid*.
- You should include discussion of the theoretical rationale behind different approaches to liability, including the justifications for liability based on a subjectivist approach.

! Don't be tempted to . . .

- You will waste time in an exam if you set out the facts of *Cunningham, Caldwell* and *G* in detail. While you may wish to refer to specific facts, such as the fact that the defendants in *G* were children, you should be able to do this without regaling all of the facts of the cases.
- Merely provide a historical account of the development of the law from *Cunningham* to *Caldwell* and *G*. The question asks you to critically evaluate the development of the law and the current position.

 Question 6

To what extent does the imposition of criminal liability without proof of fault offend traditional notions of criminal responsibility?

Answer plan

➡ Refer to the presumption of mens rea and the situations in which the presumption may be displaced.

➡ Outline the arguments in favour of imposing strict liability on an individual.

➡ Outline the arguments against strict liability, considering also the extent to which strict liability offends traditional notions of criminal responsibility.

➡ Discuss any alternatives to strict liability.

Diagram plan

A printable version of this diagram plan is available from www.pearsoned.co.uk/lawexpressqa

Answer

This question requires a critical evaluation of strict liability and whether this violates fundamental traditional principles of criminal responsibility. Strict liability offences are offences which do not require proof of mens rea in respect of at least one of the actus reus elements.[1] They are largely statutory offences and usually regulatory offences which apply to matters such as pollution, food safety, road traffic, public health, etc. It is a fundamental principle of criminal law that liability requires proof of both actus reus and mens rea elements, commonly expressed as '*actus non facit reum, nisi mens sit rea*' (an act does not make a man guilty of a crime, unless his mind be also guilty): Lord Hailsham in **Haughton v Smith** [1975] AC 476. It can be argued that imposing criminal liability upon an individual without proving a guilty mind violates traditional notions of criminal

[1] Demonstrate that you understand what strict liability is by defining it at the outset.

[2] Address the question directly in the first paragraph.

responsibility.[2] The arguments for and against the imposition of strict liability will be explored.

It is not necessarily apparent from reading a statutory provision whether an offence is one of strict liability or not. The courts have held that, where a statutory provision is silent as to mens rea, there is a presumption that mens rea elements are required: Lord Reid in **Sweet v Parsley** [1970] AC 132. However, this presumption may be displaced by the words of the statute or by the subject-matter of the offence: **Sherras v De Rutzen** [1895] 1 QB 918.

In **Gammon (Hong Kong) Ltd v Attorney General of Hong Kong** [1985] AC 1, Lord Scarman laid down guidelines in order for determining whether an offence is one of strict liability. His Lordship held that the presumption of mens rea is particularly strong where the offence is 'truly criminal' in nature, rather than merely regulatory, and it can only be displaced by clear words or if it is by necessary implication the effect of the statute. The statute must involve an issue of social concern and the imposition of strict liability must promote the object of the statute by encouraging greater vigilance to prevent the prohibited act.[3]

[3] Set out the guidelines from a leading authority in order to demonstrate your understanding of the operation of the presumption and when it may be displaced.

The main argument for the imposition of strict liability is that it provides a degree of protection to the public through the promotion of care. Strict liability operates on a utilitarian approach.[4] Wilson comments that a welfarist paradigm of criminal responsibility, '. . . does not require proof of moral wrongdoing . . . In order to live a life of relative autonomy we require certain basic welfare needs to be ministered to . . . Only the criminal law can satisfactorily ensure that these collective needs can be properly catered for and this is only possible if the criminal law requires all citizens to satisfy standards of good rather than morally blameless citizenship. The essence of such crimes is to prevent harm rather than to punish a moral wrong' (*Central Issues in Criminal Theory* (2002), Oxford: Hart Publishing, p. 72).[5] Strict liability also has a deterrent element as it encourages people to comply with regulations in order to protect people from harm.

[4] These sentences demonstrate a good understanding of the justification for strict liability offences.

[5] This quote shows that you have conducted effective research and read widely in your preparation for the examination.

Another argument in favour of strict liability relates to the ease of proof. It is much easier for the prosecution to prove criminal liability where a state of mind does not have to be proved. Strict liability offences can be further justified by reference to the sanction they carry. As they only apply to regulatory (or quasi) crimes and not true offence, offences of strict liability usually carry only a small penalty as a sanction and do not pose any risk to the liberty of individuals.

However, consideration must also be given to the arguments against the imposition of strict liability. The main argument is that it violates the principle of coincidence of actus reus and mens rea, a traditional notion of criminal responsibility.[6] A defendant should not be held to be criminally liable for any offence unless a blameworthy state of mind is also proved. This was emphasised by Lord Bingham in *G* '. . . it is a salutary principle that conviction of serious crime should depend on proof not simply that the defendant caused (by act or omission) an injurious result to another but that his state of mind when so acting was culpable. This, after all, is the meaning of '*actus non facit reum nisi mens sit rea*'. Simester and Sullivan comment that 'Parliament normally does not, and indeed should not, intend to make criminals of those who are not blameworthy and do not warrant that label' (*Criminal Law: Theory and Doctrine* (2007), Oxford: Hart Publishing, p. 169).[7]

Another argument against strict liability is that it serves to punish reasonable behaviour where the defendant has taken all reasonable steps to prevent liability and has no guilty mind. Consider the case of *Smedleys Ltd* v *Breed* [1974] AC 839, in which a caterpillar was found in a tin of peas sold by the defendant.[8] The defendant manufacturer was convicted of a strict liability offence despite the fact that this occurred once during production of millions of tins. The steps that a defendant must take to avoid such an incident from occurring and to avoid liability are highly onerous and not practicable.

The House of Lords has affirmed that the presumption of mens rea applies to all statutory offences (see *B (a minor)* v *DPP* [2000] 1 AC 428 and *K* [2002] 1 AC 462). In both cases, the House held that serious offences are likely to require proof of mens rea. The more serious the offence, the more severe the sanction and stigma of conviction, the greater the presumption that mens rea must be proved. The stigma attached to conviction might affect a defendant's reputation and livelihood. However, Hyman Gross argues that there is no such stigma attached to conviction for a strict liability offence: 'Perhaps the most prominent feature of most strict liability offences is that conviction does not affect respectability. Neither his conduct

---

[6] Address the question again midway through your answer in order to maintain focus and show that you are not simply writing everything you know about strict liability.

[7] Try to use a mixture of quotes from judgments and academic sources to support your arguments.

[8] If you do wish to state the facts of a case, do so briefly in a short sentence.

nor the punishment he receives for it stigmatizes the offender. These offences of low culpability are typically of the regulatory or public welfare variety, and so penal treatment is right viewed as simply an expedient way of encouraging or preventing certain consequences that flow from lawful activity, rather than as a public response to wrongdoing' (*A Theory of Criminal Justice* (1979), Oxford: Oxford University Press, p. 344).

Alternatives to strict liability include offences containing a requirement of negligence or a no fault defence of due diligence. Although it may be true that the imposition of strict liability violates traditional principles of criminal responsibility, there are convincing justifications for the use of strict liability in respect of regulatory offences for the protection of the public.

✓ Make your answer stand out

- Consider the alternatives to strict liability in more detail.
- You could include a comparative view of approaches to strict liability in Canada, where the prosecution need not prove mens rea, but a defendant can prove a lack of fault to escape liability.
- Make reference to the distinction between absolute liability offences and strict liability offences. Consider whether absolute liability offences violate any further principles of criminal responsibility, such as voluntariness. See *Winzar* v *Chief Constable of Kent* (1983) *The Times*, 28 March and *Larsonneur* (1933) 24 Cr App R 74.
- Refer to further academic opinion, such as Simester, A., *Appraising Strict Liability* (2006), Oxford: Oxford University Press and Horder, J., Strict liability, statutory construction, and the spirit of liberty [2002] LQR 458.

! Don't be tempted to . . .

- Wrongly define strict liability and confuse absolute liability and strict liability.
- Set out all of the facts of every case on strict liability. This question asks you to critically evaluate the concept of strict liability and the facts of the cases are not directly relevant to this. The principles and justifications for strict liability or arguments against it are more important.

 # Question 7

Explain the meaning of the Latin maxim *actus non facit reum nisi mens sit rea* and critically analyse the way in which this principle is applied in criminal law.

Answer plan

→ Explain the meaning of Latin maxim, *actus non facit reum nisi mens sit rea*.

→ Explore the principle of coincidence.

→ Consider the major exception of offences of absolute liability and strict liability.

→ Examine other exceptions to this principle, such as the doctrine of transferred malice, the continuing act theory, the 'duty' principle and the 'single transaction' principle.

Diagram plan

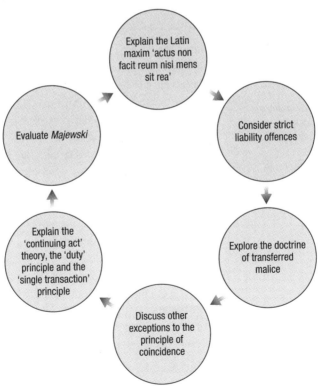

A printable version of this diagram plan is available from www.pearsoned.co.uk/lawexpressqa

Answer

Liability for a criminal offence is governed by the Latin maxim, *actus non facit reum nisi mens sit rea* which has been translated as 'an act does not make a man guilty of a crime, unless his mind be also guilty' (see Lord Hailsham in **Haughton v Smith** [1975] AC 476).[1] This means that both the actus reus (the 'guilty act') and the mens rea (the 'guilty mind') of an offence must be proved before a defendant may be convicted of a criminal offence. Thus, criminal liability usually requires proof of both actus reus and mens rea elements. This is often referred to as the principle of coincidence of actus reus and mens rea and this requires that the defendant form the requisite mens rea for the offence at some point during the actus reus. Generally speaking, if these two elements do not coincide, no offence will have been committed. However, there are a number of exceptions to this principle and situations in which the courts have circumvented the principle of coincidence in order to ensure that the defendant is held criminally liable.[2]

The first important exception to the principle of coincidence is offences of absolute liability and strict liability. A defendant may be held criminally liable for an offence of strict or absolute liability even where the actus reus and mens rea do not coincide.[3] Absolute liability offences are offences which do not require proof of any mens rea at all. Examples include the cases of **Larsonneur** (1933) 97 JP 206 and **Winzar v Chief Constable of Kent** (1983) *The Times*, 28 March. Both of these cases involve 'state of affairs' offences, where the defendant is guilty of a criminal offence simply because a state of affairs is deemed to exist. In neither case was the state of mind of the defendant relevant to their liability. Strict liability offences are offences for which at least one element of mens rea is missing. One example of a strict liability offence is assault occasioning actual bodily harm, contrary to s. 47 of the Offences Against the Person Act 1861; this offence does not require proof of mens rea in respect of the degree of harm caused: **Savage; Parmenter** [1992] 1 AC 699. Offences of strict liability violate the principle of coincidence because they do not require an element of mens rea to be proved for every element of actus reus.

In addition to this exception to the principle of coincidence, the courts have sought to circumvent the principle in other situations. The doctrine of transferred malice is one creative method used by

---

[1] Begin your answer by explaining the fundamental principle of coincidence using the Latin maxim.

[2] You should address the question directly in your introduction by mentioning the fact that the courts have sought to avoid the principle.

[3] This is the obvious example of the courts avoiding coincidence. Provide a brief explanation of offences of strict liability and the way in which they violate the principle.

the courts to circumvent the principle of coincidence. According to this doctrine, the defendant's intention in respect of one crime may be transferred to his performance of the actus reus in respect of another crime, provided that both offences are of the same type: *Latimer* (1886) 17 QBD 359. Thus, while the defendant may have the mens rea for murder in respect of A but he does not actually kill A (and thus has no actus reus in respect of A), if he accidentally kills B during his attempt to kill A, his mens rea in respect of A will be transferred to the killing of B. Thus, the actus reus and mens rea are said to coincide.[4] This, of course, is another creative way of circumventing the strict principle of coincidence.

[4] As the doctrine of transferred malice is difficult to explain, you could use an example to aid your explanation.

Another way of circumventing the principle of coincidence invented by the courts is the 'continuing act theory'. This was developed in the case of *Fagan* v *Metropolitan Police Commissioner* [1969] 1 QB 439. In this case, the defendant's act of driving on to the police officer's foot was deemed to be continuing until he later formed the mens rea when he realised and failed to drive off the officer's foot.[5] Thus, the court was 'willing to stretch the concept of an act in order to ensure that cases fall within the principle of coincidence' (Monaghan, N., *Criminal Law Directions* (2012), Oxford: Oxford University Press, p. 71). This theory was also applied in the case of *Kaitamaki* [1985] AC 147 in respect of sexual intercourse in rape. This has since been incorporated into statute under section 79(2) of the Sexual Offences Act 2003.[6]

[5] If you wish to refer to the facts of the case, then you should do so as briefly as possible and by way of explanation of your point.

[6] Demonstrate your wider knowledge of the law by providing a further example of when the continuing act theory was applied in a later authority/statute.

The courts have also avoided the principle of coincidence by the creation and application of the 'duty' principle. This was first applied in *Miller* [1983] 2 AC 161, in which it was held that where a defendant inadvertently creates a dangerous situation by his actions, the law imposes a duty on him to act to avert that danger. The defendant will be liable when he fails to act to fulfil that duty, having realised that he has caused that danger and it is only at this stage that the mens rea is formed. This approach was more recently followed by the Divisional Court in *DPP* v *Santana-Bermudez* [2003] EWHC 2908 (Admin).

The courts have circumvented the application of the coincidence principle by inventing the 'single transaction' principle, by which the courts interpret a number of consecutive events as one single transaction. This was applied in the case of *Thabo Meli* v *R* [1954]

1 WLR 288, in which the defendants tried to kill the victim and then, believing him to be dead, they rolled his body off a cliff. The victim died later. While the defendants had the mens rea for murder when they first tried to kill the victim, they did not have the mens rea for murder when they actually caused the victim's death by rolling him off the cliff. Thus, there was no coincidence of actus reus and mens rea. Nevertheless, the court held that the series of acts constituted a single transaction and that the defendants would be guilty of murder provided they formed the mens rea at some stage during that trans-action. This principle has since been applied in cases such as *Church* [1966] 1 QB 59, *Le Brun* [1991] 4 All ER 673 and *Attorney General's Reference* (No. 4 of 1980) [1981] 1 WLR 705.[7]

[7] If you have time, you could compare these cases as there are some significant differences between them, yet the courts have reached the same conclusion as to liability.

Finally, it has been argued that the rules on voluntary intoxication laid down in *DPP v Majewski* [1977] AC 443 also violate the prin-ciple of coincidence. Lord Elwyn-Jones held that a defendant who becomes intoxicated is reckless and thus he has the mens rea for any basic intent offence. The mens rea is formed before the actus reus of the offence is performed, while the defendant becomes intoxicated.[8] This rule, however, presumes that the defendant is reckless, despite a clear lack of subjective recklessness, and thus violates the principle of coincidence.

[8] Draw on your wider knowledge of the criminal law and examine the application of this defence as well. A well-voiced criticism of *Majewski* is that it violates the principle of coincidence.

In conclusion, while the principle of coincidence clearly has an important role to play in criminal law, the courts have used various inventive methods to circumvent the fundamental principle of coin-cidence in order to suit their desire to ensure criminal liability.

✓ **Make your answer stand out**

- You could consider the rationale underlying the principle of coincidence.
- You should include some discussion of the justifications for imposing criminal liability for offences of strict liability and provide some examples of cases.
- You should expand upon some of the exceptions to the principle of coincidence as well as the rationale for the courts' creative approach in each case.
- You could make reference to academic opinion on the principle of coincidence. For instance, see Sullivan, G.R., Cause and the contemporaneity of actus reus and mens rea [1993] CLJ 487 and Marston, G., Contemporaneity of act and intention in crimes (1970) 86 LQR 208.

! **Don't be tempted to . . .**

- Simply provide the facts of the cases in which the courts have avoided the strict application of the principle of coincidence, such as *Fagan* v *MPC*. There are many cases you could mention in this answer and you will waste valuable time setting out the facts of all of these cases.
- Just set out the obvious exception of strict liability offences. This is not a question on strict liability, but it is one which requires you to think more widely about the criminal law and you should incorporate as many instances of circumventing the principle of coincidence as you can.

www.pearsoned.co.uk/lawexpressqa

 Go online to access more revision support including additional essay and problem questions with diagram plans, You be the marker questions, and download all diagrams from the book.

Murder

How this topic may come up in exams

Murder could be examined by way of an essay or a problem question. Problem scenarios might ask you to discuss murder only, or you might be required to identify and apply the partial defences to murder (see Chapter 3) or other general defences such as self-defence, intoxication or duress in a mixed problem question. Essay questions on murder might ask you to consider the proposed reforms to the definition of murder and the hierarchy of the homicide offences. Alternatively, you may be asked for a critical evaluation of an aspect of the law of murder, such as causation or intention (see Chapter 1).

Attack the question

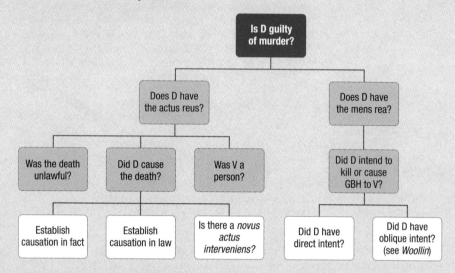

A printable version of this diagram is available from www.pearsoned.co.uk/lawexpressqa

❓ Question 1

Consider the criminal liability of Gareth and Charles for murder in the following scenarios:

(a) Five years ago, Gareth's wife, Sandra, was diagnosed as suffering from a terminal illness. Gareth is devastated at this and becomes extremely distressed while watching his wife's health deteriorate and seeing her suffer and in pain. He decides that he should end her suffering and he kills her.

(b) Charles, a disgruntled employee who was made redundant from his job, storms into his old work place and threatens to shoot staff. Lisa, an employee, panics and jumps out of the window. She dies from the fall. Charles points a gun at Tom, a manager and says 'Die!' before shooting him. Tom sustains a wound to the arm and is taken to hospital. where the severity of his injuries is not recognised and he dies from severe blood loss.

Answer plan

➡ Discuss Coke's definition of murder.

➡ Examine Gareth's liability for murder in respect of the death of his wife, Sandra, including whether Gareth caused the death and whether he had the mens rea of murder.

➡ Examine Charles's liability for murder in respect of Lisa's death and Tom's death, including whether Charles caused those deaths and whether he had the requisite mens rea of murder.

Diagram plan

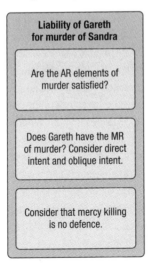

Liability of Gareth for murder of Sandra

Are the AR elements of murder satisfied?

Does Gareth have the MR of murder? Consider direct intent and oblique intent.

Consider that mercy killing is no defence.

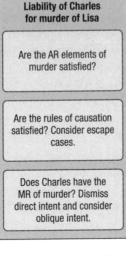

Liability of Charles for murder of Lisa

Are the AR elements of murder satisfied?

Are the rules of causation satisfied? Consider escape cases.

Does Charles have the MR of murder? Dismiss direct intent and consider oblique intent.

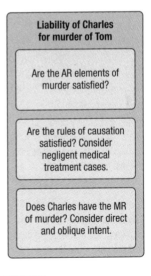

Liability of Charles for murder of Tom

Are the AR elements of murder satisfied?

Are the rules of causation satisfied? Consider negligent medical treatment cases.

Does Charles have the MR of murder? Consider direct and oblique intent.

A printable version of this diagram plan is available from www.pearsoned.co.uk/lawexpressqa

Answer

This question requires consideration of the common law offence of murder. The classic definition of murder is provided by Coke:[1] 'Murder is when a man of sound memory, and of the age of discretion, unlawfully killeth within any county of the realm any reasonable creature *in rerum natura* under the King's peace, with malice aforethought . . .' (3 Inst 47). Thus, the actus reus of murder requires proof that the defendant unlawfully caused the death of the victim (a person in being) within the Queen's peace.[2] The mens rea is 'malice aforethought', which is more commonly expressed today as intention to kill or cause GBH (*Vickers* [1957] 2 QB 664).[3]

Part (a) requires consideration of whether Gareth may be held criminally liable for the murder of his wife, Sandra. Dealing first with the actus reus of murder, the victim is a person in being, there is no evidence of self-defence, thus the killing is unlawful, and if killing occurs within the Queen's peace. Applying the tests of causation, factual causation is established because, but for Gareth's actions, Sandra would not have died. In relation to legal causation, Gareth's actions are the sole cause of death and it is clear that his actions did contribute significantly towards the death (*Pagett* [1983] 75 Cr App R 279). Thus the actus reus of murder is established.

The main question relates to the mens rea. Did Gareth have the necessary mens rea for murder? The question that must be asked is whether Gareth intended to kill Sandra or to cause her GBH? (*Vickers*) In considering direct intention first, it could be argued that Gareth's aim or purpose was not to kill or cause GBH to his wife, but it was to end her suffering. If so, then killing her or causing GBH was not his direct intention.[4] Thus, the virtual certainty test from *Woollin* [1999] AC 82 would then need to be applied in relation to oblique intention: was death or GBH virtually certain to occur and did Gareth appreciate this?[5] At this stage, it is clear that Gareth would have no defence since the Court of Appeal has held that mercy killing is no defence to a charge of murder in English law (*Inglis* [2011] 1 WLR 1110). It is clear that Gareth foresaw Sandra's death as virtually certain to occur in such circumstances; thus, at the very least, oblique intention can be established. Consequently, the mens rea for murder will be present and Gareth will be guilty of murder.

[1] As this question is about one offence, you should begin by defining the offence.

[2] This sentence shows that you have identified the actus reus elements within the definition.

[3] You should set out the mens rea in its more modern form rather than relying on the misleading phrase 'malice aforethought'.

[4] If there is clearly no direct intent, you should rule this out before discussing whether the test for oblique intent is satisfied.

[5] Ensure you state the test fully and accurately before you apply the law to the facts in the problem scenario.

Part (b) involves consideration of whether Charles may be guilty of the murders of Lisa and Tom. In relation to the death of Lisa, the actus reus of murder should be considered first. Lisa is clearly a person, there is no evidence of self-defence (thus the killing is unlawful) and the killing occurs within the Queen's peace. However, it may be difficult to establish causation. The rules of causation must be applied. Applying the test for factual causation (the 'but for' test from **White** [1910] 2 KB 124), but for Charles storming into the building and threatening to shoot, Lisa would not have jumped out the window and died, thus factual causation is established. In relation to legal causation, Charles's actions do not need to be the sole cause of death, as long as they contributed significantly towards death (**Pagett**). Alternatively, it could be asked whether Charles's actions were a 'substantial and operative cause' of death (**Smith** [1959] 2 QB 35). It is clear that although Charles's actions may not have been the only cause of death, they were a 'substantial' or 'significant' cause of death. Consideration must also be given to whether Lisa's action of jumping out of the window breaks the chain of causation. The actions of a victim will not break the chain of causation where they are reasonably foreseeable and involuntary, but they will break the chain of causation where they are 'daft' (**Roberts** (1971) 56 Cr App R 95). Applying this, Lisa's escape might be reasonably foreseeable in light of the fact that Tom was carrying a gun and threatening to use it, but it would be useful to know other facts, such as how high the window was and whether there were any other reasonable escape routes available.[6]

[6] You should never assume facts, but if your answer depends upon the existence of unknown facts you should state this.

It is also necessary to consider the mens rea or murder, which is intention to kill or cause GBH (**Vickers**). It was not Charles's direct intention to kill or cause GBH to Lisa. However, he may have oblique intent. Applying **Woollin**, it would need to be asked whether it was virtually certain that people would try to escape by jumping out of the window, and that they would suffer GBH or die. This question may also depend upon other unknown circumstances, such as whether there were other escape routes. Even if death or GBH was virtually certain, it would then need to be shown that Charles appreciated this. If oblique intention can be established, then the mens rea for murder will also be present and Charles will be guilty of Lisa's murder. However, if there is no oblique intent, he will not be guilty of murder.

In relation to Tom's death, the key issue with the actus reus for murder is causation. The other elements of the actus reus are present because Tom is a person, the death is unlawful as there is no evidence of self-defence and it occurs within the Queen's peace. Applying the test for factual causation, but for Charles shooting Tom, he would not have been misdiagnosed and would not have died (**White**). In relation to legal causation, although Charles's actions may not have been the only cause of death, Charles's act of shooting Tom was a 'substantial' cause of death (**Smith**).

The courts are reluctant to find that negligent medical treatment breaks the chain of causation so as to absolve a defendant of liability. In the exceptional case of **Jordan** [1956] 40 Cr App R 152, the chain of causation was deemed to be broken where the medical treatment was 'palpably wrong'. However, this is an extreme example and is limited to its own facts.[7] Applying the leading case of **Cheshire** [1991] 1 WLR 844, it must be asked whether the doctor's act of misdiagnosing Tom's injuries was so independent of Charles's act and so potent in causing Tom's death that it renders Charles's actions insignificant. In light of these authorities, it is very unlikely that the actions of the doctor will break the chain of causation, thus Charles was the legal cause of Tom's death.[8]

The mens rea is also present: it was Charles's direct intention to kill Tom because this was his aim or his purpose. This is evident when he says the word 'Die!' immediately before shooting Tom.[9]

[7] This sentence demonstrates that you understand the limited effect of this authority and the fact that it is unlikely to be applied.

[8] Ensure that you provide short conclusions at significant points throughout your answer, such as here after dealing with the actus reus of murder.

[9] Even though this element is obviously present, you must apply the law, i.e. explain why the element is fulfilled.

✓ **Make your answer stand out**

- Ensure that you structure your answer in a logical way. Where there is more than one defendant, deal with each defendant's liability in full before moving on to the next defendant.
- In establishing a defendant's liability, you should ensure that you have defined murder (using Coke's definition) before applying the actus reus elements, and finally the mens rea.
- Ensure that you apply both limbs of the test for oblique intent, if relevant.
- You could also incorporate some academic critique into your answer.

Question 2

The common law relating to murder and manslaughter has developed in a piecemeal way. Consequently, the current framework of homicide offences lacks coherence and is in need of reform.

Discuss.

Answer plan

→ Refer to the development of the common law, including Coke's definition of murder.

→ Examine the scope of murder, including problems defining the mens rea of murder.

→ Outline the relationship between murder and manslaughter.

→ Look at defences and partial defences which are available to a charge of murder.

→ Conclude with the Law Commission proposals for reform and academic critique.

Diagram plan

A printable version of this diagram plan is available from www.pearsoned.co.uk/lawexpressqa

Answer

There are currently two main homicide offences: murder and manslaughter. These are two of the most serious criminal offences and they carry heavy penalties: mandatory life and discretionary life imprisonment respectively. In light of their severity, it is vital that the scope of these offences and their relationship is clearly defined.[1] However, the law of homicide has been governed by a mixture of common law and statute, none of which has been coherent and systematic. The law has developed in a piecemeal way; one example is the development of the defence of provocation (now loss of control). This has led to the current framework of offences, which lacks coherent structure, and offences of murder and manslaughter which are too broad.[2] The Law Commission's recommendations for reform involves extending the two current offences into three and provides a sensible hierarchy of offences, which 'relates to the principles of fair and representative labelling'[3] (Rogers, J., 'The Law Commission's proposed restructuring of homicide' (2006) 70(3) JCL 223).

Coke's classic definition of murder is still cited today: 'Murder is when a man of sound memory, and of the age of discretion, unlawfully killeth within any county of the realm any reasonable creature *in rerum natura* under the King's peace, with malice aforethought . . .' (3 Inst 47). The common law has sought to clarify the meaning of terms such as 'reasonable creature *in rerum natura*' and 'malice aforethought' and statutory provisions have made further amendments to the scope of murder, such as the Law Reform (Year and a Day Rule) Act 1996. While the Homicide Act 1957 dealt with the partial defences to murder, it failed to provide new definitions of murder or manslaughter or to deal with the wider issue of the grading of homicide offences.[4]

For many years, the scope of murder was uncertain and confused. This was largely due to the problem the courts had in defining 'intention' within the mens rea of murder. Murder requires proof of an intention to kill or cause GBH (***Vickers*** [1957] 2 QB 664). At one stage, 'intention' was widely defined to include the defendant's foresight of the consequences as highly probable to occur (***Hyam*** [1975] AC 55). This blurred the line between intention and recklessness, and thus between the offences of murder and manslaughter. Although the law on oblique intent is currently more settled (see ***Nedrick*** [1986] 1 WLR 1025 and ***Woollin*** [1999] AC 82), the offence of murder covers too broad a range of killings. Oblique intent is currently sufficient mens rea for murder, as is an intention to cause GBH.[5] This raises questions about the current scope of murder and

Margin notes

[1] This shows that you understand why the structure and grading of homicide offences is important.

[2] Identify the key problems with the law at the start.

[3] This sentence identifies a key objective which the reforms aim to achieve.

[4] This sentence demonstrates your understanding of the development of the law and the failures of previous legislation.

[5] Show that you know why the offence of murder is deemed to be very broad in its scope. The key to this lies in the mens rea of the offence which encompasses more than a mere intention to kill.

the relationship between murder and manslaughter. A more appropriate grading system might be adopted in order to distinguish between these different degrees of culpability.

The law on voluntary manslaughter has also been plagued with problems. The defence of provocation has caused confusion in recent years; although it was recently abolished by the Coroners and Justice Act 2009, which created a new partial defence of loss of control. Similarly, diminished responsibility has been the subject of reform. These reforms, however necessary, still fail to deal with the overall structure of the law of homicide and merely add to the piecemeal developments which have taken place over the years.[6]

[6] This statement shows the examiner that your knowledge of the law is up to date. It also directly relates the recent reforms back to the title.

Involuntary manslaughter is also a very wide offence. The mens rea of unlawful act manslaughter requires proof only that the reasonable man would foresee the risk of some harm, and not that the defendant himself foresaw the risk of death: *Church* [1966] 1 QB 59. This would cover a defendant such as the 'one-punch killer' (Mitchell, B., 'Minding the gap in unlawful and dangerous act manslaughter' (2008) 72 JCL 537) as well as a defendant who foresaw a very real risk of death, such as one who set fire to a block of flats at night. According to Rogers: 'The law of involuntary manslaughter is also too broad insofar as it currently equates cases which are not far short of murder, such as those defendant who firebomb houses in order to scare . . . with cases which (absent the misfortune of death) would ordinarily be nothing more than assaults . . .' Similarly, gross negligence manslaughter contains a broad and objectively assessed requirement that the defendant's conduct is 'so bad in all the circumstances as to amount . . . to a criminal act or omission' (*Adomako* [1995] 1 AC 171). These broad offences are also accompanied by a third head of subjectively reckless manslaughter. Although a subjectively reckless killing is arguably more culpable than killing by gross negligence, both are currently sufficient for manslaughter, demonstrating further incoherence in the present framework of offences.[7]

[7] Try to make a reference to the title at the end of each paragraph, summarising how the point you have made within that paragraph is directly relevant to the question.

In 2005, the Law Commission published a Consultation Paper, *A New Homicide Act for England and Wales?* (No. 177), recommending a new Homicide Act which would provide definitions of murder, manslaughter and the partial defences to murder. The Commission recommends a grading structure of homicide offences which reflects different levels of culpability. The most serious offence of first degree murder would be reserved for intentional killings and would carry a mandatory life sentence. The next serious offence would be second degree murder, which would cover killings with the intention of causing GBH, reckless killings with an indifference to risk, and killings where there is a partial defence to first degree murder. This offence would carry a discretionary life maximum sentence. Finally, the offence of manslaughter would cover killing through gross negligence and killing through an intentional act intended to cause injury or involving recklessness as to whether injury was caused or not. This offence would carry a maximum sentence of ten years' imprisonment.

These recommendations are welcomed by academics who applaud the restriction of the scope of murder and manslaughter and the creation of a three-tier framework. While first degree murder is reserved for intentional killings, other less culpable killings are more fairly labelled as second degree murder.[8] Professor Dennis comments that the recommendations would also reduce the scope of manslaughter and 'result in a more coherent offence of manslaughter in terms of labelling' ('Reviewing the law of homicide' [2006] Crim LR 187).

[8] An ability to summarise academic opinion as well as quoting directly from journal articles demonstrates your understanding of academic literature.

However, there are some criticisms of the recommendations. Rogers calls for cases where the victim has consented to being killed to be given further consideration.[9] Under the recommendations, a mercy killing would fall under first degree murder because it is an intentional killing. Rogers argues that consent should be recognised as a partial defence to first degree murder, thus recognising the distinction between mercy killing and other types of intentional killing.

[9] This sentence provides an example of a criticism of the proposed reforms and shows that you appreciate both the positive and negative aspects of the recommendations.

The current broad homicide offences are in need of reform so that a more coherent framework of offences might be established. While the recommendations of the Law Commission are favoured by academics, Parliament has yet to make any significant movement towards reform.

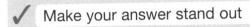

✓ Make your answer stand out

- You could critically evaluate the Law Commission's recommendation that duress may amount to a partial defence to first degree murder.

- You could consider the practical implications on plea bargaining and the argument that the proposed structure would provide defendants with more incentive to maintain a not guilty plea to first degree murder and prosecutors with more incentive to accept a guilty plea to second degree murder.

- You should refer to further academic writing on the recommendations, such as Wilson, W., The structure of criminal homicide [2006] Crim LR 471 and Ashworth, A., Principles, pragmatism and the Law Commission's recommendations on homicide law reform [2007] Crim LR 333.

- You might offer a comparative view of the structure of homicide offences in other common law countries such as the US, Australia, Canada, New Zealand.

! Don't be tempted to . . .

- Simply set out the current law on murder and manslaughter – you are being asked specifically about the framework of homicide offences and reform.

- Use this question as an excuse to just 'rant' about the law of homicide. Instead, you must provide a structured critique of the structure of homicide offences and the proposed reforms.

- Focus on just one element of murder or manslaughter. This question is looking for a much wider appreciation of the scope of murder and manslaughter and their relationship.

www.pearsoned.co.uk/lawexpressqa

Go online to access more revision support including additional essay and problem questions with diagram plans, You be the marker questions, and download all diagrams from the book.

Voluntary manslaughter

How this topic may come up in exams

Voluntary manslaughter lends itself well to both essay and problem questions. As the law on loss of control and diminished responsibility has recently been reformed by the Coroners and Justice Act 2009, this is a ripe area for an essay question requiring a critical evaluation of the new defence of loss of control and a comparison with the common law defence of provocation. Similarly, an essay question might require consideration of the reforms of diminished responsibility, or even of partial defences more generally. Alternatively, examiners may favour a problem question which deals with one or both partial defences.

Attack the question

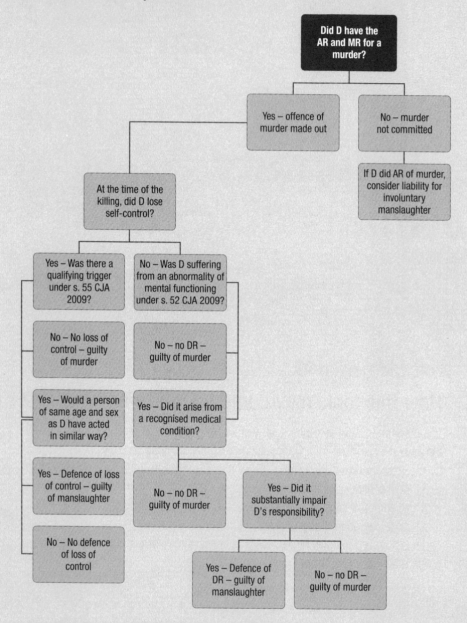

A printable version of this diagram is available from www.pearsoned.co.uk/lawexpressqa

❓ Question 1

Manisha and Angelo have been unhappily married for ten years. Angelo has often hit Manisha, causing bruising. He has also had a string of affairs and has recently begun an affair with Manisha's best friend, Rita. Manisha knows about Angelo's history of extra-marital affairs. One evening, when Angelo comes home very late, Manisha suspects that he has spent the evening with Rita. Manisha, who has drunk a bottle of vodka over the course of the evening, confronts Angelo when he returns home, asking him where he has been. At this moment, Angelo's mobile rings and Manisha notices that 'Leggy Rita' flashes up on the screen. Manisha makes a grab for the phone but Angelo strikes her and snatches the phone from Manisha, saying 'I'll give you a hiding later'. Manisha goes into the kitchen and picks up a carving knife. When she emerges, Manisha stabs Angelo repeatedly in the back, killing him.

Manisha is charged with murder. Discuss the likelihood of Manisha's defence of loss of control being successful.

Answer plan

→ Outline the effect of a successful plea of loss of control.

→ Assess the legal and evidential burdens.

→ Discuss the elements of loss of control.

→ Did Manisha suffer a loss of control?

→ Was there a qualifying trigger?

→ Assess whether a person of Manisha's sex and age, with a normal degree of tolerance and self-restraint and in the circumstances of Manisha, might have reacted in the same or a similar way to Manisha.

Diagram plan

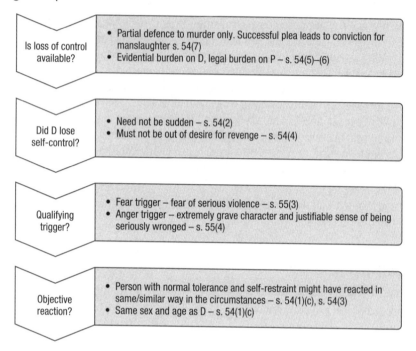

Is loss of control available?	• Partial defence to murder only. Successful plea leads to conviction for manslaughter s. 54(7) • Evidential burden on D, legal burden on P – s. 54(5)–(6)
Did D lose self-control?	• Need not be sudden – s. 54(2) • Must not be out of desire for revenge – s. 54(4)
Qualifying trigger?	• Fear trigger – fear of serious violence – s. 55(3) • Anger trigger – extremely grave character and justifiable sense of being seriously wronged – s. 55(4)
Objective reaction?	• Person with normal tolerance and self-restraint might have reacted in same/similar way in the circumstances – s. 54(1)(c), s. 54(3) • Same sex and age as D – s. 54(1)(c)

A printable version of this diagram plan is available from www.pearsoned.co.uk/lawexpressqa

Answer

¹ This statement demonstrates that you have picked up on the fact that the focus of the question is the defence of loss of control and not the offence of murder.

² Show the examiner that you have a wider understanding of practical issues such as who bears the evidential burden and who bears the legal burden.

³ Adopt a logical and clear structure. State that there are three elements and then deal with each one in turn.

As Manisha is charged with murder, she may plead loss of control, which is a defence to murder only.¹ It is a statutory defence which was created by section 54(1) of the Coroners and Justice Act 2009 ('CJA 2009'). Section 56 abolished the common law defence of provocation. Loss of control is a partial defence to murder, which, if successful, reduces liability to manslaughter (s. 54(7)). While the defence bears the evidential burden to adduce evidence with respect to the defence (s. 54(6)), the legal burden of disproving the defence beyond reasonable doubt rests with the prosecution (s. 54(5)).²

Under section 54(1), there are three main elements of the defence of loss of control:³ (a) at the time of the killing, Manisha must have suffered a loss of self-control; (b) the loss of control must have had a qualifying trigger under section 55; and (c) someone of the same age and sex as Manisha, with a normal degree of tolerance and self-restraint and in the circumstances of Manisha, might have reacted in the same or a similar way to Manisha.

The first element to consider is whether there was a loss of self-control. This is subjectively assessed – the key question is whether, in stabbing Angelo, Manisha lost self-control. It is clear on the facts that Manisha launched a frenzied attack on Angelo, stabbing him repeatedly; thus, there is evidence that Manisha did indeed lose self-control.[4] However, immediately prior to the attack and after the event which triggered the attack, Manisha went into the kitchen. This raises the question of whether there was a delay between the trigger and the killing. However, whereas the old common law defence of provocation required that the loss of self-control be 'sudden and temporary' (**Duffy** [1949] 1 All ER 932),[5] under the CJA 2009, 'it does not matter whether or not the loss of control was sudden' (s. 54(2)). Thus, any delay would not be relevant. Under section 54(4), the defence will not be available if Manisha 'acted in a considered desire for revenge'. This is consistent with the old common law which precluded the defence of provocation where the defendant had planned an attack out of revenge: **Ibrams** [1981] 74 Cr App R 154. The delay might be suggestive of planned revenge and if Manisha is acting out of revenge, rather than as a result of a loss of self-control, the defence will not be available to her. However, in the circumstances she is likely to be able to counter the suggestion that she is acting in revenge.

[4] Use the facts to apply the law to this specific problems scenario.

[5] This demonstrates an awareness of how the old defence of provocation and the new defence of loss of control differ.

As there is evidence of a loss of self-control, the next question to consider is whether there is a qualifying trigger under section 55. There are two types of qualifying trigger under the CJA 2009 and either one or a combination of both of them is sufficient for loss of control (s. 55(5)). The first is the 'fear trigger' under section 55(3), which applies where Manisha's 'loss of self-control was attributable to [her] fear of serious violence' from Angelo against Manisha.[6] Manisha has suffered an abusive relationship for years and, immediately prior to the attack, Angelo tells Manisha that he will give her 'a hiding' later. Thus, Manisha's loss of self-control may be attributable to her fear of serious violence.

[6] Deal with each type of qualifying trigger in turn, setting out the law and then applying it to the facts of the scenario.

The second trigger is the 'anger trigger',[7] which is 'attributable to a thing or things done or said (or both) which (a) constituted circumstances of an extremely grave character, and (b) caused [Manisha] to have a justifiable sense of being seriously wronged' (s. 55(4)).

[7] Use a new paragraph to deal with the second type of trigger in order to ensure your answer is easy to read.

There is some evidence that Manisha may have reacted as a result of the phone call which Angelo received from Rita. This may have fuelled Manisha's suspicions that Angelo has been having an affair with Rita. Background information about Manisha and Angelo's relationship may be taken into account as it would have been taken into account in respect of provocation (see **Humphreys** [1995] 4 All ER 889). However, sexual infidelity must be disregarded as a qualifying trigger (s. 55(6)(c)), although it may be considered as part of the contextual background to a case where there is another potential qualifying trigger (**Clinton** [2012] EWCA Crim 2). This means that any sexual infidelity by Angelo may not be taken into account as a qualifying trigger for Manisha's loss of self-control. However, if there is evidence that Manisha may have suffered a loss of self-control as a result of fear of serious violence, any sexual infidelity may be considered as part of the contextual background to the case.[8]

[8] Ensure that you include a brief conclusion at the end of your discussion about each element before you move onto the next element.

The third element of loss of control requires that someone of the same age and sex as Manisha, with a normal degree of tolerance and self-restraint and in the same circumstances as Manisha, might have reacted in the same or a similar way. This follows the approach taken in respect of the common law in **DPP v Camplin** [1978] 2 All ER 168 and **AG for Jersey v Holley** [2005] UKPC 23 and is objectively assessed.[9] The age and sex of the defendant may be taken into account. Thus, the question is whether a woman of Manisha's age, with normal levels of tolerance and self-restraint but placed in the same circumstances as Manisha, *might* have reacted in the same way, or at the very least, in a similar way.[10] According to section 54(3), the phrase 'all the circumstances' within section 54(1)(c) does not refer to circumstances which are relevant to the defendant's 'general capacity for tolerance and self-restraint'. Thus, characteristics which go to the gravity of the provocation are relevant, but characteristics which go to the level of control to be expected of the defendant are not to be taken into account. Manisha's intoxication may not be taken into account as a control characteristic, i.e. Manisha's response must be measured against a sober person of normal tolerance and self-restraint.

[9] This sentence demonstrates that you understand how the CJA 2009 has developed from the old common law defence of provocation.

[10] Rephrase the law so as to show how it will be applied in this scenario.

In conclusion, Manisha's defence of loss of control is likely to be successful if based upon her fear of serious violence. However, it will be for the jury to decide whether a woman of Manisha's age with a normal degree of tolerance and self-restraint, might have reacted in the same or a similar way.

✓ **Make your answer stand out**

- You should demonstrate very good knowledge of the new statutory provisions under sections 54 and 55 of the CJA 2009 and the way in which these provisions are applied.
- You should also refer to relevant cases relating to the old common law defence of provocation as the courts may refer to these cases in interpreting the new legislation.
- You should refer to any new cases on loss of control that are relevant, such as *Clinton* [2012] EWCA Crim 2.
- You could make reference to journal articles on the new CJA 2009 and academic opinion on how the new law will work in practice or any problems that might arise, provided this is relevant to the particular facts in the question.
- You could also explain in further detail the meaning of the evidential burden being upon the defendant – see section 54(6), CJA 2009.

❗ **Don't be tempted to . . .**

- Waste time discussing whether the elements of murder are satisfied. The question tells you that Manisha has been charged with murder and specifically asks you about the *defence* of loss of control, so you should focus on this. You must ensure that you read the instruction line carefully.
- Focus solely on explaining and applying the old law. You should refer to the old common law defence of provocation to demonstrate your knowledge of how the law has changed, and you must incorporate the new legislation on loss of control.

❓ Question 2

Percy and Coleen have been in a relationship for three years and started living together a year ago. Their relationship has always been happy one, but recently Percy was made redundant and this affected him quite badly. Coleen notices that Percy has become increasingly withdrawn and fears that he may be suffering from depression. Percy becomes more irritable and begins to snap at Coleen for seemingly trivial things. Eventually, Coleen decides to confront the issue and she tries to persuade Percy to go to see his doctor to get some help. When Percy refuses to even discuss the subject, Coleen becomes frustrated and when he turns away from her she throws a book at Percy and shouts, 'You're never going to get another job are you? You're supposed to look after me!' The book strikes Percy on the back. Percy then picks up a solid silver candlestick and throws it at Coleen. It strikes her on the head, killing her.

Consider the liability of Percy for the death of Coleen.

Answer plan

→ Examine the elements of murder and whether Percy can be charged with this offence.

→ Discuss the likelihood that Percy will successfully be able to plead loss of control under section 54, CJA 2009.

→ Could Percy plead diminished responsibility under section 52, CJA 2009?

Diagram plan

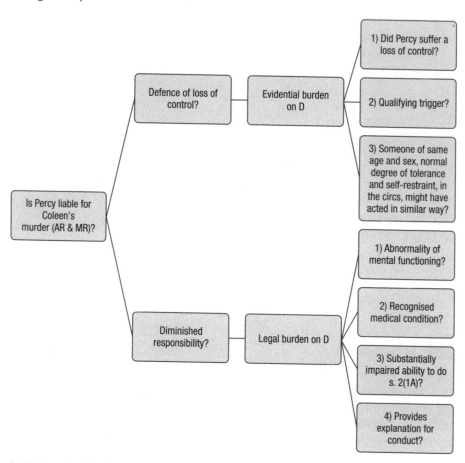

A printable version of this diagram plan is available from www.pearsoned.co.uk/lawexpressqa

Answer

As Percy has killed Coleen, he will most likely be charged with her murder.[1] Percy is both the factual and legal cause of Coleen's death. 'But for' his actions, she would not have died (*White* [1910] 2 KB 124) and his actions were an operating and substantial cause of her death (*Smith* [1959] 2 QB 35).[2] The mens rea for murder will be established by evidence of Percy's act of throwing a solid silver candlestick directly at Coleen. This demonstrates at least an intention to cause GBH, and possibly an intention to kill, thus it seems most likely that Percy would be charged with murder. However, he may plead the partial defences of loss of control or diminished responsibility. These are both statutory defences and they are defences to murder only. If Percy is successful in pleading either loss of control or diminished responsibility he will be convicted of manslaughter instead of murder.[3]

[1] As the question does not specify an offence with which Percy has been charged but asks you to consider his liability, you should begin by identifying the offence he will likely be charged with.

[2] This sentence applies the rules of causation succinctly and is all that you need bearing in mind the number of issues in the question and the fact that causation is not really controversial here.

[3] This sentence shows that you understand the implications of a successful plea of these defences.

Loss of control is a partial defence under section 54(1) of the Coroners and Justice Act 2009 ('CJA 2009'). There are three main elements of the defence of loss of control: (a) at the time of the killing, Percy must have suffered a loss of self-control; (b) the loss of control must have had a qualifying trigger under section 55; and (c) someone of the same age and sex as Percy, with a normal degree of tolerance and self-restraint and in the circumstances of Percy, might have reacted in the same or a similar way to Percy. Percy will bear the evidential burden to adduce evidence with respect to the defence. This means that he must adduce sufficient evidence 'to raise an issue with respect to the defence . . . which, in the opinion of the trial judge, a jury, properly directed, could reasonably conclude that the defence might apply' (s. 54(6)). However, the legal burden of disproving the defence beyond reasonable doubt rests with the prosecution (s. 54(5)).

The first element requires proof that Percy suffered a loss of self-control. This is subjectively assessed. There is certainly evidence of a loss of self-control. There is no delay between the trigger and Percy's act of throwing the candlestick, and in fact under the CJA 2009, 'it does not matter whether or not the loss of control was sudden' (s. 54(2)). Percy's defence would be negated by any evidence that he 'acted in a considered desire for revenge' (s. 54(4)).

If there is a loss of control, it must also be shown that there is a qualifying trigger under section 55. Under section 55(5), CJA 2009 either the 'fear trigger' or the 'anger trigger' or both is sufficient for the defence of loss of control. The 'fear trigger' (s. 55(3)) applies if Percy's 'loss of self-control was attributable to [his] fear of serious violence' from Coleen. Percy might argue that his loss of self-control was attributable to his fear of serious violence after Coleen throws a book at him. However, this is unlikely to succeed as it is not likely that Percy feared serious violence from the single act of the book being thrown at him. Furthermore, there is no evidence of previous abuse within the relationship. Nevertheless, this is a subjective test, so this would depend upon whether Percy honestly feared serious violence.

The 'anger trigger' is one which is 'attributable to a thing or things done or said (or both) which (a) constituted circumstances of an extremely grave character, and (b) caused [Percy] to have a justifiable sense of being seriously wronged' (s. 55(4)). It is not clear what exactly constitutes things said and done of an extremely grave character, which cause a justifiable sense of being seriously wronged. Only if Coleen's act of throwing the book at Percy and taunting him with being unable to get a job and not looking after her is of extremely grave character and caused him a justifiable sense of being seriously wronged could it be said that the 'anger trigger' applies. This is quite unlikely on the facts, and here there is no clear evidence of either trigger.

In the event that a trigger can be established, the third element of loss of control requires that someone of the same age and sex as Percy, with a normal degree of tolerance and self-restraint and in the same circumstances as Percy, might have reacted in the same or a similar way. This element is objectively assessed and only the age and sex of the defendant may be taken into account, along with the circumstances of the defendant which do not bear on the defendant's 'general capacity for tolerance and self-restraint' (s. 54(3)). Thus, the fact that Percy suffers from depression will not be a relevant consideration, as he is expected to exercise the level of control of a person of his age and sex of normal tolerance and self-restraint.[4] The defence of loss of control is unlikely to be successful.

However, there is another partial defence open to Percy, that of diminished responsibility under section 2(1) of the Homicide Act 1957 ('HA 1957') (as amended by s. 52 of the CJA 2009).[5] Unlike the defence of loss of control, the burden of proving diminished responsibility is on the defence (s. 2(2), HA 1957) and the elements

[4] Ensure that you notice any characteristics that are mentioned within the question and explain whether these will be taken into account and why.

[5] Show the examiner that you understand that the CJA 2009 does not create a new defence but merely amends the existing defence under section 2(1), HA 1957.

of diminished responsibility must be proved on a balance of probabilities (The defendant must prove that at the time of the killing: (i) he was suffering from an abnormality of mental functioning, (ii) which arose from a recognised medical condition (s. 2(1)(a)), (iii) substantially impaired the defendant's ability to understand the nature of his conduct, to form a rational judgment, or to exercise self-control (s. 2(1)(b) and s. 2(1A)), and (iv) which provides an explanation for the defendant's acts and omissions in the killing (s. 2(1)(c)). On the facts, Percy is suffering from depression, which is likely to constitute an abnormality of mental functioning arising from a recognised medical condition (**Seers** (1984) 79 Cr App R 26).[6] It is also likely that the defence will be able to prove that this substantially impaired Percy's ability to form a rational judgment or to exercise self-control. Finally, under section 2(1B), this will provide an explanation for Percy's conduct in throwing the candlestick if it causes, or is a significant contributory factor in causing, him to carry out that conduct. On the facts, the defence of diminished responsibility is likely to be successful.

[6] Use existing case law to support your argument that depression amounts to an abnormality of mental functioning.

In conclusion,[7] Percy caused the death of Coleen and had the requisite mens rea for murder. He is more likely to be successful with a plea of diminished responsibility, although it will be for the jury to decide whether his depression caused, or was a significant contributory factor in causing, him to throw the candlestick. It is likely that he will be convicted of manslaughter.

[7] Use the conclusion to briefly summarise the issues, but do not regurgitate your arguments all over again.

✓ Make your answer stand out

- Ensure that you adopt an appropriate and clear structure. You should deal with offences before looking at the elements of the possible defences.

- If you are not permitted to take your statute book into the exam with you, you should learn the important parts of the statutory provisions so that you can quote from the relevant sections. If you are permitted a statute book in the exam, you should still ensure that you are familiar with the sections to save yourself time in the exam.

- Ensure that you understand the effect of the new law under the CJA 2009 to both defences. While the CJA 2009 created the new defence of loss of control (abolishing provocation), it merely amends the HA 1957 in respect of diminished responsibility.

- Refer to case law where appropriate. In order to do this you will need to be familiar with the various principles which have remained the same and those which have changed as a result of the 2009 Act.

! **Don't be tempted to . . .**

■ Spend too much time setting out the definition and elements of murder, and do not labour over the rules of causation as they are relatively uncontroversial here and there are many other more important issues to discuss.

■ Make the mistake of using this question as a forum for comparing the old and the new law, although you do need to show an awareness of the old law. This is a problem question and you are expected to explain how the current law will affect Percy.

🔯 Question 3

Critically evaluate the new defence of loss of control. To what extent has the defence improved the law?

Answer plan

→ Consider the rationale behind the reforms and the abolition of the defence of provocation.

→ Discuss the subjective requirement of a loss of control which need not be sudden.

→ Refer to the new requirement of a qualifying trigger.

→ Examine the specific exclusion of sexual infidelity as a qualifying trigger and the case of *Clinton* [2012] EWCA Crim 2.

→ Discuss the objective question which takes into account the age, sex and circumstances of the defendant.

→ Evaluate academic opinion on the new defence.

Diagram plan

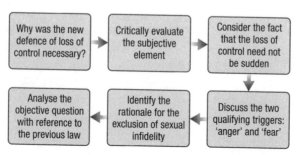

A printable version of this diagram plan is available from www.pearsoned.co.uk/lawexpressqa

Answer

The Coroners and Justice Act 2009 has made fundamental changes to the partial defences to murder. Section 54(1) created a new partial defence of loss of control and section 56 abolished the old common law defence of provocation and repealed section 3 of the Homicide Act 1957. The defence of provocation has always been the subject of criticism. The subjective limb of the defence, which required proof that the defendant suffered a 'sudden and temporary' loss of self-control (**Duffy** [1949] 1 All ER 932), was criticised for failing to protect women in abusive relationships who lashed out as a result of a relatively minor incident of provoking conduct (the 'last straw').[1] There was no guarantee that women suffering from 'battered woman syndrome' would be able to successfully rely upon the defence where there was a delay between the provoking conduct and the killing, and such women would often be left with no choice but to plead diminished responsibility (**Ahluwalia** [1992] 4 All ER 889). The objective limb of the defence has caused the courts considerable confusion for over 60 years, although the situation intensified in the last nine years with conflicting House of Lords and Privy Council decisions in **Smith (Morgan James)** [2000] 4 All ER 289 and **A-G for Jersey v Holley**.[2] Therefore, these reforms were intended to redress the gender imbalance and clarify the law,[3] hopefully putting an end to the criticism and confusion. However, in its short life to date, the new defence of loss of control has already been the subject of academic criticism.

According to section 54(1), the defence of loss of control contains three elements: (i) the defendant's acts or omissions in doing the killing resulted from the defendant's loss of self-control; (ii) the loss of self-control had a qualifying trigger; and (iii) a person of the defendant's sex and age, with a normal degree of tolerance and self-restraint and in the circumstances of the defendant, might have reacted in the same or a similar way.

The first element contains the subjective question: whether the defendant actually lost self-control. Under the new law, there is no requirement that the loss of control was sudden (s. 54(2)). Leigh argues that:[4] 'The implications of this are obscure . . . One can readily see how cumulative abuse might lead to a loss of self-control, but

[1] Having stated that the old law has been criticised, this sentence explains some of the problems with the subjective limb of the old law.

[2] This sentence demonstrates your awareness of some of the problems with the objective limb.

[3] You should show the examiner that you are aware of the reasons for the reforms.

[4] Include academic commentary to show that you have read more than just your textbook.

the notion of loss of self-control as such does rather suggest a sudden point of explosion.' ('Two new partial defences to murder' (2010) 174 JPN 53.) The purpose of the removal of the requirement of suddenness was to protect those who have suffered cumulative abuse, who react after a minor incident (the 'last straw', as in **Humphreys** [1995] 4 All ER 889). This provision is a peculiar addition to a defence dealing with 'loss of control' because, as Leigh points out: 'It is . . . difficult to see how a killing that does not involve a sudden loss of control involves a loss of control at all'.

Section 54(4) stipulates that the defence does not apply if the defendant killed the victim 'in a considered desire for revenge'. This is similar to the case of **Ibrams** [1981] 74 Cr App R 154, which precluded the defence of provocation where the killing was a pre-planned revenge attack; however, one question which remains unanswered is the meaning of 'considered'.[5] Leigh questions 'what degree of deliberation is required in order to exclude [the defence]'. This will be a question for the jury to determine on a case-by-case basis.

[5] This sentence shows you are able to compare both the old and new law and evaluate the new defence.

The second requirement is that the loss of control has a qualifying trigger. Section 55 specifies two types of qualifying trigger which are based upon highly emotional states: the first is the 'fear trigger' under section 55(3), which applies where the 'loss of self-control was attributable to [the defendant's] fear of serious violence' from the victim against the defendant or another identified person. This trigger is similar to self-defence; however, unlike self-defence, it is not available if the defendant was the initial aggressor (s. 55(6)(a)).[6] The second trigger is the 'anger trigger', which is 'attributable to a thing or things done or said (or both) which (a) constituted circumstances of an extremely grave character, and (b) caused [the defendant] to have a justifiable sense of being seriously wronged' (s. 55(4)). Either of these qualifying triggers will be sufficient, or a combination of both of them. It is also notable that the key phrases within these provisions ('serious violence', 'extremely grave character' and 'justifiable sense of being seriously wronged') have not been further defined under the Act and will be left open to interpretation by the courts. Section 55 marks a significant departure from the old law which was much less restrictive in terms of the provoking words or conduct permitted. It seems rather odd that cases such as **Doughty** (1986) 83 Cr App R 319 will no longer be protected by the new defence.[7]

[6] This demonstrates a wider knowledge of the comparative rules relating to general defences in criminal law.

[7] Using an example is an effective way of demonstrating how these reforms will affect the law.

One highly controversial provision is section 55(6)(c), which states that, in determining whether there was a qualifying trigger, sexual infidelity is to be disregarded. The Court of Appeal has recently ruled that while sexual infidelity must be disregarded as a qualifying trigger, it may be considered as part of the contextual background to a case where there is another potential qualifying trigger (*Clinton* [2012] EWCA Crim 2). Section 55(6)(c) was introduced in order to preclude husbands who kill their unfaithful wives from relying upon the defence. This provision was strongly contested in the House of Commons and the government's arguments have been labelled as 'incoherent' (Leigh (2010)). It is difficult to see why sexual infidelity (something which is likely to incite a highly emotional reaction) may not constitute a qualifying trigger, while words spoken of a highly offensive or insulting nature may.[8] The government's objective in ensuring gender equality could be said to have swung too far the other way as a result of this provision.

[8] This sentence provides support for the opinion of the author which is expressed in the next sentence. Ensure that you express the reasons for your opinion.

The final element of loss of control is the objective question which calls for consideration of the reasonableness of the defendant's response. In line with *DPP v Camplin* [1978] 2 All ER 168, two subjective characteristics can be taken into account: sex and age. However, as Norrie points out, 'it is unclear what role "sex" should play' ('The Coroners and Justice Act – partial defences to murder (1) Loss of control' [2010] Crim LR 275). Norrie observes that there is no explanation as to how exactly sex is thought to affect the capacity for self-control. Leigh (2010) states that 'The reference to sex . . . reflects anachronistic views' and argues that 'The relevant factors seem to lie in . . . the relative size and strength of the parties and the existence or not of a state of dependency . . .' Norrie also criticises the reference to age: 'Capacity for self-control is indeed an aspect of maturity, but age is not then the main issue, maturity is.'[9] Thus, problems are also evident with the 'objective' question.

[9] This paragraph contains several references to academic opinion. You will gain marks for crediting the relevant author with their academic opinion as this shows that you are widely read. You run the risk of falling foul of allegations of plagiarism if you do not reference properly.

Although the CJA 2009 may have clarified the law in some respects, the new defence of loss of control is open to significant criticisms and has arguably shifted the 'gender balance' too far.[10]

[10] Ensure that you link your conclusion back to the title and briefly summarise your view.

Make your answer stand out

- You should read the House of Commons debates in Hansard and incorporate the arguments put forward by Claire Ward MP for the government and Dominic Grieve QC MP in opposition into your answer.

- You could also incorporate references to recommendations made by the Law Commission in 2005 and consider the extent to which these reflect the current law.

- You should discuss the theoretical justifications behind the reforms. See Norrie, A., The Coroners and Justice Act 2009 – partial defences to murder (1) Loss of control [2010] Crim LR 275 for a detailed discussion.

- You must discuss the old law on provocation as part of your answer as you need to be able to compare and contrast the old and new law.

- Discuss in more detail the ways in which the new law has improved the law, by creating clarity.

! **Don't be tempted to . . .**

- Spend a disproportionate amount of time discussing the old law and previous cases because you must also show the examiner that you are familiar with the new law.

- Merely set out the new and old law in a narrative fashion. You are required to critically evaluate the new law and this requires you to demonstrate that you are aware of the problems with the old law as well as improvements made by the new law and any problematic areas that you foresee might arise with the new law.

www.pearsoned.co.uk/lawexpressqa

 Go online to access more revision support including additional essay and problem questions with diagram plans, You be the marker questions, and download all diagrams from the book.

Involuntary manslaughter

How this topic may come up in exams

Forms of involuntary manslaughter, such as unlawful act manslaughter, reckless manslaughter and gross negligence manslaughter are popular with examiners and often appear in exam papers in problem scenarios. A problem question would expect you to identify the relevant offences and apply the elements of the offence to the facts in the question. An essay question could ask for a critical evaluation of any offence of involuntary manslaughter. Corporate manslaughter is currently a popular topic for essay questions.

Attack the question

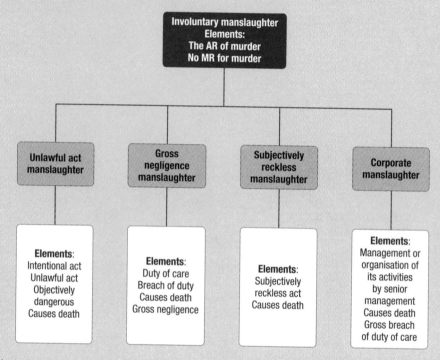

A printable version of this diagram is available from www.pearsoned.co.uk/lawexpressqa

? Question 1

Tom decides to attend his friend's fancy dress Halloween party dressed as an axe murderer. He doesn't have any money to buy some drinks to take with him, so he decides to steal some bottles of beer from an off-licence. He enters the off-licence wielding his axe and shouts at the shopkeeper, 'Don't move or I'll kill you.' The shopkeeper, who has a heart condition, suffers a heart attack due to stress. Tom takes the beer and runs out of the shop. He bumps into an elderly lady on his way out, knocking her to the floor. She sustains a broken leg.

Steve is a newly qualified paramedic who arrives at the scene. He considers the shopkeeper to be a more urgent medical emergency and he steps over the elderly lady in order to go and provide medical assistance to the shopkeeper. Unfortunately, Steve is unable to revive the shopkeeper, who dies. Steve is so traumatised by this experience that he forgets to treat the elderly lady and she dies of hypothermia.

Discuss the criminal liability of Tom and Steve for the deaths of the shopkeeper and the elderly lady only.

Answer plan

→ Consider Tom's liability for unlawful act manslaughter in respect of the death of the shopkeeper.

→ Consider Tom's liability for unlawful act manslaughter or gross negligence manslaughter in respect of the death of the elderly lady.

→ Examine Steve's liability for gross negligence manslaughter in respect of the death of the elderly lady.

Diagram plan

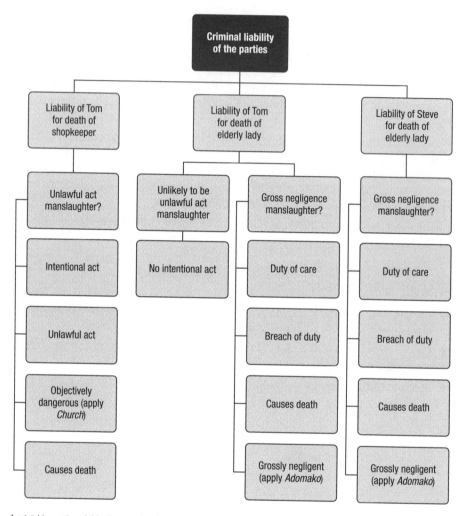

A printable version of this diagram plan is available from www.pearsoned.co.uk/lawexpressqa

[1] As the question specifically asks you to consider the parties' liability for the deaths, there is no need to consider other offences, unless they constitute the unlawful act in unlawful act manslaughter.

Answer

Involuntary manslaughter[1] is charged when the mens rea of murder cannot be established. Neither Tom nor Steve intended to kill or cause GBH (***Vickers*** [1957] 2 QB 664) to the shopkeeper or the elderly lady.[2]

Tom's liability re the shopkeeper

Tom might be guilty of unlawful act manslaughter. This offence was defined in **Larkin** (1944) 29 Cr App R 18: there must be an intentional act, which is unlawful, objectively dangerous and which causes death[3] (Lord Salmon, **DPP v Newbury & Jones** [1977] AC 50).

The prosecution must prove that Tom intentionally did an act. This must be a positive act and not an omission: **Lowe** [1976] QB 702. Tom's act is intentionally entering the shop wielding an axe and shouting threats.

The act must be unlawful in the sense that it must constitute a criminal offence: **Franklin** (1883) 15 Cox CC 163. The criminal act here is robbery. Both the actus reus and mens rea elements of the unlawful act must be established: **Lamb** [1967] 2 QB 981. The elements of robbery under section 8 of the Theft Act 1968 are satisfied. Tom commits theft by stealing bottles of beer and immediately before or at the time of doing so, and in order to do so, he puts or seeks to put the shopkeeper in fear of being then and there subjected to force by shouting threats and wielding an axe.[4]

It must also be proved that the act was objectively dangerous. The test was laid down in **Church** [1966] 1 QB 59, in which it was stated that 'the unlawful act must be such as all sober and reasonable people would inevitably recognise must subject the other person to, at least, the risk of some harm . . . albeit not serious harm' (Edmund Davies J).[5] The reasonable man is deemed to have the knowledge that the defendant had or ought to have had at the time of the offence: **Dawson** (1985) 81 Cr App R 150. If the risk of harm becomes obvious during the commission of the offence, the reasonable man is attributed with that knowledge: **Watson** [1989] 1 WLR 684. It is not clear whether Tom was aware of the shopkeeper's heart condition, although this is unlikely. If he was not aware and ought not to have been aware of the heart condition, then the dangerous element of the offence is not satisfied and Tom will not be liable for unlawful act manslaughter. However, if, after entering the shop, it became apparent that the shopkeeper was a very old and frail man, then Tom ought to have been aware of the risk of some harm, and thus the reasonable man would be attributed with such knowledge and the act would be a dangerous one.[6]

Finally, it must be proved that the robbery caused death. The usual rules of causation apply. Applying the test for factual causation: but for Tom's act of robbery, the shopkeeper would not have died: *White* [1910] 2 KB 124. Tom's act of robbery was also a more than minimal cause of the shopkeeper's death: *Cato* [1976] 1 WLR 110 and there is no intervening event as the defendant must take his victim as he finds him: *Blaue* [1975] 1 WLR 1411.[7] Thus, Tom is likely to be guilty of unlawful act manslaughter.

[7] If causation is easily established, do not waste time writing everything you know about causation. Simply apply the relevant tests succinctly.

Tom's liability re the elderly lady

Tom will probably not be guilty of unlawful act manslaughter re the elderly lady, but he may be convicted of gross negligence manslaughter.

Tom is unlikely to be guilty of unlawful act manslaughter because his act of bumping into the elderly lady and knocking her over is probably not intentional.[8] However, if it were intentional, it is an unlawful act (battery), which is objectively dangerous because a reasonable person would inevitably recognise the risk of some harm, albeit not serious harm: *Church*, and it can be said that he causes her death. The argument that the negligent omission of the paramedic breaks the chain of causation is unlikely to be successful: *Cheshire* [1991] 1 WLR 844.

[8] If there is unlikely to be a conviction for a particular offence, state this at the start of the paragraph and explain why.

Tom is likely to be convicted of gross negligence manslaughter. The prosecution would need to prove that Tom owed her a duty of care, that he breached this duty, that the breach caused her death and that his act or omission was grossly negligent: *Adomako* [1995] 1 AC 171. Whether or not Tom owed the elderly lady a duty of care is a question of law (*Willoughby* [2004] EWCA Crim 3365 and *Evans* [2009] EWCA Crim 650). The judge will direct the jury as to the law and explain that a duty will exist if the jury find certain facts. The ordinary principles of negligence apply to the meaning of 'duty of care' (Lord Mackay in *Adomako*). As there is no existing precedent here, the court will consider the reasonable foreseeability that the elderly lady would be harmed by Tom's conduct, the proximity of their relationship and whether it would be fair, just and reasonable to impose a duty: *Caparo Industries plc v Dickman* [1990] 2 AC 605.

It must be established whether Tom breached his duty. Breach requires that Tom's conduct fell below that to be expected of a reasonable man. The usual rules of causation apply and would be satisfied here:

but for Tom's act of bumping into the elderly lady, she would not have fallen and she would not have died (**White**). Tom's act was a more than minimal cause of death (**Cato**) and the negligence of the paramedic is unlikely to break the chain of causation (**Cheshire**).

Finally, it must be established that Tom's conduct was grossly negligent. This is a question of fact. The jury should consider 'whether having regard to the risk of death involved, the conduct of the defendant was so bad in all the circumstances as to amount in their judgment to a criminal act or omission'[9] (per Lord Mackay). A reasonably prudent person must have foreseen a serious risk of death: **Misra** [2004] EWCA Crim 2375. If Tom's conduct was grossly negligent, Tom will be convicted of gross negligent manslaughter.

[9] This is a key quote which you should learn.

Steve's liability re the elderly lady

Steve might be guilty of gross negligence manslaughter. As a paramedic called to the scene, he owed her a duty of care, which he breached by failing to attend to her. It could be argued that but for his breach she would not have died (**White**) and that this was a more than minimal cause of death (**Cato**). The jury would have to consider whether his omission was grossly negligent. Applying **Adomako**, having regard to the high risk of death, the jury might find that Steve's conduct was so bad as to amount to a criminal omission.

✓ Make your answer stand out

- Adopt a clear and logical structure. These offences each contain four elements which provide the structure of your answer for you. You simply need to define the offence and then apply each element in turn to the problem scenario.

- You should use headings to break up your answer and to ensure that you keep your focus and stick to your structure.

- You could draw upon academic opinion relating to involuntary manslaughter and/or comment upon the basis of criminal blameworthiness in respect of both unlawful act manslaughter and gross negligence manslaughter.

- Use key quotes from leading authorities where you can. It is suggested that in respect of unlawful act manslaughter, you learn the quote by Edmund Davies J in *Church* on the meaning of dangerousness.

> **! Don't be tempted to . . .**
>
> - Provide a lengthy narrative on the law of causation. Although the usual rules of causation apply, you only need to apply the principles and cases on causation which are directly relevant to the problem scenario.
> - Confuse the test for dangerousness with the thin skull rule (which relates to causation). Many students fail to deal with these tests separately. You should apply the test for dangerousness from *Church* before dealing with causation as a completely separate element of unlawful act manslaughter. It helps if you adopt a methodical approach to this offence, dealing with each element separately and in turn.

❓ Question 2

David and Jenny are both drug addicts. They ask Samantha, a drug dealer, to get them some heroin. Samantha hands over a quantity of heroin to both David and Jenny. They decide to sample the heroin in Samantha's presence in order to check the quality of the heroin. David prepares a syringe and asks Samantha to hold a tourniquet around his arm while he injects himself. Samantha does so and David takes the drugs. Jenny prepares a syringe and injects herself. Both David and Jenny fall unconscious. Samantha does not call for a doctor, but decides to leave them for a while in order that the effects of the drugs can wear off. Samantha goes to visit another client of hers, Ian. She prepares a syringe with a mixture of heroin and water for Ian and injects Ian with the substance. David, Jenny and Ian all die from the effects of the drugs.

Discuss Samantha's criminal liability for the deaths of David, Jenny and Ian.

Answer plan

→ Examine Samantha's liability for unlawful act manslaughter in respect of the death of David.

→ Consider Samantha's liability for unlawful act manslaughter or gross negligence manslaughter in respect of the death of Jenny.

→ Discuss Samantha's liability for unlawful act manslaughter in respect of the death of Ian.

Diagram plan

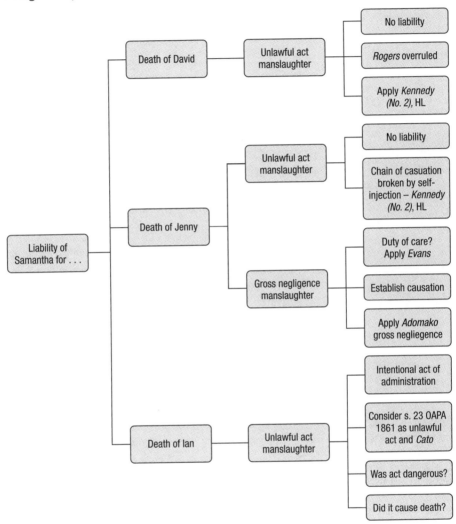

A printable version of this diagram plan is available from www.pearsoned.co.uk/lawexpressqa

Answer

It is unlikely that Samantha will be convicted of murder, because there is no evidence that she intended to kill or cause GBH to David, Jenny or Ian. Thus, she has no mens rea for murder. However, she might be convicted of offences of involuntary manslaughter, namely unlawful act manslaughter and gross negligence manslaughter.

Samantha might be charged with unlawful act manslaughter in relation to David's death. Unlawful act manslaughter was defined in *Larkin* [1944] 29 Cr App R 18 and requires proof of four elements: there must be an intentional act, rather than an omission (*Lowe* [1976] QB 702), which is unlawful, objectively dangerous and which causes death (per Lord Salmon in *DPP* v *Newbury & Jones* [1977] AC 50).

However, although Samantha does an intentional act here by holding the tourniquet for David while he injects himself with the heroin, on the facts there are problems in establishing guilt here. The offence of unlawful act manslaughter requires that there is an unlawful act which is a criminal offence: *Franklin* [1883] 15 Cox CC 163. It could be argued that the criminal act here is assisting the malicious administration of a poison or noxious thing so as to endanger life or inflict GBH and in *Rogers* [2003] EWCA Crim 945, the Court of Appeal held that a defendant could be guilty of unlawful act manslaughter where he held a tourniquet around the victim's arm while the victim injected himself with a drug because the defendant had played a part in the mechanics of the injection.[1] However, this was rejected by the House of Lords in *Kennedy (No. 2)*, in which Lord Bingham stated that: 'the crucial question is not whether the defendant facilitated or contributed to administration of the noxious thing but whether he went further and administered it. What matters . . . is whether the injection itself was the result of a voluntary and informed decision by the person injecting himself.'[2] Lord Bingham concluded that the voluntary act of self-administration precluded a finding of guilt. Thus, Samantha will not be convicted of unlawful act manslaughter in respect of David's death.

Samantha is also unlikely to be convicted of unlawful act manslaughter in respect of Jenny's death because Jenny self-injects. Consequently, it is difficult to ascertain what the unlawful act would be that Samantha does which causes Jenny's death. If the act is the

[1] Although this case has been overruled, it is worth mentioning because it is factually very similar to the problem scenario.

[2] It is worth learning a few key quotes from leading judgments for use in your examination. At the very least, you should be able to paraphrase key principles.

possession of drugs or the supply of drugs, proving causation is problematic. In fact, the House of Lords has now held that the free and voluntary self-administration of heroin by a fully informed and responsible adult would break the chain of causation: *Kennedy (No. 2)* [2007] UKHL 38.[3] Thus, provided that Jenny was acting freely and voluntarily in injecting herself and that she was a fully informed and responsible adult, Samantha will not be guilty of unlawful act manslaughter here.[4]

Furthermore, Samantha cannot be convicted of unlawful act manslaughter for the failure to summon medical assistance as this offence requires a positive act: *Lowe*.[5]

However, Samantha may be convicted of gross negligence manslaughter on the basis that she left Jenny unconscious without summoning medical help. The offence of gross negligence manslaughter may be committed by either an act or an omission, so Samantha might be convicted on the basis that she failed to summon medical assistance or because she acted by walking off and leaving Jenny to die. The prosecution would need to prove that Samantha owed Jenny a duty of care, she breached this duty, the breach caused Jenny's death and that Samantha's omission was grossly negligent: *Adomako* [1995] 1 AC 171. The duty to act giving rise to criminal liability for omission is narrower than the civil duty of care.

Whether or not Samantha owed Jenny a duty of care is a question of law according to *Willoughby* [2004] EWCA Crim 3365 and *Evans* [2009] EWCA Crim 650. The judge will direct the jury as to the law in this regard. According to Lord Mackay in *Adomako*, the ordinary principles of negligence apply to the meaning of 'duty of care'. This scenario is factually similar to the case of *Evans*, in which the Court of Appeal held that the defendant did owe the victim a duty of care despite the fact that their relationship was not one upon which the law already imposed a familial duty. Lord Judge CJ stated that: '. . . when a person has created or contributed to the creation of a state of affairs which he knows, or ought reasonably to know, has become life threatening, a consequent duty on him to act by taking reasonable steps to save the other's life will normally arise.'[6] Thus, applying this case, it is likely that a duty of care will be imposed upon Samantha to take reasonable steps to save Jenny's life when she realises (as she ought reasonably to) that Jenny is unconscious.

[3] As this is the leading authority on this point now, there is no need to trawl through the previous drugs cases.

[4] This sentence is important as it provides the application of the law to the problem scenario.

[5] If it is clear that unlawful act manslaughter does not apply, rule it out and move on to a more appropriate offence.

[6] This quote supports the argument that there is a duty of care here and is a useful application of the *Miller* principle by the Court of Appeal.

Next it must be established whether Samantha breached this duty. Breach requires that Samantha's conduct fell below that to be expected of a reasonable person. This is likely to be the case here, as the reasonable person would have summoned medical assistance and not simply walked off and left Jenny.[7]

[7] This sentence demonstrates application to the problem scenario.

The usual rules of causation apply. But for Samantha's act of supplying the heroin and then failing to summon medical assistance, leaving Jenny unconscious, Jenny would not have died: **White**. Samantha's omission was also a more than minimal cause of death: **Cato** and there was no intervening event.

Finally, it must be established that Samantha's conduct was grossly negligent. This is a question of fact and the jury should consider 'whether having regard to the risk of death involved, the conduct of the defendant was so bad in all the circumstances as to amount in their judgment to a criminal act or omission' (Lord Mackay in **Adomako**). A reasonably prudent person must have foreseen a serious risk of death: **Misra**. If Samantha's conduct was grossly negligent, she will be convicted of gross negligent manslaughter.

Samantha might be convicted of unlawful act manslaughter in relation to Ian's death. The intentional act here occurs when Samantha injects Ian with the heroin. This is a criminal offence (**Franklin** [1883] 15 Cox CC 163) under section 23 of the Offences Against the Person Act 1861, namely the malicious administration of a poison or noxious thing so as to endanger life or inflict GBH (see **Cato** [1976] 1 WLR 110).[8] The administration of the drug is an objectively dangerous act because it was such as 'all sober and reasonable people would inevitably recognise must subject the other person to, at least, the risk of some harm . . . albeit not serious harm' (Edmund Davies J in **Church** [1966] 1 QB 59). Finally, in order to establish Samantha's liability for unlawful act manslaughter in respect of Ian, it must be proved that Samantha's act of injecting Ian caused his death. The usual rules of causation apply. Applying the test for factual causation: but for Samantha's act of injecting Ian, he would not have died: **White** [1910] 2 KB 124. Samantha's act was also a more than minimal cause of Ian's death (**Cato**) and there is no novus actus interveniens to break the chain of causation. Thus, Samantha is likely to be guilty of unlawful act manslaughter in respect of Ian's death.

[8] Refer to factually similar authorities to demonstrate how liability will be established.

Make your answer stand out

- Refer to specific statements made by judges in leading authorities. If you cannot remember quotes verbatim, you should be able to paraphrase the principles. In fact, the ability to accurately paraphrase a point made in a judgment demonstrates a better understanding of the specific issue.
- Refer to academic opinion where appropriate. You might consider referring to Heaton, R., Dealing in death [2003] Crim LR 497 (although be aware that this article was obviously written prior to the decision of the House of Lords in *Kennedy (No. 2)*, which was decided in 2007). You might also refer to Leigh, L., Duty of care and manslaughter (2009) 173 JPN 296.
- You should be able to distinguish between all of the drugs cases, but you should demonstrate particularly good knowledge of the House of Lords' decision in *Kennedy (No. 2)*.
- Consider exploring further the extent to which criminal law relies upon definitions of civil law in defining the offence of gross negligence manslaughter and whether this is satisfactory in light of the severity of the offence.

 Don't be tempted to . . .

- Waste time going through all of the previous cases on the supply of drugs. In a problem question, you are expected to apply the current law and now that the law is settled as a result of *Kennedy (No. 2)*, this is the case you should apply. However, if the facts of a previous authority are directly relevant, you may make brief reference to it.
- Forget that some of the previous case law has been overruled by *Kennedy (No. 2)*. Make sure that you are aware which cases are still good law and which have been overruled so as to avoid applying incorrect law.

Question 3

Critically evaluate the extent to which a conviction for unlawful act manslaughter necessarily reflects the moral culpability of the offender.

Answer plan

→ Outline the elements of unlawful act manslaughter.

→ Discuss the problem of the potential gap between moral culpability and death within the offence of unlawful act manslaughter.

→ Consider the objectives of criminal law.

→ Assess whether the moral culpability of an offender is proportionate in other forms of involuntary manslaughter.

→ Evaluate academic opinions of the current law and suggestions for reform.

Diagram plan

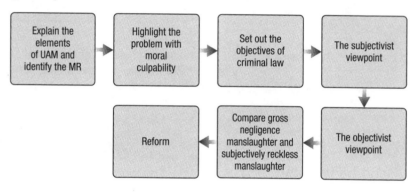

A printable version of this diagram plan is available from www.pearsoned.co.uk/lawexpressqa

Answer

Unlawful act manslaughter (UAM) does not require proof of an intention to kill or cause GBH. Criminal liability for manslaughter is constructed out of a lesser unlawful act (such as an assault) which causes the death of the victim even though that death is neither intended nor foreseen by the defendant. Thus, the defendant may be convicted in respect of unforeseen consequences.[1] This offence was described as 'unjustifiable in principle' by the Law Commission (*Legislating the Criminal Code: Involuntary Manslaughter*, Law Com. No. 237 (1996), para. 5.15). In its current form, this offence raises the question of whether the moral culpability of the defendant is too remote from the death of the victim to justify a conviction for UAM with a potentially lengthy sentence of imprisonment.[2]

[1] This sentence demonstrates immediately that you have identified the key issue and understand the problems associated with unlawful act manslaughter.

[2] You should address the question directly in your introduction.

The offence of UAM requires proof of four elements: (i) an intentional act; (ii) which is unlawful; (iii) the act must be objectively dangerous; and (iv) it must cause death (*Larkin* (1944) 29 Cr App R 18 and *DPP v Newbury & Jones* [1977] AC 50). Although it is necessary to prove a causal link between the actions of the defendant and the death of the victim, there is no need to prove that the defendant intended or foresaw the risk of death or even harm. The dangerousness element is objectively assessed, such that it must be questioned whether the act was 'such as all sober and reasonable people would inevitably recognise must subject the other person to, at least, the risk of some harm resulting therefrom, albeit not serious harm' (*Church* [1966] 1 QB 59).[3]

[3] This is a key quote which you should learn.

Thus, a defendant might be convicted of UAM where a reasonable person would foresee the risk of some harm resulting from the defendant's actions, irrespective of whether the actual defendant foresaw any risk of harm. The offence has a very broad scope and even on this objective assessment it is clear that the reasonable person need not foresee the risk of death or serious harm. Thus, the mens rea element of UAM is reduced to three requirements: (i) the defendant must intentionally do an act; (ii) the mens rea for the lesser unlawful act must be proved (the subjective elements); and (iii) the reasonable man would foresee the risk of some harm (the objective element). The scope of this offence has been criticised because it allows conviction for a serious criminal offence in respect of accidental and negligent deaths,[4] as in the case of *Meeking* [2012] EWCA Crim 641 where the defendant was convicted of manslaughter on the basis of the unlawful act of interfering with a motor vehicle (s. 22(a) Road Traffic Act 1988), by pulling the handbrake of a car being driven at 60 mph. Another example is provided by Mitchell, where 'in the course of a drunken fight, D punches V who falls over, hits his head on a hard surface causing a fractured skull from which V subsequently dies' ('Minding the gap in unlawful and dangerous act manslaughter: a moral defence of one-punch killers' (2008) 72 JCL 537). A similar defendant in a case where the victim does not die would be charged with unlawfully inflicting GBH under section 20 of the Offences Against the Person Act 1861. Thus, the liability of the defendant is determined by the consequences of his actions, whether foreseen or not, and ultimately is based on luck. Professor Mitchell argues that the gap between what was foreseen or foreseeable and the death of

[4] This sentence (and those that follow) demonstrate your appreciation of the academic criticism surrounding this offence.

the victim is 'too great'. Simester and Sullivan state that 'the connection between the unlawfulness of D's act and its dangerousness may be extremely tenuous' (*Criminal Law: Theory and Doctrine*, 3rd edn (2007), p. 378). The question of whether there should be a minimum threshold of moral culpability for a conviction for manslaughter requires consideration of the objectives of the criminal law and the criminal justice system[5] and a comparison with other forms of manslaughter.[5]

[5] Relate back to the title during your answer in order to ensure that you maintain your focus.

One of the aims of criminal law is to ensure that culpable conduct is met with a proportionate response by the criminal justice system. This means that both the offence which the defendant is convicted of and the punishment imposed must be proportionate to the moral culpability of the defendant. The principle of fair labelling requires that offences 'should be categorized and labelled for symbolic reasons to capture the essence of the wrongdoing involved and to convey the level of rejection of the activity involved' (Clarkson, C., 'Context and culpability in involuntary manslaughter', in A. Ashworth (ed.), *Rethinking English Homicide Law* (2000), pp. 141–2). Clarkson argues that offences should be 'defined with sufficient specificity' to reflect the moral significance of the offence and 'structured to reflect a hierarchy of seriousness'. Clarkson suggests that the offence of UAM 'fails both tests' (p. 142).

[6] This sentence (and the rest of this paragraph) sets out one side of the argument, criticising the current law.

Subjectivists would argue that a conviction for manslaughter should only be possible if the defendant foresaw a risk of harm at the very least,[6] and that the current offence of UAM is 'contrary to principle' (Ashworth, A., 'Taking the consequences', in S. Shute (ed.), *Action and Value in Criminal Law* (1993), p. 118). From a subjectivist standpoint, the culpability of the 'one-punch killer' who did not foresee a risk of harm, let alone death, is not so great as to warrant the label of 'manslaughter'. As far back as 1980 the Criminal Law Revision Committee recommended reform, criticising the current law because 'the offender's fault falls too far short of the unlucky result' (14th Report, *Offences Against the Person* (1980), para. 120). Wilson points out that, while the objective approach adopted in relation to the meaning of intention in murder was corrected, the objective approach in respect of the meaning of 'dangerous' in UAM has not been corrected[7] (*Criminal Law: Doctrine and Theory*, 4th edn (2011), p. 386).

[7] This sentence demonstrates a wider understanding of criminal law by incorporating the approach taken by the courts in respect of the meaning of intention.

[8] This paragraph presents the opposing view – that supporting the current law.

Ashworth outlines the reasons objectivists would give to support the argument that the actions of the defendant should be labelled as manslaughter:[8] (i) the moral difference between the one-punch killer and a defendant who punches the victim without causing death. While the former feels 'morally burdened with the death', the latter does not; (ii) the one-punch killer 'cannot undo the results of his act'; and (iii) he 'should be censured for causing the death, since a law which convicted him merely of battery . . . would be suggesting that the death did not matter' (p. 119).

Some consideration should be given to other forms of involuntary manslaughter. Gross negligence manslaughter requires that a risk of death be objectively foreseeable (**Adomako** [1995] 1 AC 171), thus carrying greater moral culpability than UAM which merely requires that a risk of harm be objectively foreseeable.[9] Subjectively reckless manslaughter requires the defendant to foresee a risk of death or serious harm (**Lidar**, unreported, 11 November 1999), also carrying greater moral culpability than UAM because it is subjectively assessed and requires foresight of a risk of death or serious injury.

[9] You should compare other related offences in order to demonstrate a wider understanding of the criminal law.

It is true to say that there is too great a gap between the moral culpability of the defendant and UAM. A more satisfactory approach would require subjective foresight of a risk of at least some harm.[10]

[10] This final sentence ties your answer back to the question and sets out a recommendation for reform.

✓ Make your answer stand out

- Refer to a number of different academic sources and opinions to demonstrate your appreciation of the wide range of academic literature available.
- Present both sides of the argument. You should also consider the arguments in favour of having a low threshold for unlawful act manslaughter.
- If you have time, you might explore further the recommendations for reform made by the Law Commission.
- You might also consider where the offence of causing death by dangerous driving fits into the current framework of offences.

! Don't be tempted to . . .

- Simply set out the law on unlawful act manslaughter. The examiner is looking for an appreciation of the peculiarities of the mens rea of unlawful act manslaughter and the extent to which the offence reflects the moral culpability of the defendant.
- Just simply set out one side of the argument. You should explore both sides of the argument.

Question 4

'Despite a gestation period extending over thirteen years, the Corporate Manslaughter and Corporate Homicide Act 2007 is a disappointment. It is limited in its scope, restricted in its range of potential defendants and regressive to the extent that . . . it allows its focus to be deflected from systematic fault to individual fault.' (Gobert, J., 'The Corporate Manslaughter and Corporate Homicide Act' (2008) 71(3) MLR 413–63.)
Critically evaluate the above statement.

Answer plan

➜ Discuss the background to the 2007 Act and gross negligence manslaughter.

➜ Consider the scope of the offence of corporate manslaughter.

➜ Address criticisms of the new legislation.

Diagram plan

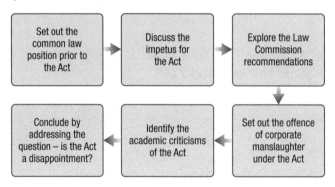

A printable version of this diagram plan is available from www.pearsoned.co.uk/lawexpressqa

Answer

The long overdue Corporate Manslaughter and Corporate Homicide Act 2007 ('CMCHA 2007') came into force in April 2008, over a decade after corporate responsibility for causing deaths was initially considered by the Law Commission[1] (*Criminal Law: Involuntary Manslaughter*, Consultation Paper No. 135 (1994b)). In 1996, the Law Commission recommended the creation of an offence of 'corporate killing' (*Legislating the Criminal Code: Involuntary Manslaughter*, Law

[1] This sentence demonstrates your wider knowledge of the background to this piece of legislation.

Commission Report No. 237) and this led to a consultation paper in 2000 and the Act in 2007. However, despite over a decade of consultation and drafting, the CMCHA 2007 has attracted criticism from academics and been labelled a 'disappointment'.[2]

[2] Ensure that you address the question directly in your introduction.

Prior to the Act, a corporation could be guilty of gross negligence manslaughter subject to the identification of an individual who represented the embodiment of the company and who could be said to be responsible for the acts and state of mind of the company (*Tesco Supermarkets Ltd* v *Nattrass* [1972] AC 153). However, problems with the application of the identification doctrine led to unsuccessful attempts at prosecution.[3] Various sea and rail disasters from the late 1980s onwards and the failure to secure convictions for gross negligence manslaughter for the deaths of the victims led to public calls for a new offence of corporate killing. Whilst it had been possible in some cases to bring successful prosecutions for health and safety offences, this was an unsatisfactory conclusion to such large scale disasters as such convictions failed to adequately represent the severity of the offence which had in fact occurred. In the interests of fair labelling, the Law Commission recommended that a specific statutory offence of corporate manslaughter be created to increase the social stigma of conviction.[4]

[3] This shows the examiner that you understand the context within which the legislation was created as well as the problems with the old law.

[4] Explain why it was still necessary to create an offence of corporate manslaughter even though prosecutions for other offences were possible.

Although the common law offence of gross negligence manslaughter still exists, section 20 of the CMCHA 2007 abolishes the application of the common law offence to corporations and any other body to which the 2007 Act now applies. Thus, the offence of gross negligence manslaughter now only applies to individuals. Section 1 of the CMCHA 2007 creates a new homicide offence which can only be committed by an organisation. Under section 1(1), an organisation is guilty of corporate manslaughter if the management or organisation of its activities by senior management causes the death of a person and amounts to a gross breach of a duty of care owed to the victim. Under section 1(3), an organisation is guilty only if the way in which its activities are managed or organised by its senior management is a substantial element in the breach. This is a complex offence which requires a number of elements to be proved before liability can be established: the body in question must constitute an organisation under the Act, there must be a relevant duty of care owed to the victim, there must be a gross breach of that duty, the management or organisation of the activities of the organisation must cause the death of the victim, the offence must be due to the way in which the activities of the organisation are managed or organised and senior management must contribute substantial elements in the breach.

Both the scope of the Act and that of the offence of corporate manslaughter require further consideration. While the Act has been criticised for its restrictive focus on just one offence (manslaughter) and its failure to deal with principles of corporate liability as a whole,[5] the specific offence under section 1 is broad in scope. The organisations it applies to is widely construed in section 1(2) and goes beyond liability of a corporation. Thus, as Ormerod and Taylor state, 'Calling the offence "corporate manslaughter" is somewhat misleading' ('The Corporate Manslaughter and Corporate Homicide Act 2007' [2008] Crim LR 589). The offence applies to police forces, partnerships, government departments and trade unions and Ormerod and Taylor welcome the breadth of the definition of organisation. By contrast, Gobert comments that 'the extension of the Act to so diverse an array of organisations may be too broad'.[6] The list of government departments in Schedule 1 to which the offence applies extends to the Ministry of Justice and Department of Health, thus a prison may be convicted in respect of the death of a prisoner in custody and hospital trusts may be convicted in respect of the death of a patient.[7] Gobert concedes that 'Criminal laws can and should be constructed to cover these types of situations', but he argues that 'a law of corporate manslaughter arguably is aimed at a more specific and quite different problem – that of companies which allow their pursuit of profit to blind them to concerns of safety'.

Some elements requiring proof under the Act resemble elements required for the common law offence of gross negligence manslaughter, such as duty of care and gross breach. Both these elements have been questioned within the context of the common law: first, proof of a duty of care leads to concepts of civil law being adopted by criminal law despite the fact that each system has distinct and clearly defined aims. This requirement did not form part of the Law Commission recommendations in 1996 and Gobert questions whether it is in fact 'otiose' and 'simply provides defendants with another avenue for deflecting the trial from its main objective'. Secondly, the test for 'gross breach' is ambiguous. Section 1(4)(b) refers to conduct which falls far below what can reasonably be expected of the organisation in the circumstances. The test for gross

[5] This enables you to provide a further criticism of the Act that it only deals with one aspect of corporate liability and does not develop general principles of corporate liability.

[6] These sentences show that you are able to compare and contrast differing academic opinions.

[7] Demonstrate to the examiner that you are familiar with the legislation and the extent of the impact that it may have.

negligence from **Adomako** [1995] 1 AC 171 has endured criticism for its circularity and it appears similar criticism may be levelled at the meaning given to 'gross breach' under the Act.[8]

[8] This sentence demonstrates that you are able to integrate criticisms of other areas of law into your argument where appropriate.

One of the reasons for the implementation of the 2007 Act was to avoid the evidential problems posed by the identification doctrine. However, the Act requires proof that individuals who amount to 'senior management' contribute a 'substantial element' to the breach. Gobert argues that this is not consistent with the recommendations made by the Law Commission which focused exclusively on 'systematic failure', rather than on 'individual failings'. Ormerod and Taylor comment that this is 'a further limiting factor to the offence and one which brings with it the potential for time consuming technical arguments'. Nevertheless, despite identifying individual failings, the Act does not permit individual liability, either as a principal or as an accessory to an offence committed by the organisation.

There are several criticisms which may be levelled at the 2007 Act which is indeed disappointing in a piece of legislation which was over a decade in the making. Nevertheless, this was a long overdue piece of legislation and as Gobert suggests: 'The symbolic effects of the 2007 Act may in the long run overshadow [its] deficiencies.'

✓ Make your answer stand out

- Cite academic opinion in your answer. You could refer to other academic literature on this topic, such as O'Doherty, S., The Corporate Manslaughter and Corporate Homicide Act 2007 (2008) 172 JPN 244.
- If you have time you could explore further the background to the legislation (see Wells, C., The Law Commission Report on Involuntary Manslaughter [1996] Crim LR 545), or look more specifically at the impact of the Act (see Griffin, S. and Moran, J., Accountability for deaths attributable to the gross negligent act or omission of a police force: the impact of the Corporate Manslaughter and Corporate Homicide Act 2007 (2010) 74 JCL 358).
- You could consider further the common law prior to the 2007 Act and the reasons why the common law was unsatisfactory in dealing with corporate liability.
- You could explore the identification doctrine and academic opinion relating to this.

! **Don't be tempted to . . .**

■ Simply set out the statutory provisions of the Act. This question asks you to explore the criticisms of the legislation rather than provide a narrative of the law.

■ Spend too much time setting out the law relating to gross negligence manslaughter and the identification doctrine. Neither should your answer be solely a critique of the old law. You need to critically evaluate the new law (albeit with reference to the old law where appropriate).

www.pearsoned.co.uk/lawexpressqa

 Go online to access more revision support including additional essay and problem questions with diagram plans, You be the marker questions, and download all diagrams from the book.

Non-fatal offences against the person

How this topic may come up in exams

The non-fatal offences against the person could be examined by way of either a problem scenario or an essay question. A problem question would expect you to identify any of the five main non-fatal offences against the person and/or the sexual offences (covered in Chapter 6, with a mixed question in Chapter 13). You might also be expected to apply the law relating to consent and self-defence. An essay question could ask for a critical evaluation of the general area or it might focus on a specific issue, such as consent.

■ Attack the question

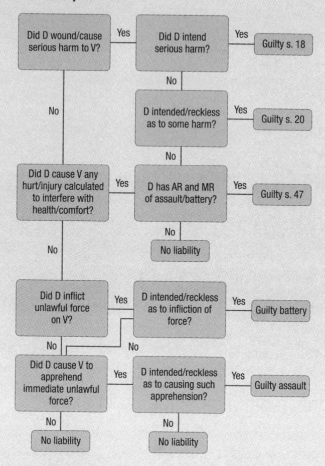

A printable version of this diagram is available from www.pearsoned.co.uk/lawexpressqa

❓ Question 1

After they meet at a party, Claire becomes 'friends' with Abraham on Facebook. Over the next few weeks, they send each other flirtatious messages on Facebook. Encouraged by this, Abraham decides to ask Claire if she would go on a date with him. Claire rejects Abraham's offer of a date and tells him that she is not interested in him romantically. Confused by Claire's flirtatious behaviour and rejection, and angry at being used, Abraham starts sending Claire threatening messages on Facebook. After receiving several threatening and abusive messages from Abraham over the course of two weeks, Claire suffers an anxiety disorder.

Claire's friends decide to take her out to cheer her up. However, on the night out with her friends, Claire runs into Abraham in a nightclub. Abraham is delighted to see Claire and he starts dancing with her before touching her on the back. Claire is frightened at seeing Abraham and doesn't like him touching her, so she pushes him away from her. He stumbles backwards and falls to the floor, but is not injured.

The following day, Abraham meets up with his friends and they go out paintballing. As a joke, Abraham's friends decide to gang up against him and they all target him by shooting him with paintballs. One of his friends, Matthew, shoots paintballs at Abraham's back at close range, causing severe bruises.

Discuss the criminal liability of the parties.

Answer plan

→ Discuss the liability of Abraham for assault in respect of the Facebook messages.

→ Consider Abraham's liability for battery and implied consent.

→ Explore Claire's potential liability for battery and her use of self-defence.

→ Consider Abraham's consent to the paintballing, and thus to the infliction of ABH or GBH.

Diagram plan

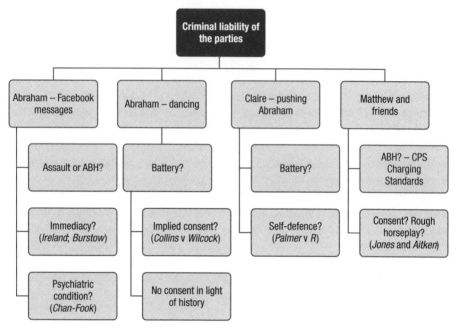

A printable version of this diagram plan is available from www.pearsoned.co.uk/lawexpressqa

Answer

This question requires consideration of the liabilities of the parties for non-fatal offences against the person and the issue of consent.

Facebook messages

Abraham may be charged with assault in respect of the threatening Facebook messages he sent to Claire. Assault is charged contrary to section 39 of the Criminal Justice Act 1988 (CJA) and involves intentionally or recklessly causing a person to apprehend immediate and unlawful personal violence: **Fagan v MPC** [1969] 1 QB 439.[1] An assault may be committed by words alone: **Ireland; Burstow** [1998] AC 147. It must also be proved that the Facebook messages caused Claire to apprehend immediate and unlawful personal violence. This is likely to be satisfied since the messages were threatening and they caused Claire to suffer anxiety. This is evidence that she was

[1] There is no need to set out the facts of the case here. The legal principle is more important and you will waste time going through the facts of cases.

worried about the threats being carried out, although it is less clear whether the apprehension was of immediate personal violence since the messages were sent through a social networking website and there is no evidence that Abraham was anywhere near Claire at the time. However, 'immediacy' has been widely construed. In *Constanza* [1997] 2 Cr App R 492, it was held that immediacy meant any time 'not excluding the immediate future'. In *Ireland; Burstow*, Lord Steyn held that silent telephone calls could be sufficient to satisfy the requirement of immediacy. In light of these authorities, messages sent via Facebook could potentially be sufficiently immediate.[2]

[2] Use the facts of a key case and the principle derived from that case to reach a sensible conclusion on slightly different facts.

The mens rea of assault is also present because Abraham intends to cause such apprehension. He is likely to be subjectively reckless because he must have recognised the risk that sending threatening Facebook messages might cause such apprehension, and he went ahead and took that risk (*Cunningham* [1957] 2 QB 396).[3]

[3] Try to set out the principle of law and apply it in one sentence as this demonstrates a more sophisticated style of writing as well as saving you time in the exam.

Finally, Abraham might be guilty of assault occasioning ABH (s. 47, Offences Against the Person Act (OAPA) 1861). A clinically recognised psychiatric injury may amount to ABH, but this does not include mere emotions: *Chan-Fook* [1994] 1 WLR 689. The effect of the Facebook messages was to cause Claire to suffer an anxiety disorder. Provided the anxiety disorder is deemed to be a clinically recognised psychiatric condition, this will be sufficient to constitute ABH.

Abraham dancing and touching Claire

Abraham could be charged with assault and battery. The assault might be based upon Abraham's act of dancing near Claire. Taking into account their history and the Facebook messages, Claire may have apprehended immediate and unlawful personal violence, and Abraham is likely to have been reckless as to such apprehension at the very least. In respect of Abraham touching Claire's back, there may be a battery. Battery is charged contrary to section 39 of the CJA.

[4] Where it is less obvious, ensure that you set out the definition of the key offence at the start and cite appropriate authorities.

It is defined under common law as intentionally or recklessly inflicting unlawful force on a person without consent: *Collins v Wilcock* [1984] 1 WLR 1172.[4] 'Force' merely requires 'the least touching of another': *Cole v Turner* (1705) 6 Mod Rep 149, thus when Abraham touches Claire on the back, this is sufficient. The mens rea of battery is also present because it is clear that Abraham intends to apply force to (or touch) Claire.[5] It could be argued that the touching was

[5] Do not forget to state and apply the mens rea of the offence.

not unlawful because Claire had impliedly consented to it. According to Robert Goff LJ in *Collins* v *Wilcock*, most of the physical contacts of everyday life are impliedly consented to. While this defence applies to accidental contact, such as bumping into someone, it is not clear that it would apply to this type of touching, especially in light of the history between them.[6] It is unlikely that Claire will be deemed to have consented to this touching as she has previously rejected Abraham's advances.

[6] Use the facts to reach a sensible conclusion.

Claire pushing Abraham

When Claire pushes Abraham away, this might also amount to a battery and the main issue here is one of self-defence. Claire is unlikely to attract any liability for battery when she pushes Abraham away, as she is clearly acting in defence of herself here.[7] She honestly believes that the use of force is necessary to defend herself from being touched by Abraham and she only uses reasonable force in pushing him away: *Palmer* v *R* [1971] AC 814.

[7] Where it is obvious that no offence has been committed, get to the point and explain why at the start.

Paintballing

Matthew (and Abraham's other friends) might be guilty of assault occasioning actual bodily harm (s. 47 of the Offences Against the Person Act 1861). This offence requires proof of either an assault or a battery, which causes actual bodily harm. There may be an assault here as Abraham does apprehend that he will be struck with paintballs and the friends and Matthew are, at the very least, reckless as to causing such apprehension. There is also a battery because striking Abraham with the paintballs involves intentionally or recklessly inflicting unlawful force. There need only be the least touching to constitute 'force' and this is evident here. 'Actual bodily harm' is defined under *Miller* [1954] 2 WLR 138 as 'any hurt or injury calculated to interfere with health or comfort'.[8] According to the most recent CPS Charging Standards (http://www.cps.gov.uk/legal/l_to_o/offences_against_the_person/#a24), the injuries must be 'serious' to constitute ABH and 'relevant factors may include, for example, the fact that there has been significant medical intervention and/or permanent effects have resulted'.[9] There is no evidence on the facts that Abraham has had to receive any medical treatment in relation to the bruising, nor is there any evidence of permanent scarring.

[8] This is a good quote to remember. Try to remember key quotes from judgments which define the crucial elements of the offences.

[9] Refer to relevant parts of the CPS Charging Standards in questions on non-fatal offences against the person in order to show that you are familiar with them.

Nevertheless, these factors serve only as examples and since the bruises are stated to be severe bruising, it might be that this is enough to constitute ABH.[10]

[10] Ensure you explain why/how the principle could be extended to apply to the specific problem scenario you are dealing with.

The mens rea required is the mens rea for the assault or battery. No additional mens rea in respect of the degree of harm caused need be proved according to *Roberts* (1971) 56 Cr App R 95 and *Savage; Parmenter* [1992] 1 AC 699.[11] Here, the mens rea of the battery must be proved, and it is clear that Matthew and the other friends intended to inflict force on Abraham (i.e., touch him).

[11] Correctly state the mens rea for this offence. Students often make the mistake of thinking that additional mens rea is required.

As the injuries were sustained during a game of paintballing, Matthew and the other friends might try to argue that Abraham consented to the injury by relying on 'rough horseplay'. The general rule is that a person may not consent to the infliction of actual bodily harm or grievous bodily harm: *Donovan* [1934] All ER 207. However, such injuries inflicted during 'rough horseplay' are consented to. However, this exception applies to injuries sustained during horseplay which were not intentionally inflicted: *Jones* (1986) 83 Cr App R 375; *Aitken* [1992] 1 WLR 1006. It could be argued that the injuries here were inflicted intentionally, thus the defence of consent is unlikely to be available here and Matthew and the other friends may be guilty of assault occasioning ABH.

✓ Make your answer stand out

- Each time you set out a relevant legal principle, you should cite an authority which supports that principle and then apply it to the facts in the problem scenario.

- In your revision you should choose some key quotes and names of judges who gave leading judgments in key cases to refer to (only where appropriate) in the exam.

- You could discuss any potential liability under the Protection from Harassment Act 1997 in respect of the Facebook messages.

- You should develop your discussion of the issue of self-defence in respect of the push and provide further detail about this defence.

- You could provide reference to some academic opinion on issues such as consent or immediacy to make your answer stand out. For instance, read Ormerod, D., *Smith and Hogan Criminal Law*, 12th edn, pp. 600–4. You could also make reference to the Law Commission Consultation Paper No. 134, *Consent and Offences Against the Person* (1994a).

> ! **Don't be tempted to . . .**
>
> ■ Forget to apply the principles of law relating to the mens rea. If you merely establish the actus reus you have only really dealt with half of the question. In order to establish liability, both the actus reus and mens rea must be satisfied.
>
> ■ Make the mistake of writing everything you know about any offence that you have identified without referring to the problem scenario. The examiner does not want to read two pages of description before you refer to the facts of the problem scenario. You must refer to the facts in the problem scenario from the very start of your answer and combine statements of law with application to the facts.

? Question 2

Amanda and Owen are unhappily married. In a bid to spice up their sex life, Owen asks Amanda if she will let him whip her on the buttocks. Amanda reluctantly agrees and she sustains a number of cuts which require medical treatment. Amanda has been having an affair with Paolo for the past six months. Paolo is jealous of Owen and he puts pressure on Amanda to leave Owen for him. Paolo has tested HIV positive but does not tell Amanda about this. Impatient with Amanda's indecision and becoming increasingly angry, Paolo persuades Amanda to have unprotected sex with him hoping to transmit the virus to Amanda. Amanda later tests positive for HIV.

Discuss the criminal liability of the parties.

Answer plan

→ Discuss Owen's potential liability for assault occasioning ABH under section 47, OAPA 1861 in respect of the injuries caused to Amanda's buttocks.

→ Consider whether the elements of maliciously wounding or inflicting GBH under section 20, OAPA 1861 are satisfied.

→ Consider whether consent applies and the cases of *Brown* [1994] 1 AC 212 and *Wilson* [1997] 1 QB 47.

→ Evaluate Paolo's liability for maliciously wounding or inflicting GBH under section 20, OAPA 1861 in respect of the transmission of HIV to Amanda.

→ Explore the issue of consent and the cases of *Dica* [2004] QB 1257 and *Konzani* [2005] EWCA Crim 706.

Diagram plan

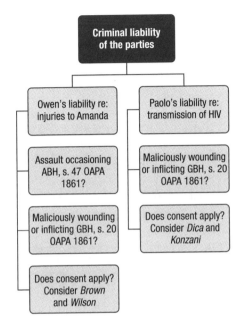

A printable version of this diagram plan is available from www.pearsoned.co.uk/lawexpressqa

Answer

This question requires consideration of the liability of Owen and Paolo for various non-fatal offences against the person. In particular, Owen might be criminally liable for the injuries to Amanda's buttocks and Paolo might be criminally liable for the transmission of HIV to Amanda. Both cases also require consideration of the issue of consent.[1]

[1] Use your introduction to briefly set out the key issues that you will be addressing.

Injuries to Amanda

In respect of the injuries to Amanda's buttocks, Owen could be charged with assault occasioning actual bodily harm under section 47, OAPA 1861.[2] This offence requires proof of an assault or battery which causes ABH. There is clearly a battery here. Battery is defined as intentionally or recklessly inflicting unlawful force on a person without consent: **Collins v Wilcock** [1984] 1 WLR 1172. 'Force' merely requires 'the least touching of another': **Cole v Turner** (1705)

[2] Begin by clearly identifying the most relevant offence which might apply.

93

6 Mod Rep 149, thus when Owen strikes Amanda with the whip, this is sufficient. The mens rea of battery is also present because it is clear that Owen intends to apply force to Amanda. 'Actual bodily harm' is defined under **Miller** [1954] 2 WLR 138 as 'any hurt or injury calculated to interfere with health or comfort'. The Crown Prosecution Service Charging Standards suggest that the injuries must be 'serious' to constitute ABH and 'relevant factors may include, for example, the fact that there has been significant medical intervention and/or permanent effects have resulted.' Since Amanda's injuries required medical treatment, it is clear that Amanda's injuries constitute ABH under the Charging Standards.[3] The mens rea required is the mens rea for the assault or battery. No additional mens rea in respect of the degree of harm caused need be proved according to **Roberts** (1971) 56 Cr App R 95 and **Savage; Parmenter** [1992] 1 AC 699. Here, the mens rea of the battery must be proved, and it is clear that Owen intended to inflict force on Amanda.

[3] Be aware of the CPS Charging Standards, as these are used to determine the charge and this demonstrates some knowledge of legal practice.

However, if the injuries to Amanda are more serious, Owen might be charged with maliciously wounding or inflicting grievous bodily harm under section 20, OAPA 1861.[4] The actus reus of this offence requires proof that Owen wounded or inflicted GBH to Amanda. A wound is a break in the continuity of the skin: **Moriarty v Brookes** (1834) 6 C & P 684. Amanda has sustained cuts which could satisfy the actus reus of an offence under section 20. The mens rea of this offence is intention or recklessness as to whether some harm was caused: **Savage; Parmenter**.[5] Even if Owen does not intend to cause some harm to Amanda, he is likely to be subjectively reckless as to whether some harm would be caused. This is because he must recognise the risk of causing some harm to her when he strikes her, and he takes that risk: **Cunningham** [1957] 2 QB 396. In fact, if Owen intends to cause Amanda GBH, he will be guilty of the more serious offence of wounding or causing GBH under section 18, OAPA 1861.

[4] Once you have dealt with the offence that is most likely to apply, you should consider other relevant offences.

[5] Ensure that you correctly state the mens rea of section 20. Many students misstate this crucial element.

Owen might try to rely on consent in order to avoid liability. The general rule is that consent is only a defence to assault and battery and will provide no defence to ABH or GBH: see **Donovan** [1934] All ER 207 and **Attorney General's Reference** (No. 6 of 1980) [1981] 2 All ER 1057. There are a number of exceptions to this rule. Owen would seek to rely on the case of **Wilson** in order to support his argument that consent absolves him of liability. In this case, the Court of Appeal compared the act of branding to tattooing, which is rendered lawful

[6] Set out the arguments that would be put forward in Owen's defence along with supporting authorities.

[7] You should then set out the counter arguments which would be relied upon by the prosecution. This demonstrates your ability to explore both sides of a legal argument.

[8] Make reference to the rationale for the decision to demonstrate your understanding of the decision of the court and the wider factors which were considered.

[9] Try to remember key quotes from leading authorities to demonstrate detailed knowledge.

by consent. The court held that consensual activity between husband and wife in the privacy of the matrimonial home should not be prosecuted.[6]

However, the prosecution might seek to distinguish Wilson on the basis that the injuries in that case were not inflicted for sexual gratification.[7] In this case, the injuries have been inflicted in order to gratify Owen and spice up their sex life. The prosecution would seek to equate this conduct to sado-masochism and rely on **Brown** [1994] 1 AC 212, in which the House of Lords refused to allow the defence of consent for reasons of public policy, namely the protection of the public against 'a cult of violence'.[8] Lord Templeman stated that sex was no excuse for violence and he was 'not prepared to invent a defence of consent for sado-masochist encounters which breed and glorify cruelty'.[9] Similarly, in **Emmett** (1999) *The Times*, 15 October, consent was no defence where the injuries sustained were more serious than those inflicted in **Wilson**. The approach taken by the courts in respect of Owen's potential liability may depend upon the number and severity of the injuries sustained by Amanda.

Transmission of HIV

Paolo may be convicted of maliciously wounding or inflicting GBH under section 20, OAPA 1861. The actus reus of this offence is satisfied because Paolo has inflicted GBH on Amanda by transmitting HIV to her. GBH means 'really serious harm': **DPP v Smith** [1961] AC 290. The infliction of GBH does not require proof of an assault: **Wilson (Clarence)** [1984] AC 242. In **Dica** [2004] QB 1257, the Court of Appeal held that the reckless transmission of HIV could amount to an offence under section 20. The mens rea of the offence under section 20 requires proof that Paolo intended or was reckless as to whether some harm was caused: **Savage; Parmenter** [1992] 1 AC 699. Paolo hopes to transmit HIV to Amanda, so it could be said that he intended to cause some harm to Amanda. If this cannot be established, he is likely to be subjectively reckless as to whether some harm would be caused because he recognises the risk of causing some harm to her when he has unprotected sexual intercourse with her, and he takes that risk: **Cunningham**. In fact, if Paolo intends to cause Amanda GBH, he may be guilty of wounding or causing GBH under section 18, OAPA 1861.

Consent will provide no defence to Paolo because Amanda did not consent to running the risk of the transmission of HIV. Her consent to having sexual intercourse is not a defence to a charge of section 20. Amanda was not aware that Paolo was HIV positive and by consenting to sexual intercourse Amanda is not to be taken to be consenting to the risk of HIV: **Dica**. This is supported by the case of **Konzani**, in which Lord Judge CJ reiterated the fact that the defence of consent would only be available where the victim knew about the risk of HIV and gave his/her informed consent to running the risk of transmission.[10] However, as Amanda was not aware that Paolo had tested HIV positive, she did not provide any informed consent to run such a risk. Thus, the defence of consent will not be available to Paolo and he will be guilty of maliciously wounding or inflicting GBH under section 20, OAPA 1861.

[10] Cite supporting authorities without repeating yourself, by referring to a specific point made by a judge.

✓ Make your answer stand out

- Where there are a number of offences which might apply, you should deal with the most appropriate offence first before also exploring the alternative potential offences.
- Ensure that you fully define the offences setting out both the actus reus and mens rea elements.
- Make reference to the CPS Charging Standards when choosing the most appropriate charge as this demonstrates your knowledge of the way in which the offences will be charged in practice.
- You should also make reference to specific points made by judges or quotes from judgments in order to demonstrate a wide and detailed knowledge of the area.
- Refer to academic opinion if you can, particularly in relation to issues of consent. Consider Ryan, Reckless transmission of HIV: knowledge and culpability [2006] Crim LR 981.

! Don't be tempted to . . .

- Misstate the mens rea for maliciously wounding or inflicting GBH under section 20, OAPA 1861. This is a mistake made by many students in criminal law exams every year.
- Provide a recitation of the facts of key cases simply because the case is relevant. For instance, in this question, repeating in detail the facts of *Brown* or *Dica* adds nothing of substance to your answer and wastes valuable time in the exam. You should instead focus on applying the relevant legal principles to the facts of the problem scenario.

📝 Question 3

'The history of our law upon personal injuries is certainly not creditable to the legislature, and the result at which we have at present arrived is extremely clumsy' (Sir James Fitzjames Stephen, *A History of the Criminal Law of England*, 1883)

To what extent does this statement reflect the current law on non-fatal offences against the person?

Answer plan

➜ Critically evaluate the OAPA 1861.

➜ Discuss the fact that defining key elements has been left to the courts.

➜ Explore the conflict between definitions and practical application.

➜ Consider the need for reform.

Diagram plan

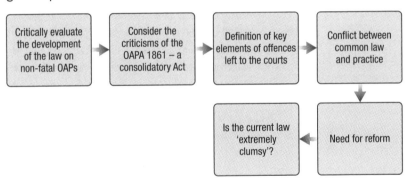

A printable version of this diagram plan is available from www.pearsoned.co.uk/lawexpressqa

Answer

[1] Refer directly to the quote in your introduction to show your engagement with the question and that you are not about to set out everything you know about the offences.

The quote by Stephen is highly critical of the contributions made by the legislature to the non-fatal offences against the person. It is agreed that the law is not creditable to the legislature; it is submitted that the judiciary has coped well in the circumstances by providing good interpretations to a very poorly drafted statute. The current law is in an 'extremely clumsy' state and in need of reform.[1]

It is surprising that the legislation to which Stephen refers is the same piece of legislation which governs the law on non-fatal offences against the person today. The Offences Against the Person Act 1861 (OAPA) 'is much disparaged by today's criminal lawyers' (Gardner, J., 'Rationality and the rule of law in offences against the person' (1994) 53 CLJ 502).[2] When it was initially drafted, the Act was a consolidatory Act. It was acknowledged by the draftsman that '[n]one of [the sections were] rewritten; on the contrary, each contains enactments taken from different Acts passed at different times and with different views, and frequently varying from each other in phraseology' (Greaves, *The Criminal Law Consolidation and Amendment Acts* (1862)).[3] Gardner argues that, while 'the Act as a whole is often found guilty by association, these serious accusations are being levelled, for the most part, at just a few of its provisions'. The provisions in question are three of the main non-fatal offences against the person: assault occasioning actual bodily harm under section 47, maliciously wounding or inflicting grievous bodily harm under section 20 and maliciously wounding or causing grievous bodily harm with intent under section 18.

[2] Make reference to excellent academic sources where you can to provide evidence of your wider reading.

[3] This demonstrates your understanding of the background to the OAPA 1861 and the reasons why the law has developed in the way that it has.

The OAPA did not create new offences but consolidated those that already existed in various other pieces of legislation into one Act. Section 39 of the Criminal Justice Act 1988 (CJA) is a further statutory provision which provides for the sentences for the summary offences of assault and battery. These legislative provisions provide the statutory framework for the five main non-fatal offences against the person. It is unfortunate that these provisions fail to provide a clear legislative hierarchy of offences: not only are the five offences spread over two different Acts, but the section numbers themselves are not set out in any logical sequence.[4] The most serious of the five offences is maliciously wounding or causing GBH with intent under section 18, OAPA, the next offence decreasing in severity is maliciously wounding or inflicting GBH under section 20, OAPA, the next offence is assault occasioning ABH under section 47, OAPA and the least serious offences are battery and then assault under section 39, CJA. It is abundantly clear that the OAPA is not logically drafted and there is no clear hierarchy.

[4] This sentence sets out a key criticism of the OAPA 1861 and provides reasoning for the critique.

A further, related criticism is that there is no logical distinction between the maximum sentences available for each offence. While the most serious offence under section 18 carries a discretionary life sentence of imprisonment, the offences under sections 20 and 47 both carry a maximum sentence of five years' imprisonment. This is so despite a clear distinction in severity between the actus reus elements:[5] section 47 requires actual bodily harm, while section 20 requires proof of a higher degree of harm, grievous bodily harm (or 'really serious harm': **DPP v Smith** [1961] AC 290). Assault and battery also both carry the same maximum sentence of six months' imprisonment; although perhaps this is more justifiable as neither offence requires proof of any harm being caused.

[5] Explain why the maximum sentences for these offences are illogical.

Another problem with the legislative provisions is that they fail to define the offences adequately. It is not clear from simply reading the relevant statutory provisions what the elements of the offences are; thus, the law is inaccessible and uncertain. Sections 47 and 20, OAPA do not clearly set out what the mens rea of these offences are. The mens rea elements have instead been established by case law: **Savage; Parmenter** [1992] 1 AC 699. Further, section 47, which necessarily requires proof of an assault, does not specify the elements of this lesser, inherent offence. Section 39, CJA makes no reference to any of the elements of assault and battery. Thus, the definition of the elements of these offences is left to the courts to develop. As the provisions of the OAPA and CJA fail to provide adequate detail regarding the elements of these offences, there is necessarily a large base of common law which explains the terms used in the Acts. Thus, it can be said that the history of the non-fatal offences against the person is not creditable to the legislature, but has been moulded and created by the judiciary through the development of the common law.[6]

[6] Refer back to the quote in the question in order to maintain the focus of your answer.

The two offences of GBH are distinguishable by their mens rea. However, the actus reus elements are also expressed in different terms. While section 20 requires the 'infliction' of GBH, section 18 requires that GBH is 'caused'. This lack of consistency is explained by the manner in which the Act was drafted. As a consolidating piece of legislation, it cannot be argued that there was any intended distinction between the different terms used: Lord Steyn states, '[t]he difference in language is . . . not a significant factor' (**Ireland; Burstow** [1998] AC 147).[7]

[7] Try to remember some key parts of important cases. This is a House of Lords authority and clearly an important case in this area of law.

The use and meaning of the word 'maliciously' in sections 20 and 18, OAPA has caused problems in application and required clarification from the courts. In respect of section 20, 'maliciously' means 'intentionally or recklessly' (**Savage; Parmenter**). However, recklessness is not sufficient for an offence under section 18 (**Belfon**

[1976] 1 WLR 714), thus the word 'maliciously' is rendered redundant where the charge is maliciously wounding or causing GBH with intent to cause GBH. However, 'maliciously' does have practical application where the charge involves an intention to resist or prevent arrest under section 18, although academics' opinions differ on the degree of harm which must be foreseen.[8]

[8] This demonstrates a nuanced understanding of the elements of the section 18 offence and the mens rea requirements.

There is further difficulty in the practicality of charging these offences because the theoretical interpretation of the law is not easily reconcilable with the CPS Charging Standards.[9] A 'wound' is a break in the continuity of the skin (*Moriarty v Brookes* (1834) 6 C & P 684), thus stabbing someone with a pin and drawing blood technically constitutes a wound and could be charged under section 20. Yet, causing a victim to lose consciousness would only attract a charge under section 47. In practice, stabbing a person with a pin would never be charged under section 20 and would be more likely to be a battery.

[9] Demonstrate your awareness of the practical application of the offences by referring to the CPS Charging Standards.

[10] Refer back to the quote again in your conclusion to show how your answer is relevant to the title.

In conclusion, the offences are in need of reform in order to create consistency and certainty in the law. It is agreed that the law is not creditable to the legislature, and the current position is extremely clumsy.[10] The hierarchy of these offences is confusing and it is surprising that the criminal justice system is still so heavily reliant upon a 150-year-old piece of legislation.[11]

[11] This sentence provides the author's concluding opinion in order to enhance the answer and make it stand out from other answers.

✓ Make your answer stand out

- Add further reference to judicial comment to your answer. For instance, you could refer to the fact that Lord Diplock states that the word maliciously 'adds nothing' to section 18 (see *Mowatt* [1967] 3 WLR 1192).

- You could also refer to the academic opinion on the degree of harm which must be foreseen for a conviction under section 18 where the charge involves an intention to resist or prevent arrest. Ormerod states that there must be proof that the defendant foresaw the specified result (*Smith and Hogan Criminal Law* (2011), Oxford: Oxford University Press).

- You could contrast differing academic opinion. In contrast with Ormerod's approach, Jefferson states that the defendant must merely foresee some harm (*Criminal Law* (2011), London: Pearson Longman).

- Provide your opinion to demonstrate to the examiner that you are capable of independent thought and to make your answer stand out from other answers which merely regurgitate the law.

! Don't be tempted to . . .

- Set out everything you know about the non-fatal offences against the person. This question is very specific and does not ask you for a recitation of the elements of each of the offences. Instead, you must demonstrate a critical appreciation of the law and select some of the key problem areas.
- Recite the facts of the cases. There is a lot that could be discussed in this answer and you will waste time by regaling the facts of cases which are not relevant to the question.

Question 4

To what extent do policy considerations influence the use of consent as a defence to non-fatal offences against the person?

Answer plan

→ Briefly outline the general rule that consent is a defence to assault and battery only.

→ Explain the exceptions to this and the rationale for these exceptions.

→ Consider problematic areas, such as consent and sexual gratification and the conflict between *Brown*, *Wilson* and *Emmett*.

→ Explore whether consent plays a part in the transmission of HIV through consensual sex and *Dica* and *Konzani*.

→ Discuss the role of policy considerations and the public interest.

Diagram plan

A printable version of this diagram plan is available from www.pearsoned.co.uk/lawexpressqa

Answer

Public policy considerations play a significant role in the law on consent and non-fatal offences against the person. There are two conflicting principles: the protection of the public from harmful conduct and respect for individual bodily autonomy.[1] The law faces the precarious task of finding a suitable balance between allowing dangerous consensual activity and restricting individual autonomy. The courts are not willing to permit one person to lawfully cause actual or grievous bodily harm to another unless it is in the public interest that such harm be caused. Thus, policy considerations are taken into account in deciding whether in certain circumstances an individual should be permitted to consent to activity which causes harm and would otherwise be a criminal offence.[2]

The general rule is that consent is no defence to assault or battery: ***Donovan*** and ***Attorney General's Reference*** (No. 6 of 1980) [1981] 2 All ER 1057. These are both offences which require no proof of any harm being caused to the victim.[3] However, the courts are stricter when a degree of harm is actually caused; thus, consent is no defence to charges of assault occasioning actual bodily harm (s. 47, OAPA 1861), maliciously wounding or inflicting grievous bodily harm (s. 20) and wounding or causing GBH with intent (s. 18). The law also dictates that we impliedly consent to physical contact of everyday life: ***Collins* v *Wilcock*** [1984] 1 WLR 1172.

However, the law would be incredibly restrictive on our daily lives if it did not permit some deviations from this general rule. Thus, there are certain socially acceptable exceptions when the law allows such harm in the public interest. These exceptions were outlined by Lord Lane CJ in ***Attorney General's Reference*** (No. 6 of 1980) and each is justifiable on grounds of public policy. For instance, reasonable surgical intervention must be permissible for the protection of the health of individuals and to protect the sanctity of life. This exception also includes cosmetic surgery, but the justifications for permitting cosmetic surgery are different and must concern the protection of individual bodily autonomy.[4] Similarly, forms of body adornment, such as tattooing and body piercing are permissible to protect individual autonomy. Since cutting a substantial amount of hair off a person's head was deemed to constitute ABH in ***DPP* v *Smith*** [1961] AC 290, hairdressing must also fall under these exceptions.

Margin notes:

[1] This sentence shows that you have identified the competing interests at the very start.

[2] Address the question directly in your introduction.

[3] This sentence demonstrates that you understand the rationale for the general rule.

[4] Show the examiner that you are able to distinguish between the different justifications for the different exceptions to the general rule.

Injuries caused during properly regulated sports are not subject to criminal sanction because the promotion of exercise is in the greater public interest and sport is a socially acceptable form of entertainment. The Court of Appeal has held that prosecutions for injuries sustained during properly regulated sports should be reserved for grave conduct which is sufficiently serious to be criminal: see **Barnes** [2004] EWCA Crim 3246. While injuries caused unintentionally as an incidental by-product of sports such as rugby and football are easy to justify, it is much harder to justify the use of consent to render lawful injuries intentionally inflicted during sports such as boxing.[5]

[5] Including this reference to boxing shows that you appreciate that the legality of boxing is not necessarily justified using policy considerations.

Unintentional injuries sustained during 'rough horseplay' are deemed to be consented to: see **Jones** (1986) 83 Cr App R 375 and **Aitken** [1992] 1 WLR 1006. The rationale for this lies in the often used phrase 'boys will be boys'. The law would be too restrictive if criminal liability was imposed on individuals for unintentionally causing harm during rough horseplay amongst willing participants. Other exceptions include: lawful chastisement, dangerous exhibitions, ritual circumcision and religious flagellation, which was deemed necessary to avoid a conflict with Article 9 of the European Convention on Human Rights (see Lord Mustill in **Brown**).

One problematic area is that involving injuries inflicted during sexual activity. The House of Lords has ruled that consent is no defence to harm deliberately inflicted for sexual gratification: **Brown** [1994] 1 AC 212. This case involved sado-masochistic conduct between a group of consenting men. The men sustained wounds and injuries which had deliberately been inflicted, and their conduct was videoed and videos were circulated amongst members. The defendants' convictions for offences under section 47 and section 20, OAPA 1861 were upheld in the Court of Appeal and House of Lords. The rationale for imposing criminal liability upon a defendant in such circumstances was expressed by Lord Templeman as the need to protect society against a 'cult of violence' which would 'breed and glorify cruelty'.[6] His Lordship was also concerned by the risk of transmission of HIV and other STDs and the corrupting effect that such behaviour could have on younger members of society.[7] However, this decision of the House of Lords may be criticised for casting moralistic judgments on the defendants in question.[8] The protection of the public was the overriding consideration in this case, and this outweighed respect

[6] Try to remember short key quotes from relevant judgments.

[7] This shows that you have read the opinion and understood the reasoning provided by the judge.

[8] This sentence demonstrates your ability to question (rather than merely accept) the decision of the judge.

for individual autonomy. By contrast, later cases involving hetero-sexual couples have confused the issue by taking the opposite approach.

In **Slingsby** [1995] Crim LR 570, consent was a valid defence where the victim accidentally sustained an internal wound caused by vigorous consensual sexual activity and which ultimately led to her death. Similarly, in **Wilson** [1997] 1 QB 47, **Brown** was distin-guished on the basis that branding with a hot knife constituted body adornment. This act was committed with full consent but was not done for purposes of sexual gratification, and thus can be distin-guished on this basis. The Court of Appeal was keen to emphasise the fact that consensual sexual activity between husband and wife which takes place in private is not a matter for criminal investigation; thus, placing great weight on personal autonomy and privacy. However, this approach was not followed in **Emmett** (1999) *The Times*, 15 October, a case involving sado-masochistic activity between an engaged couple. The Court of Appeal held that the severity of the injuries meant that intervention by the law was in the public interest.

It must be asked whether the law should be able to restrict the behaviour of consenting adults, thus overriding individual autonomy and the freedom to be able to consent to injury or the risk thereof. According to Ashworth, consent 'embodies a recognition that the autonomy of the other person is involved, and that if that person agrees to the conduct there should be no offence' (*Principles of Criminal Law*, 6th edn (2009), OUP at p. 318). This freedom appears to have been respected in both **Dica** and **Konzani** in respect of the risk of transmission of HIV. In both cases, the Court of Appeal held that an informed consent to the risks of having unprotected sexual intercourse with a partner infected with HIV would be a valid defence to a charge under section 20, OAPA 1861 in the event of the virus being transmitted.

In conclusion, policy considerations clearly influence the use of con-sent as a defence. The courts face the difficult task of finding a suitable and consistent balance between the competing principles of the protection of the public and respect for individual autonomy.

✓ Make your answer stand out

- You should explore in more detail the reasoning of the judges in the House of Lords in *Brown*.
- You should compare the opinions of the majority in *Brown* with the dissenting opinion of Lord Mustill. You should refer to Malcolm, T., 'How far is too far? – The extent to which consent is a defence to non-fatal offences against the person' in Geach and Monaghan, *Dissenting Judgments in the Law* (2012, Wildy, Simmonds and Hill) at p. 317 for academic commentary on Lord Mustill's dissenting opinion.
- You could elaborate on the issue of to what extent morality should influence the decisions of judges and include reference to the Hart–Devlin debate.
- You should refer to academic opinion, such as Weait, M., Knowledge, autonomy and consent: *R* v *Konzani* [2005] Crim LR 763; Bamforth, N., Sado-masochism and consent [1994] Crim LR 661; and Gunn, M. and Ormerod, D., The legality of boxing (1995) 15 Legal Studies 181.

! Don't be tempted to . . .

- There is no need to provide factual accounts of all of the cases as you will not have time to do this and address the issue of policy in the exam.
- Set out the elements of the offences. This question asks you specifically about consent and you will waste time by setting out the actus reus and mens rea elements of the non-fatal offences against the person.
- Forget to address the question directly throughout your answer, as well as in your introduction and conclusion.

www.pearsoned.co.uk/lawexpressqa

 Go online to access more revision support including additional essay and problem questions with diagram plans, You be the marker questions, and download all diagrams from the book.

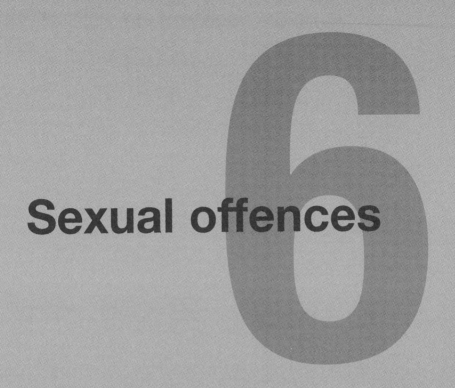

Sexual offences

How this topic may come up in exams

Sexual offences could be examined by way of an essay or a problem question. Essay questions might require you to compare the old law with that under the Sexual Offences Act 2003, or to critically evaluate the meaning of consent. Problem questions will require you to have good knowledge of all elements of the offences and of the law on consent. You should check your syllabus so that you know whether you could be examined on the four main sexual offences, whether your syllabus includes child sex offences, or whether you will only be examined on the offence of rape.

■ Attack the question

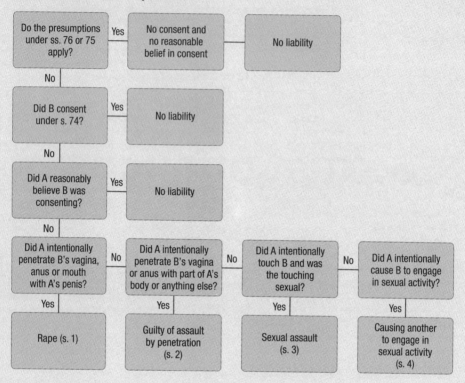

A printable version of this diagram is available from www.pearsoned.co.uk/lawexpressqa

 # Question 1

Prior to the Sexual Offences Act 2003, the law on sexual offences was 'archaic, incoherent and discriminatory' and failed to 'reflect the changes in society and social attitudes' (Home Office White Paper, *Protecting the Public* (2002)).

Critically evaluate the law on rape and the extent to which the law has been improved.

Answer plan

→ Outline the offence of rape under the SOA 2003.

→ Analyse the changes to the elements of rape.

→ Explore the meaning of consent.

→ Discuss whether the SOA 2003 has improved the law.

→ Consider whether the law is coherent and reflects changes in society.

Diagram plan

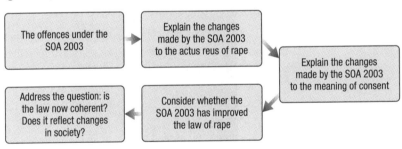

A printable version of this diagram plan is available from www.pearsoned.co.uk/lawexpressqa

Answer

This question requires a critical evaluation of the Sexual Offences Act 2003 ('SOA 2003'). The law on rape underwent radical reform when the SOA 2003 came into force. The Act intended to modernise the law and add coherence and clarity to an area which had developed in a piecemeal fashion.[1] Rape is defined under section 1(1). The actus reus requires the penile penetration of the vagina, anus or mouth, without consent. The mens rea requires intentional penetration, where the defendant had no reasonable belief in consent.

[1] State the aims of the SOA 2003 to demonstrate wider knowledge beyond the elements of the offence.

The actus reus of rape has been extended to cover non-consensual oral sex (previously indecent assault), which was deemed to be serious enough to amount to rape because it is just 'as abhorrent, demeaning and traumatising' as vaginal and anal rape and 'equally, if not more, psychologically harmful' (Government Reply to the Fifth Report from the Home Affairs Committee Session 2002–2003).[2] The Act dispenses with the phrase 'sexual intercourse', which was used to define rape under the SOA 1956. This phrase was incredibly vague as to when intercourse begins. The SOA 2003 is clear in only requiring slight penetration (s. 79(9)). The Act also places the authority of **Kaitamaki** [1985] AC 147 on a statutory footing by stating that penetration is a continuing act (s. 79(2)).

[2] Use key quotes from government publications where appropriate to show awareness of the lead up to enactment.

Another notable change is the use of gender neutral terminology. The SOA 2003 dispenses with gender-specific words, to ensure that the offence of rape can apply to those who have undergone gender reassignment surgery. The old law was discriminatory in this respect and failed to reflect changes in society and social attitudes. The reforms to the actus reus of rape are a welcome improvement to the outdated and vague definition of rape which existed previously.[3]

[3] Provide your opinion at a midway point of your answer to maintain focus.

The SOA 2003 defines consent for the first time (s. 74) and provides for evidential and conclusive presumptions relating to consent (ss. 75 and 76). Sections 75 and 76 place the common law onto a statutory footing. The conclusive presumptions under section 76(1) that the complainant did not consent and that the defendant did not believe that she consented are relevant where: (a) A intentionally deceived B as to the nature or purpose of the act; or (b) A intentionally induced B to have sex by impersonating a person known personally to B. This section places cases such as **Flattery** [1877] 2 QBD 410, **Williams** [1923] 1 KB 340 and **Linekar** [1995] QB 250 onto a statutory footing, whilst incorporating the approach adopted in **Tabassum** [2000] 2 Cr App R 328 in relation to fraud as to the purpose of the act. In relation to fraud as to the identity of the defendant, the case of **Elbekkay** [1995] Crim LR 163 has been placed on a statutory footing but extends the law beyond the impersonation of a spouse or partner.[4]

[4] Compare and contrast the law to show that you are aware of the effects of the SOA 2003.

Section 75(1) sets out evidential presumptions that the complainant did not consent and that the defendant did not reasonably believe that she consented, which are relevant where one of the circumstances in section 75(2) applies and A knew this. The presumptions are rebuttable, so where A adduces some evidence to rebut the presumptions, it will be for the prosecution to prove beyond reason-able doubt that there was no consent and that A did not reasonably believe B was consenting. Section 75 has placed cases such as *Larter* [1995] Crim LR 75 on a statutory footing.

The SOA 2003 has codified much existing case law, but the pre-sumptions are not easy to explain to a jury. It is difficult to explain why deception qualifies as a conclusive presumption, but the use of violence only an evidential presumption. This difficulty is especially evident when one considers the approach taken by the House of Lords towards sexual gratification by violence in *Brown* [1994] 1 AC 212.[5] One might also question whether the use of conclusive presumptions is a satisfactory method of securing convictions.

[5] This sentence demonstrates your ability to think critically and to link this topic to other topics in criminal law.

One problem which has not been addressed by the Act is that of intoxication and consent. Although the Act deals with cases where the complainant is unconscious or asleep and 'date rape' situations through the use of evidential presumptions under section 75, situa-tions in which the defendant has sex with an intoxicated complainant have not been directly addressed (*Bree* [2008] QB 131).[6] As such, the issue of consent is left to the jury and recourse must be had to the definition of consent. Consent has been defined under section 74 as agreeing by choice, having the capacity and freedom to make that choice. Consent is a question for the jury who will receive no detailed direction on consent from the trial judge.

[6] This paragraph demonstrates your awareness of topical problems as well as up-to-date case law.

Another problem concerns submission and consent. Whether sub-mitting to sexual intercourse as a result of non-violent threats con-stitutes consent is not addressed by the Act (*Olugboja* [1982] QB 32). Although the Act is to be commended for codifying existing legal principles which have evolved under the common law, it leaves many situations unexplored which must now be dealt with by broad defini-tion of consent under section 74 and the interpretation given by the jury.

Under the common law there was no definition of consent, conse-quently, the 'parameters [of rape were] unclear' (Temkin, J., *Rape and the Legal Process* (2002) Oxford: Oxford University Press). However, the definition under section 74 is very broad and leaves much to the interpretation of the jury. It has been criticised for being 'vague in its terms' and for leaving 'too much uncertainty in the application of the law to a whole range of familiar situations' (Temkin, J. and Ashworth, A., 'Rape, sexual assaults and the problems

[7] Cite academic opinion where appropriate to show that you have read widely.

of consent' [2004] Crim LR 328).[7] This is certainly true in respect of intoxication and consent and cases of submission. The extent to which the Act has achieved its aim of clarifying the law by explaining what behaviour is and is not acceptable must be questioned.

Another significant amendment to the definition of rape concerns the mens rea. The SOA 2003 contains no mention of the concept of recklessness, but rape requires a reasonable belief that the complainant was consenting. It dispenses with the subjective test under **DPP v Morgan** [1976] AC 182 in relation to a mistaken belief in consent. The old law requiring an honest belief in consent has been replaced by an objective requirement that the belief is reasonable.

[8] Link your conclusion back to the question.

In conclusion, although certain aspects of the SOA 2003 are welcomed, such as the extension of the actus reus of rape, the Act is disappointing in other respects. The law on consent is confusing and the long-awaited definition is too broad and leaves much to the interpretation of the jury. Thus, the SOA 2003 has not provided the clarity craved by the law on rape.[8]

 Make your answer stand out

- Develop the discussion about intoxication and consent and *Bree*. You could also discuss cases such as *Jheeta* [2007] EWCA Crim 1699 and *Zhang* [2007] EWCA Crim 2018 on consent.

- Expand upon the issue of submission and consent and refer to the article by Gardner, S., Appreciating *Olugboja* (1996) 16 Legal Studies 275.

- Expand upon the discussion of consent and fraud, discussing cases such as *Tabassum* and the difference between fraud as to the 'quality' of the act and fraud as to the 'purpose' of the act.

- Discuss the question raised by Temkin and Ashworth in [2004] Crim LR 328, as to whether the categories of presumptions are 'intended to reflect some kind of moral hierarchy' or simply organised to ensure 'clarity and certainty' or a mixture of the two 'with an added element of common law history'.

- Elaborate upon the change to the test applied to mistaken belief in consent. Consider whether the introduction of an objective approach is in line with the subjectivist nature of criminal law. Read Wells, C., Swatting the subjectivist bug [1982] Crim LR 209.

- Consider whether the actus reus of rape should have been extended to cover non-consensual oral sex or whether this should have been categorised as assault by penetration.

! Don't be tempted to . . .

- Discuss other offences such as assault by penetration, sexual assault and causing a person to engage in sexual activity without consent. The question is limited to the offence of rape, so do not waste valuable time.

- There is no need to write out large swathes of statute. It is better to ensure that you understand the meaning of the relevant sections, and to learn short extracts of the sections by heart. This question requires a critical appreciation of the law rather than a mere recital of the law.

? Question 2

Answer **ALL** parts.

Discuss the criminal liability of the parties for rape in the following scenarios:

(a) During the night, Gerry decides to sneak into his flatmate Suzy's room. He climbs into bed with her and begins to have sexual intercourse with her. Suzy wakes up during the act and, believing Gerry is her boyfriend, allows Gerry to have anal intercourse with her.

AND

(b) Jasper, a student, decides to attend his university's annual winter ball which is being held at a hotel in London. After dinner he meets Amy, another student, with whom he spends several hours, dancing and drinking. Just before the end of the evening, Jasper buys Amy a drink. He places a quantity of rohypnol, a hypnotic drug which is a powerful sedative, in Amy's glass of wine. Amy drinks the wine and becomes drowsy. Jasper leads Amy to his hotel room where she collapses on the bed, unconscious and unable to move. Jasper proceeds to have sexual intercourse with Amy.

AND

(c) Damian threatens to call off his engagement to his girlfriend unless she performs an act of oral sex on him. His girlfriend, afraid that Damian will carry out his threat, agrees to perform the act of oral sex.

Answer plan

→ Consider the liability of Gerry for the vaginal and anal rape of Suzy. In particular, you will need to address the issue of consent and the conclusive presumptions under section 76(1) triggered by section 76(2)(b), SOA 2003 and the evidential presumptions under section 75(1) triggered by section 75(2)(d).

➜ Explore the liability of Jasper for the rape of Amy. In particular, you will need to address the issue of consent and the evidential presumptions under section 75(1) triggered by section 75(2)(d) and section 75(2)(f).

➜ Discuss the liability of Damian for oral rape in respect of his girlfriend. In particular, you will need to address the definition of consent under section 74 and the issue of consent and submission. Make reference to the cases of *Olugboja* and *McAllister* [1997] Crim LR 233.

Diagram plan

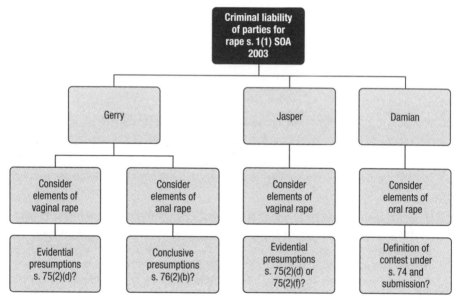

A printable version of this diagram plan is available from www.pearsoned.co.uk/lawexpressqa

Answer

This question requires consideration of the liability of Gerry, Jasper and Damian for the offence of rape. Rape is defined under section 1(1) of the Sexual Offences Act 2003 ('SOA 2003'). The actus reus requires the penetration of the vagina, anus or mouth, with the defendant's penis, where the complainant does not consent. The mens rea is intentional penetration, where the defendant had no reasonable belief in consent.[1]

[1] Set out the definition of rape at the start so that you do not need to do this throughout the answer.

(a) Gerry

Gerry may be guilty of two offences of rape against Suzy – one involving vaginal intercourse and the other anal intercourse. Both incidents of intercourse involve the penetration of the vagina or anus of Suzy with Gerry's penis. It is also clear that the penetration is intentional;[2] thus, the issue here is really one of consent. In order to secure convictions, the prosecution must establish that Suzy was not consenting and that Gerry did not reasonably believe that she was consenting.[3] Consideration must be given to the evidential and conclusive presumptions under section 75(1) and section 76(1), SOA 2003.

In respect of the vaginal intercourse, the evidential presumptions under section 75(1) apply. Section 75(1) sets out two evidential presumptions: that the complainant did not consent and that D did not reasonably believe that she consented. These are relevant where one of the circumstances under section 75(2) is applicable and D knew this. These presumptions may apply due to the fact that Suzy is asleep when Gerry begins to have intercourse with her (s. 75(2)(d)).[4] If Gerry is aware that Suzy is asleep, the evidential presumptions under section 75(1) are triggered, which means that Suzy is presumed not to have consented and it is presumed that Gerry did not reasonably believe that she was consenting. These presumptions are rebuttable and Gerry may adduce evidence to the contrary, however, he is unlikely to be able to in this scenario.[5]

The second incident, that of anal rape, requires consideration of the conclusive presumptions under section 76(1). Section 76(1) sets out two conclusive presumptions: that the complainant did not consent and that D did not believe that she consented. These are relevant where one of the circumstances under section 76(2) is applicable. Gerry has intentionally deceived Suzy into having anal sex by impersonating a person known personally to her, namely her boyfriend. According to section 76(2)(b), the conclusive presumptions under section 76(1) will be triggered. This means that it is presumed that Suzy did not consent and that Gerry did not believe she was consenting. As conclusive presumptions, these may not be rebutted by Gerry.[6]

Thus, Gerry will be guilty of the anal rape of Suzy due to the application of the conclusive presumptions under section 76(1). He will also be guilty of vaginal rape, unless he can adduce evidence to rebut the evidential presumptions under section 75(1).[7]

[2] Although you do not need to define rape again here, you must apply the elements to the facts.

[3] Identify the key issues at the beginning of your answer.

[4] There is no need to list all of the circumstances under section 75(2). Choose the most appropriate circumstance on the facts.

[5] Do not forget to explain the effect of an evidential presumption.

[6] This sentence shows your awareness of the distinction between the evidential and conclusive presumptions.

[7] Provide a short conclusion to part (a) before moving on to part (b).

(b) Jasper

Jasper may be convicted of the rape of Amy. There is clear evidence on the facts that Jasper has penetrated the vagina, anus or mouth of Amy with his penis. This is likely to be a case of vaginal rape. The penetration would also appear to be intentional, thus, the issue here is also that of consent.

The evidential presumptions under section 75(1) may apply. In this case, section 75(2)(f) applies, as Jasper caused a drug to be administered to Amy without her consent, which was capable of causing her to be stupefied or overpowered. It is also the case that Jasper knew of this circumstance at the time of intercourse. Alternatively, section 75(2)(d) could apply as Amy was unconscious or asleep at the time of intercourse and Jasper must have known this.[8] The presumptions under section 75(1) are only evidential, which means they are rebuttable. Jasper bears only the evidential burden: it is for Jasper to raise some evidence to rebut the presumptions, but it is for the prosecution to prove beyond reasonable doubt that there was no consent and that Jasper did not reasonably believe Amy was consenting.

It is unlikely that Jasper will be able to adduce any evidence to rebut the presumptions and it is likely that the prosecution will secure a conviction for rape here.

[8] Ensure that you discuss all of the circumstances under section 75(2) that apply to demonstrate your knowledge.

(c) Damian

Damian may be guilty of the rape of his girlfriend. Non-consensual oral sex is now included in the offence of rape. It is clear on the facts that Damian has penetrated his girlfriend's mouth with his penis. It is also clear that the penetration is intentional. Thus, the issue here is again one of consent. This will only amount to rape if it is proved that the girlfriend was not consenting and that Damian did not reasonably believe that she was consenting. However, the presumptions under sections 76 and 75 will not apply here as none of the circumstances under sections 75(2) and 76(2) exist.[9] Consequently, the definition under section 74 will need to be applied in order to establish whether or not the girlfriend was consenting. If it is established that the girlfriend did not consent to the oral sex, it must also be established that Damian did not reasonably believe that she was consenting. Whether a belief is reasonable is to be determined having regard to all the circumstances, including any steps Damian has taken to ascertain whether she is consenting (s. 1(2)).

[9] If the presumptions do not apply, rule them out at the start.

Section 74 defines consent as agreeing by choice, with the capacity and freedom to make that choice. The facts here raise the issue of whether submission amounts to consent or not. Under section 75(2) (a), threats of violence would trigger the evidential presumptions under section 75(1). However, the law is less clear in relation to non-violent threats. In *Olugboja* [1982] QB 32, the Court of Appeal held that it was up to the jury to decide whether there was consent on a case-by-case basis. In *McAllister* [1997] Crim LR 233, it was held that the judge was not required to direct the jury that reluctant acqui-escence amounted to consent. Although these were cases decided before the enactment of the SOA 2003, they follow the approach adopted today.[10] Consent is a question for the jury and they will receive no detailed direction on consent from the trial judge. It is questionable whether the girlfriend in this scenario agreed by choice. She has been given a choice between two evils and has made a choice between them. The proportionality between the threat and the act of sex must be explored. The gravity of the threat must also be considered. It could be argued that the threat issued here was not sufficiently grave to warrant the girlfriend acceding to it.[11] It may be necessary to know a little more about the circumstances of their relationship. However, on the facts it is likely that the jury will consider consent to be present, and thus there will be no conviction for rape.

[10] This demonstrates your awareness that the pre-SOA 2003 cases may apply here and why.

[11] These few sentences justify your conclusion on this point.

✓ Make your answer stand out

- Although the law on rape is now contained within the SOA 2003, you should apply any pre-2003 cases which might be relevant, particularly in relation to consent and submission.

- Demonstrate a clear understanding of how the presumptions work in practice and the distinction between the evidential and the conclusive presumptions under sections 75(1) and 76(1) respectively.

- You could incorporate some academic opinion into your answer, particularly relating to contentious issues that arise on the facts of the problem question. For instance, in this question you could also consider academic opinion on submission, such as Gardner, S., Appreciating *Olugboja* (1996) 16 Legal Studies 275.

- Although the main issues in this question require a discussion of the provisions relating to consent, you must also apply the other elements of rape in order to provide a complete answer and to demonstrate a rounded knowledge of the SOA 2003.

! **Don't be tempted to . . .**

- Forget that the presumptions under section 75(1) require not only the existence of a circumstance under section 75(2), but also require the defendant to be aware of the existence of that circumstance.

- Confuse an evidential burden and a legal burden. The evidential presumptions may be rebutted. This requires the defendant to discharge an evidential burden (raise some evidence to rebut the presumptions). This is not a burden of proof. The legal burden still rests with the prosecution to prove (beyond reasonable doubt) that there was no consent and that the defendant had no reasonable belief in consent.

- Set out the circumstances under sections 75(2) and 76(2) which do not apply to the particular problem scenario you are dealing with. You will gain no extra marks for providing irrelevant information and you will merely highlight your inability to distinguish between relevant and irrelevant information.

? Question 3

Answer **ALL** parts.

Consider the criminal liability of the parties for any sexual offences in ALL of the following scenarios:

(a) Richard sees Natalia walking down the street towards him. As she passes him Richard says to her, "You're sexy. Fancy a shag?" and he stretches his leg out and catches the hem of her skirt, lifting it.

AND

(b) Alicia tells Jamie to masturbate himself in front of a camera while she takes photographs of him. When Jamie refuses to comply, Alicia says, "Don't make me call Bruiser. He's a huge bloke and he will do you some serious damage". Fearful of an attack, Jamie masturbates in front of the camera.

AND

(c) Owen threatens Katrina that unless she allows him to penetrate her vagina with his fingers, he will kill her family. Katrina is afraid that Owen will carry out his threat and allows him to penetrate her digitally.

AND

(d) Tim kidnaps Mike, who suffers from motor neurone disease and is paralysed from the neck down. Tim has sexual intercourse with Mike. Mike is not a willing participant but, due to his condition he is unable to tell Tim to stop.

Answer plan

→ Explore the liability of Richard for sexual assault under section 3, SOA 2003 in respect of Natalia. In particular, you will need to address the meaning of 'sexual' under section 78.

→ Discuss the liability of Alicia for the offence of causing a person to engage in sexual activity without consent under section 4, SOA 2003. The issue of consent and the evidential presumptions under section 75(1) triggered by section 75(2)(a) will be important here. You should also refer here to the meaning of 'sexual' under section 78.

→ Consider the liability of Katrina for the offence of assault by penetration under section 2, SOA 2003. The issue of consent and the evidential presumptions under section 75(1) triggered by section 75(2)(b) will be important here.

→ Consider Tim's liability for the rape of Mike under section 1, SOA 2003. You will need to consider here the issue of consent and the possibility of the evidential presumptions under section 75(1) being triggered by section 75(2)(c) or (e).

Diagram plan

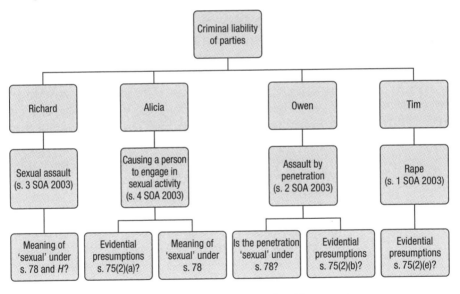

A printable version of this diagram plan is available from www.pearsoned.co.uk/lawexpressqa

Answer

This question involves the following sexual offences: rape, assault by penetration, sexual assault and causing a person to engage in sexual

[1] List the offences that you will be discussing at the very start to demonstrate that you have identified the key offences.

[2] This question provides your structure for you. Ensure you divide your answer into parts (a) to (d).

[3] Cite any relevant definition sections to demonstrate your wider knowledge of the statute.

[4] Ensure that you apply the law using the specific facts in the problem scenario.

[5] This sentence and the following paragraph incorporate both the relevant statutory provision and case law to demonstrate wider knowledge.

activity under sections 1–4, SOA 2003.[1] The liability of Richard, Alicia, Katrina and Tim will be explored.[2]

(a) Richard

Richard could be guilty of sexual assault (s. 3(1)). This offence requires proof that Richard intentionally touched Natalia without her consent and that the touching was sexual. It must also be proved that Richard did not reasonably believe that Natalia consented. Richard does intentionally touch Natalia as he lifts her skirt with his foot. According to the case of **Thomas** (1985) 81 Cr App R 331, touching the hem of a girl's skirt is sufficient for battery and under section 79(8), 'touching' includes touching with any part of the body and through anything.[3] Thus, the fact that Richard has touched Natalia's clothing with his foot is likely to be sufficient to constitute an assault.[4] It is necessary to consider whether the touching was 'sexual' under section 78. Section 78 defines the word 'sexual' and the Court of Appeal examined its meaning in **H** [2005] 1 WLR 2005.[5] The jury must consider: (i) would the reasonable person consider that the touching could be sexual? and (ii) would the reasonable person, in the circumstances, consider that due to the purpose of the defendant, the touching was sexual? The first question deals with the meaning of sexual under section 78(a), which states that an act is sexual if a reasonable person would consider that because of its nature, it is sexual, irrespective of its circumstances or any person's purpose in relation to the act. Touching the hem of a person's skirt is not inherently sexual, so section 78(a) will not apply. Section 78(b) provides that an act is sexual if a reasonable person would consider that because of its nature it may be sexual and because of its circumstances or the purpose of any person in relation to it, it is sexual. The nature of lifting the hem of a person's skirt is such that objectively speaking, it 'may' be sexual, so if Richard's purpose is sexual, section 78(b) will be satisfied. The facts state that Richard did tell Natalia that he thought that she was sexy and he asked her for 'a shag'. Thus, it may well be that Richard's purpose is sexual, and thus, the touching will be sexual.

None of the presumptions under sections 75 and 76 apply, so recourse must be had to the definition of consent under section 74. Natalia did not agree to Richard touching her and confronts him after he does so. Under section 3(2), whether a belief is reasonable is to be determined having regard to all the circumstances, including any steps that Richard has taken to ascertain whether Natalia consents. Richard appears to have no reasonable belief in consent and he has certainly taken no steps to ascertain that she consents to the touching. He is likely to be guilty of sexual assault.

(b) Alicia

Alicia could be guilty of causing a person to engage in sexual activity (s. 4(1)). This offence requires proof that Alicia intentionally caused Jamie to engage in a sexual activity without consent and that the defendant did not reasonably believe that the complainant was consenting. It is clear that Alicia intentionally caused Jamie to engage in a sexual activity. Masturbation is inherently sexual under section 78(a) and **H**.

The main issue here is one of consent. The evidential presumptions under section 75(1) are likely to apply here. The circumstances under section 75(2)(a) exist because Alicia has threatened Jamie with violence. Since Alicia was aware of the existence of these circumstances (having made the threat herself), the rebuttable presumptions under section 75(1) are triggered. So, it is presumed that Jamie did not consent and that Alicia did not reasonably believe that Jamie was consenting. Alicia will be guilty of causing a person to engage in sexual activity unless she can rebut these presumptions. There is no evidence to rebut these on the facts.

(c) Owen

When Owen penetrates Katrina's vagina with his fingers, he is guilty of assault by penetration (s. 2(1)). This offence requires proof that the defendant intentionally penetrated the vagina or anus of the complainant with a part of his body or anything else. The intentional penetration of Katrina's vagina with Owen's fingers satisfies this. The penetration must be sexual under section 78. If the penetration of a person's vagina with another's fingers is inherently sexual, then it will fall under the meaning of sexual under section 78(a). If not, it is at least clear that Owen's purpose here is sexual, thus section 78(b) is satisfied.

The offence of assault by penetration also requires that the penetration takes place without Katrina's consent and Owen must have no reasonable belief in consent. The circumstances under section 75(2)(b) exist because Owen has threatened to kill Katrina's family. Thus, the rebuttable presumptions under section 75(1) are triggered. So, it is presumed that Katrina did not consent, and that Owen did not reasonably believe that she was consenting. Owen will be guilty of assault by penetration unless he can rebut these presumptions. It is unlikely that he will be able to do so on the facts.

(d) Tim

Tim could be charged with raping Mike. Rape is defined under section 1(1). The actus reus is penetration of the vagina, anus or mouth, with the defendant's penis, where the complainant does not consent. The mens rea is intentional penetration, where the defendant had no reasonable belief in consent. Intentional penile penetration of the anus seems to have occurred here.[6] Thus, the main issue is one of consent. Consent is defined under section 74 as agreeing by choice, having the freedom and capacity to make that choice. On the facts, it is clear that Mike does not agree by choice to the intercourse. Additionally, the evidential presumptions under section 75(1) could apply because Mike has been unlawfully detained by Tim and Tim is not detained (s. 75(2)(c)). It is also clear that Tim knew that Mike was unlawfully detained because the facts state that Tim kidnapped Mike.[7] Consequently, under section 75(1) it is presumed that Mike did not consent, and that Tim did not reasonably believe he was consenting. Thus, Tim will be guilty of rape unless he can rebut these presumptions. He only bears the evidential burden, so he must raise some evidence in rebuttal. There appears to be no such evidence on the facts. Section 75(2)(e) might also apply because Mike suffers from motor neurone disease and paralysis, if his physical disability means he would have been unable to communicate consent.[8]

[6] Do not labour over these elements if they are quite clearly satisfied.

[7] This demonstrates that you have fully understood that both the circumstances under section 75(2)(c) must be present and the defendant must have known about the existence of those circumstances.

[8] If there is an alternative paragraph which might apply, mention this too.

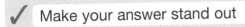

✓ Make your answer stand out

- Demonstrate a clear understanding of the distinction between the four different offences under the SOA 2003. Many of the elements for each offence are different and examiners will be looking to see if you are aware of the elements of each offence.

- Ensure that you cite key case law, such as *H* in respect of the meaning of 'sexual'. You must explain why you are mentioning the case.

- Ensure that you apply the law to the facts of the problem scenario throughout your answer. This question addresses all four main offences and is quite technical in some respects, but you must apply all elements rather than simply deal with the contentious ones.

- You could incorporate some academic opinion into your answer, such as Bantekas, I., Can touching always be sexual when there is no sexual intent? (2008) 73 *Journal of Criminal Law* 251 on the meaning of sexual for the purposes of section 78, SOA 2003.

! Don't be tempted to . . .

- Gloss over the meaning of 'sexual', which is defined under section 78.

- Write out the relevant statutory provisions verbatim. You will gain no extra marks for remembering the precise wording of the statute and you will waste valuable time writing it out. Instead you should ensure that you know all of the required elements for each offence and the meaning of the key terms. The examiner is looking for evidence of your understanding and application of the law, not a fantastic memory.

www.pearsoned.co.uk/lawexpressqa

Go online to access more revision support including additional essay and problem questions with diagram plans, You be the marker questions, and download all diagrams from the book.

7

Theft

How this topic may come up in exams

Theft is one of the main offences against property and is a popular topic with examiners and students. Theft may be examined by way of a problem question which requires students to identify any relevant areas of law and apply the law to the factual scenario. Alternatively, it may be examined by way of an essay question which requires a critical appreciation of the topic and might focus in more detail on particular elements of theft, such as appropriation or dishonesty. You should pay particular attention to the structure of answers to both problem questions and essay questions on theft.

Attack the question

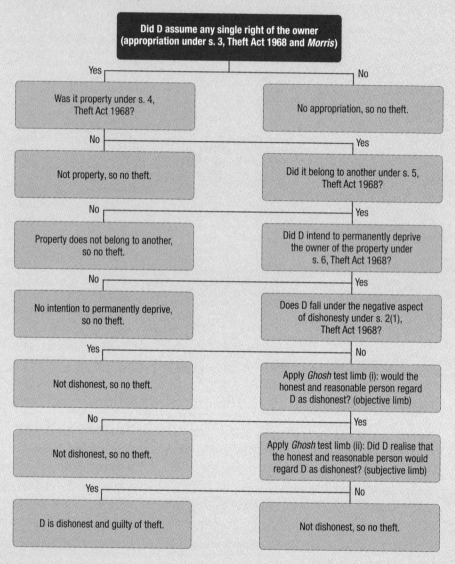

A printable version of this diagram is available from www.pearsoned.co.uk/lawexpressqa

 Question 1

Critically evaluate the assertion that the actus reus of theft has been 'reduced to vanishing point' (Ormerod, D. and Williams, D., *Smith's Law of Theft*, 9th edn, OUP, p. 20).

Answer plan

→ Discuss the meaning of appropriation under section 3(1), Theft Act 1968 and the common law.

→ Apply the approach of the courts to consent and appropriation in *Lawrence* v *MPC*, *Gomez* and *Hinks*.

→ Conclude that such a wide interpretation of the actus reus renders the mens rea (i.e. dishonesty) particularly important.

→ Discuss that liability is largely determined by application of the *Ghosh* test of dishonesty.

Diagram plan

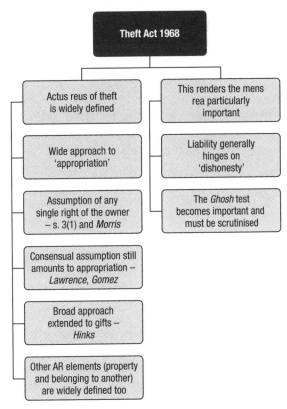

A printable version of this diagram plan is available from www.pearsoned.co.uk/lawexpressqa

Answer

This question requires a critical evaluation of the assertion that the actus reus elements of theft are so widely construed that the actus reus has now reached 'vanishing point'. It is true that the actus reus elements of theft have been very widely interpreted by the courts. Ormerod and Williams make their assertion in respect of the meaning given to 'appropriation'.[1] Such a wide interpretation of the actus reus means that liability for theft will generally be determined by the mens rea elements. This in turn requires attention to be given to the law relating to the mens rea elements; in particular, the *Ghosh* [1982] 2 All ER 689 test applied in respect of dishonesty must be scrutinised.[2]

[1] Ensure that you address the question directly in your introduction in order to demonstrate that you are able to engage with the question.

[2] These two sentences draw further on the consequences of the observation made by Ormerod and Williams. The explanation put forward here demonstrates a very good degree of knowledge and appreciation of the subject and will gain you higher marks.

Theft is defined in section 1(1), Theft Act 1968 as the dishonest appropriation of property belonging to another with the intention to permanently deprive the other of it.[3] The prosecution must prove all five elements in order to secure a conviction: *Lawrence v MPC* [1971] 2 All ER 1253. The actus reus elements of 'appropriation', 'property' and 'belonging to another' have been widely interpreted.

[3] This paragraph provides a brief overview of the elements of the offence and where it comes from.

'Appropriation' is partially defined under section 3(1), Theft Act 1968 and involves any assumption of the rights of the owner over the property. This means that the defendant appropriates property by doing something with the property that the owner has the right to do. Many different forms of conduct may constitute appropriation, such as using the property, keeping it, lending it to someone else, selling it, destroying it, etc. Under section 3(1), a later appropriation is also sufficient; thus, where the defendant comes by the property innocently but later does something with it by which he assumes the rights of the owner, he appropriates it. The law does not restrict liability by requiring a defendant to assume all of the rights of the owner, but takes a broader approach by requiring the assumption of any single right: *Morris* [1983] 3 All ER 288.[4]

[4] This paragraph focuses specifically on the element of appropriation, the scope of which has been the subject of much debate. This part of the answer provides some evidence of the wide interpretation of appropriation.

The relationship between appropriation and consent has been the subject of much debate. There are a number of cases which relate to the question of whether an authorised assumption of the owner's rights could amount to appropriation. In *Lawrence*, the House of Lords held that an authorised assumption of the rights of the owner could amount to appropriation. The House held that the defendant had appropriated money from a student's wallet, despite the fact that the student had consented to him taking money from his wallet. Viscount Dilhorne[5] stated that the absence of any words in section 3(1) of the Theft Act 1968 requiring the appropriation to take place without consent meant that Parliament had relieved the prosecution of having to prove that the appropriation took place without the owner's consent. Thus, consent was unequivocally deemed to be irrelevant to appropriation.

[5] Use the name of the relevant judge where possible in order to demonstrate the detail of your knowledge to the examiner.

However, the House of Lords reconsidered this issue in **Morris** and, confusingly, reached a different conclusion. In this case, Lord Roskill stated *obiter* that 'an act expressly or impliedly authorised by the owner' did not constitute appropriation, but appropriation did involve 'an act by way of adverse interference with or usurpation of [the owner's] rights'. According to Lord Roskill in **Morris**, an authorised act could not amount to appropriation, thus picking up goods to buy in a supermarket would not constitute appropriation, neither would the act in **Lawrence**. After **Morris**, there existed a clear conflict on the issue of consent in appropriation between two House of Lords' authorities. However, it should be noted that **Morris** was only persuasive on this point as Lord Roskill's statement was an *obiter dictum*, whereas **Lawrence** laid down a binding *ratio decidendi*.[6]

[6] Ensure you acknowledge the fact that Lord Roskill's comment in *Morris* was only an *obiter* statement in order to demonstrate to the examiner that you understand that the statement was only persuasive. By contrast, the fact that *Lawrence* provided a binding *ratio* is also highlighted.

The conflict between these authorities was resolved by the House of Lords in **Gomez** [1993] 1 All ER 1. In this case, the House of Lords held that **Lawrence** and **Morris** could not be reconciled. The House followed **Lawrence** and held that consent was irrelevant to appropriation, thus appropriation did not require an unauthorised assumption of the rights of the owner. Lord Browne-Wilkinson considered the word 'appropriation' in isolation as 'an objective description of the act done' irrespective of the mental state of the defendant. In his commentary to **Gomez** in the Criminal Law Review, Professor Smith (1993) stated that 'anyone doing anything whatever to property . . . with or without the authority or consent of the owner, appropriates it'.[7] Consequently, the element of appropriation has been widely construed.[8]

[7] This key quote from a highly esteemed academic is worth remembering.

[8] The final sentence here refers back to the question in order to ensure that the focus of the essay is the quote in the title.

[9] Examine the gift cases after considering the cases on consent and appropriation. This chronological approach provides the ideal structure for this question.

This broad approach was later extended to apply to situations where the defendant receives a gift from a suggestible or vulnerable donor.[9]

In **Mazo** (1997) 2 Cr App R 518, the Court of Appeal held that property given to the defendant with consent could be appropriated if the consent was obtained by fraud. However, this narrow interpretation of **Gomez** meant that there could be no appropriation where a valid gift was given *inter vivos*. In **Hopkins and Kendrick** [1997] 2 Cr App R 524, the Court of Appeal criticised **Mazo**. The position was finally considered by the House of Lords in **Hinks** [2001] 2 AC 241. The House extended the approach taken in **Gomez** and held that a valid gift could be appropriated. This decision has been criticised for extending the scope of appropriation too far and creating a conflict between criminal and civil law.

It is clear that a very wide interpretation is applied to 'appropriation'. A broad approach is also taken in respect of the remaining actus reus elements of theft: 'property' and 'belonging to another'.[10] 'Property' is partially defined in section 4(1) of the Theft Act 1968 and includes money, real and personal property as well as things in action and other intangible property. Under section 5(1) of the Theft Act 1968, 'belonging to another' is also widely construed; this element extends to someone in possession or control of the property, as well as the owner of the property. There is even case law to suggest that it is possible to steal property you own if someone else has possession or control over it: **Turner** (No. 2) [1971] 2 All ER 441.

In conclusion, it is quite clear that the actus reus elements of theft are widely interpreted and the assertion that the actus reus has been reduced to 'vanishing point' is certainly justifiable.[11] This renders the mens rea elements of theft particularly important. As liability will hinge upon proof of dishonesty and the intention to permanently deprive, it is important that the law relating to these elements is beyond criticism. However, the suitability of the **Ghosh** test for dishonesty sparks another debate. The importance placed upon the mens rea of theft means that the jury's application of **Ghosh** and its interpretation of 'honesty' dictate the fate of the defendant.[12]

[10] Do not forget to address the other actus reus elements of theft. Property and belonging to another have also been widely construed, despite not receiving quite as much judicial and academic attention as appropriation.

[11] In your conclusion, refer directly to the quote from Ormerod and Williams. Very good answers will provide a reasoned opinion on the assertion.

[12] The last lines of this paragraph go further than simply agreeing or disagreeing with the quote. They acknowledge the consequences of such a wide interpretation of the actus reus of theft. However, as the criticisms of *Ghosh* are not within the scope of this essay (and in fact provide a whole essay themselves), you are unlikely to have time to discuss them here.

✓ Make your answer stand out

- Refer to opinions of specific judges in cases such as *Lawrence*, *Morris* and *Gomez*.
- Refer to academic opinion. In particular, note Professor J.C. Smith's commentary to *Gomez* in [1993] Crim LR 304 (learn the key quote from this commentary) and Professor A.T.H. Smith's comments in Theft or sharp practice: who cares now? [2001] CLJ 21.
- Explain how the 'gifts cases' extended the scope of appropriation.
- Remember to discuss the remaining actus reus elements which also warrant brief mention.
- Relate each paragraph back to the question and explain how the case law supports the assertion.
- Critically evaluate the effect that this has on the mens rea. Explain that liability is consequential upon the jury's interpretation of 'honesty'.

! Don't be tempted to . . .

- Confuse the distinction between the *ratio* in *Lawrence* and the *obiter* statement in *Morris*.
- When discussing consent and appropriation, do not mention section 2(1) of the Theft Act 1968 and dishonesty. Students often confuse appropriation and dishonesty, because while consent is irrelevant to appropriation, an honest belief in consent may negate the dishonesty aspect (s. 2(1)(b), Theft Act 1968). These are two entirely distinct issues. Appropriation is an actus reus element and should be considered in isolation from the mental state of the defendant.
- Recite the facts of *Lawrence*, *Morris*, *Gomez* and *Hinks* in laborious detail. If you need to refer to the facts, do so briefly. Remember that as this essay requires an evaluation of the law, the principles from the cases are far more important.
- Go through the law relating to dishonesty and intention to permanently deprive in detail. Do not simply write everything you know on theft.

❓ Question 2

After checking her pay slip, Samantha notices that she has been overpaid by £200. She arranges an appointment to see her line manager, Thomas, the following day in order to report the error. However, later that day an email is sent to all staff detailing proposals for pay cuts for all employees. Angry at this, Samantha decides to keep the £200 overpayment.

In the evening, Samantha goes shopping for an outfit for her friend's birthday party. She decides to splash out on a designer dress with matching shoes and handbag. The outfit costs £1,000 at full price, but Samantha removes a '50% off' label from a different dress and places it on the outfit she wants to buy. She takes this to the cashier and pays £500 for the whole outfit. At the cash desk, Samantha notices a catalogue. Believing it to be free, she takes one. In fact, the catalogue costs £3.50.

On her way out of the shop, Samantha notices a £10 note on the floor. After looking around to see who might have dropped it, she picks it up and puts it in her purse.

Discuss Samantha's liability for the offence of theft.

Answer plan

→ Define theft and state where it comes from.

→ Discuss whether Samantha is liable for theft of the overpayment. In particular, you should consider section 5(4) of the Theft Act 1968.

→ Consider the theft arising from Samantha's conduct in placing a 50% off label on the outfit. This requires consideration of appropriation.

→ Discuss whether Samantha has stolen the catalogue. Section 2(1) of the Theft Act 1968 will be important here.

→ Consider whether there was a theft of the £10 note. Who does this belong to? Is Samantha dishonest?

Diagram plan

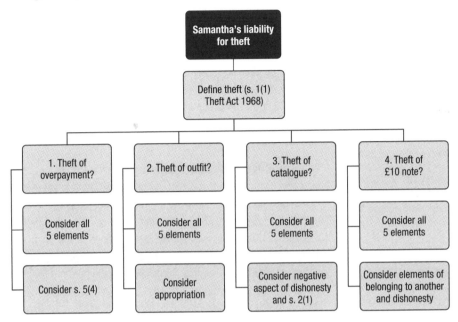

A printable version of this diagram plan is available from www.pearsoned.co.uk/lawexpressqa

Answer

[1] As the question asks specifically about theft, you should restrict your answer to theft. You will gain no extra marks for discussing the offences of burglary or fraud. If the question is more general and asks you simply to discuss the relevant party's criminal liability, then you should consider all offences which arise in the question. See the mixed questions in Chapter 13 for examples.

Samantha could be liable for theft of the £200 overpayment, the outfit, the catalogue and the £10 note.[1] Theft is defined under section 1(1) of the Theft Act 1968 as the dishonest appropriation of property belonging to another with the intention to permanently deprive the other of it. The prosecution must prove all five elements in order to secure a conviction: **Lawrence v MPC** [1971] 2 All ER 1253.

The £200 overpayment[2]

[2] Use a logical and clear structure, dealing with each incident of theft in turn and use headings to maintain focus.

By keeping the £200, Samantha may have committed theft. She has appropriated the money. Appropriation is partially defined under section 3(1) of the Theft Act 1968 as assuming the rights of the owner. The case of **Morris** [1983] 3 All ER 288 confirmed that the defendant need not assume all of the owner's rights, but any single right will

[3] Set out the law relating to appropriation briefly and cite the relevant statutory provision and any relevant case law.

[4] This demonstrates to an examiner that you are aware of the two different appropriations, the first of which is an innocent one, the second will form the basis of the conviction for theft.

[5] Deal with the actus reus elements first, before considering whether the mens rea is satisfied.

[6] As it does not apply, you should not go through all of the paragraphs under section 2(1). It is still worth mentioning the section though in order to demonstrate to the examiner that you have considered and rejected the provision.

[7] Set out the *Ghosh* test in full. Students often misstate the test, so ensure that you learn the full test and explain it accurately.

[8] Once you have set out the law relating to dishonesty, apply it to the problem scenario.

[9] If you want to mention the facts or *Morris* here in order to acknowledge the similarity between them and those in the problem scenario, do so very briefly.

do.[3] When Samantha takes possession of the money, she appropriates it. She assumes a further right of the owner (that of possession) by keeping the money.[4] Whether or not Samantha has the consent of her employers in respect of either of these assumptions is irrelevant to appropriation: *Lawrence* [1982] 1 AC 510 and *Gomez* [1993] 1 All ER 1. The £200 is property under section 4(1) of the Theft Act 1968, as it is a 'thing in action' – Samantha has a right to payment by her bank of £200. The property belongs to her employers because, under section 5(4) of the Theft Act 1968, it is property obtained by mistake. Thus, the actus reus elements of theft are satisfied.[5]

Although at first Samantha intends to pay back this money, her intention changes after she receives the email. At this stage she forms the intention to permanently deprive her employer of the money by keeping it. The remaining question then is whether Samantha is dishonest. Dishonesty is not defined in the Theft Act 1968. Section 2(1) does provide a partial definition of the negative aspect of dishonesty, but this is unlikely to apply here.[6] Therefore, the test for dishonesty under *Ghosh* [1982] 2 All ER 689 should be applied. This test requires the jury to consider: (i) whether the honest and reasonable person would regard what Samantha did as dishonest; and (ii) whether Samantha realised that the honest and reasonable person would regard her conduct as dishonest.[7] The first limb is objective and the second is subjective. Samantha's conduct is likely to be dishonest according to *Ghosh* because the honest and reasonable person would regard keeping the money as dishonest and the fact that Samantha initially intends to report the overpayment indicates that she probably realises this.[8] Thus, the mens rea is likely to be satisfied.

The outfit

Samantha is likely to be guilty of theft of the outfit. She appropriates it when she picks it up and then again when she places the 50% off label on it. This is an assumption of a right of the owner: section 3(1); *Morris*. This scenario is similar to that in *Morris*, where the defendant swapped the labels on goods in a shop.[9] Although Samantha had the consent of the shop to pick up the outfit, she had no consent to put the label on the outfit. Nevertheless, consent is not relevant to appropriation: *Lawrence* and *Gomez*. The outfit is personal property under section 4(1) and it belongs to the shop: section 5(1). Thus, the actus reus elements of theft are satisfied.

Samantha clearly intends to permanently deprive the shop of the outfit. The negative aspect of dishonest under section 2(1) is unlikely to apply here. Applying **Ghosh**, the honest and reasonable person would regard Samantha's act of applying the '50% off' label to the outfit in order to pay half the cost dishonest. Samantha must have realised this or she would have simply asked for the discount. Thus, the mens rea elements of theft are satisfied.

The catalogue

In relation to the catalogue, Samantha may have a defence to a charge of theft. The actus reus elements of the offence are clearly satisfied, but the mens rea might be disputed. Samantha has appropriated the catalogue by taking and keeping it. This amounts to an assumption of a right of the owner – that of possession: section 3(1); **Morris**. Whether or not she had consent to take the catalogue is relevant to the question of appropriation: **Gomez**. The catalogue is personal property under section 4(1) and it belongs to the shop. Thus, the actus reus elements are satisfied.

Samantha intended to permanently deprive the shop of the catalogue. However, in respect of dishonesty, she may be able to rely upon section 2(1)(a) or (b) in her defence.[10] Under section 2(1)(a), Samantha will not be dishonest if she honestly believed that she had a right in law to take the catalogue. She may have such a belief if she honestly thought that the catalogues were free for customers. Alternatively, under section 2(1)(b), Samantha will not be dishonest if she honestly believed that she had the consent of the shop to take the catalogue. It is likely that at least one of these provisions will apply. However, if they do not, the jury will determine dishonesty using the **Ghosh** test.[11] It is unlikely that Samantha was dishonest here.

[10] If you think that both of these provisions might apply, mention them both. However, as section 2(1)(c) does not apply here, do not mention that provision.

[11] You should still mention the fact that the *Ghosh* test will apply in the absence of the provision under section 2(1) in order to demonstrate to the examiner that you understand the way in which section 2(1) and *Ghosh* work in practice.

£10 note

By keeping the £10 note, Samantha may have committed theft. She appropriates it when she picks it up and assumes the right of possession: section 3(1); **Morris**. Under section 4(1), property includes money. It is difficult to know who the £10 belongs to. The owner has lost it, but this is unlikely to be abandoned property. It is very difficult to abandon property, because this requires an indifference to the property. The owner is unlikely to be indifferent to the money. Thus, the £10 must belong to somebody for the purposes of theft. Under section 5(1), property belongs to anybody in possession or control of it. By taking it into her possession, Samantha has acquired a right of possession of the £10. The shop may also have possession or control of the £10 if it demonstrates an intention to exercise control over the shop and the things in it: **Hibbert v McKiernan** [1948] 2 KB 142 and **Parker v British Airways** [1982] QB 1004.

[12] Ensure that you read the precise wording of section 2(1)(c) and understand it. Students often make the mistake of thinking that reasonable steps actually have to be taken, when they do not. The defendant must merely hold an *honest belief* that the owner could not be found *if* reasonable steps *were* taken.

If the actus reus elements are satisfied, consideration must be given to the mens rea. Samantha clearly intends to permanently deprive the owner of the money as she intends to keep it, but is she dishonest? She might argue that she honestly believed she had a right in law to the money (s. 2(1)(a)), or that she honestly believed that the owner could not be found even if all reasonable steps were taken (s. 2(1)(c)).[12] If either of these apply, she will not be dishonest. If they do not, the **Ghosh** test will be applied. If the jury think that the honest and reasonable man would regard keeping the £10 as dishonest, and that Samantha knew this, she will be convicted of theft.

✓ Make your answer stand out

- Adopt a clear structure. Use headings if necessary in order to ensure you remain focused on the potential theft in question. Headings may also assist the examiner by adding clarity to your answer.
- You should deal with each of the incidents of theft in turn and consider whether the actus reus is satisfied before moving on to the mens rea.
- Cite only the relevant principles of law and do not use your answer to regurgitate everything you know about theft.
- Apply the law to the problem scenario as you go. As a general guide you should try to apply the law every time you state a relevant principle of law.
- Refer to any relevant academic opinion. In particular, you could mention the key quote describing appropriation from Professor J.C. Smith's commentary to *Gomez* in [1993] Crim LR 304. You should also make reference to any judicial comment which may be relevant.

! Don't be tempted to . . .

- Set out all of the relevant law on theft in the first half of your answer and do not leave your application of the law to the problem scenario until the end of your answer. This practice of simply writing everything you know about theft and adding a cursory paragraph of application at the end of your answer will gravely affect your chances of passing the exam.
- Neglect correctly stating and applying both the objective and the subjective limbs of the *Ghosh* test.
- Forget that section 2(1)(c) of the Theft Act 1968 does not actually require the defendant to take reasonable steps to find the owner. He must merely hold an honest belief that the owner could not be found if reasonable steps were taken.

❓ Question 3

Jonathan, a law lecturer, decides to borrow his colleague, Professor Williams's, criminal law textbook overnight in order to prepare for a lecture. Jonathan takes the book from Professor Williams's desk and leaves a note saying 'Just borrowed a book. Hope you don't mind. Jonathan'. In fact, Professor Williams needed the textbook overnight and would not have lent it to Jonathan. Whilst in Professor Williams's office, Jonathan also notices a Dictaphone which he had lent Professor Williams months ago. Jonathan takes the Dictaphone.

The following day, after his lecture, Jonathan is approached by Nadine, a student. Nadine tells Jonathan about her ideas for reforming the law relating to dishonesty in theft. Jonathan is impressed with Nadine's ideas and decides to use them in an article that he is writing.

A retired Crown Court judge, H.H.J. Monaghan, contacts Jonathan and explains that she would like to give Jonathan £30,000 for all his dedication to teaching criminal law. H.H.J. Monaghan is very elderly, vulnerable and suggestible. Jonathan suspects that H.H.J. Monaghan is confused about the amount of money she is handing over but he accepts the £30,000 and spends it on a sports car.

Discuss Jonathan's liability for the offence of theft.

Answer plan

→ Define theft and state where it comes from.

→ Discuss whether Jonathan is liable for theft of the textbook. You should consider whether, and in what circumstances, borrowing may amount to theft.

➜ Consider the theft arising from Jonathan's conduct in taking back the Dictaphone he lent Professor Williams. This requires consideration of the meaning of property and dishonesty.

➜ Discuss whether Jonathan has stolen Nadine's ideas. The meaning of property will need to be considered here.

➜ Finally, discuss whether there was a theft of the £30,000 gift from H.H.J. Monaghan. Is it possible to steal a gift? Is Jonathan dishonest?

Diagram plan

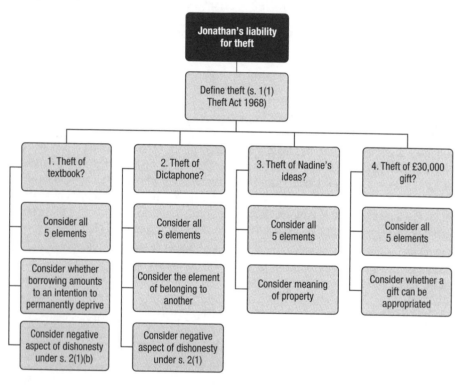

A printable version of this diagram plan is available from www.pearsoned.co.uk/lawexpressqa

Answer

Jonathan might be liable for theft of the textbook, the Dictaphone, Nadine's ideas and the £30,000 gift. Theft is defined under section 1(1), of the Theft Act 1968 as the dishonest appropriation of property belonging to another with the intention to permanently deprive the other of it.[1] The prosecution must prove all five elements in order to secure a conviction: *Lawrence v MPC* [1971] 2 All ER 1253.

[1] As with the problem question on theft above, this question specifically asks about theft, so you should restrict your answer to theft. You will gain no extra marks under the circumstances for discussing burglary.

Textbook[2]

Jonathan is unlikely to be guilty of theft of the textbook.[3] It is first necessary to establish the actus reus elements. Jonathan has appropriated the textbook. Appropriation is partially defined under section 3(1) as an assumption of the rights of the owner. According to *Morris* [1983] 3 All ER 288, the defendant need not assume all the owner's rights, just one single right. When Jonathan picks up the textbook, he assumes possession of it, and thus appropriates it. He does not appear to have the consent of Professor Williams to take the book, but consent is irrelevant to appropriation: *Lawrence* and *Gomez* [1993] 1 All ER 1. The textbook is property under section 4(1) as it is 'personal property'. The property clearly belongs to another, namely Professor Williams. Thus, the actus reus elements of theft are satisfied.

[2] Use a logical and clear structure, dealing with each incident of theft in turn.

[3] If you have planned your answer properly before you started writing, you should be able to state at the outset whether Jonathan is likely to be guilty of theft or not. You should then justify this statement in the proceeding paragraphs.

It is now necessary to establish whether the mens rea elements are present. Jonathan is borrowing the book. Under section 6, a borrowing or lending may amount to such an intention where it is equivalent to an outright taking or disposal.[4] According to *DPP v Lavender* [1994] Crim LR 297, 'to dispose of' means 'to deal with', thus dealing with property could be sufficient. This is a wide approach under which Jonathan has the necessary intention. By contrast,[5] in *Lloyd* [1985] QB 829, Lord Lane CJ[6] gave this element a narrow interpretation, stating that what was required was an intention to return the thing in such a changed state that it can be said that all its goodness or virtue has gone. As Jonathan plans to return the book with some of its goodness and virtue, Jonathan does not have the necessary intention under the narrow approach.

[4] Set out the law relating to whether borrowing amounts to an intention to permanently deprive briefly and cite the key statutory provision.

[5] Where there are two conflicting lines of authorities, apply both in the alternative to demonstrate to the examiner your knowledge of the area.

[6] Be specific about the name of the judge if you can. You should remember to use Lord Lane CJ in respect of *Lloyd*.

Dishonesty is not defined in the Theft Act 1968. However, section 2(1) provides a partial definition of the negative aspect of dishonesty. Under section 2(1)(b), a defendant is not dishonest if he honestly believes he would have had the consent of the owner. Jonathan could argue that he honestly believed that he would have had Professor Williams's consent to borrow the textbook. This is a purely subjective test; hence it does not matter if his belief was not reasonable or mistaken. Thus, the fact that Professor Williams would not in

139

fact have lent Jonathan the book is not relevant; Jonathan will have a defence provided his belief was honestly held. If Jonathan had no such belief, section 2(1) will not apply and the test for dishonesty under **Ghosh** [1982] 2 All ER 689 should be applied. This test requires the jury to consider: (i) whether the honest and reasonable person would regard what Jonathan did as dishonest; and (ii) whether Jonathan realised that the honest and reasonable person would regard his conduct as dishonest.[7] The first limb is objective and the second is subjective.[8] Jonathan's conduct is not likely to be dishonest according to **Ghosh** if the honest and reasonable person would not regard borrowing the textbook as dishonest. It would appear that Jonathan and Professor Williams are in the habit of borrowing items from each other as the professor has borrowed Jonathan's Dictaphone. Even if the objective limb is satisfied, Jonathan does not appear to realise that his conduct is objectively dishonest, as he leaves a note for Professor Williams.[9] Thus, the mens rea is not likely to be satisfied.

[7] As with the answer to question 2 above, you should set out the *Ghosh* test in full and accurately.

[8] This sentence demonstrates that you understand the distinction between the two limbs of the *Ghosh* test.

[9] Use the facts given in the problem scenario to justify your conclusions.

Dictaphone

Jonathan is not likely to be guilty of theft of the Dictaphone. He appropriates it when he takes possession of it. This is an assumption of a right of the owner: section 3(1); **Morris**. Jonathan has no consent to take the Dictaphone, but consent is not relevant to appropriation: **Gomez**. The Dictaphone is personal property under section 4(1). Although Jonathan owns the Dictaphone, under section 5(1), 'belonging to another' is concerned with possession or control. It is possible to be guilty of theft of your own property (**Turner** (No. 2) [1971] 2 All ER 441), although there is also authority to the contrary (**Meredith** [1973] Crim LR 253). The Dictaphone belongs to Professor Williams in the sense that the Professor has possession or control over it. Thus, the actus reus elements of theft may be satisfied.

Jonathan intends to permanently deprive Professor Williams of the Dictaphone. The negative aspect of dishonesty is likely to apply. Under section 2(1)(a), Jonathan may honestly believe he has a right in law to take the property as he owns it. Jonathan may believe that Professor Williams would have consented to Jonathan taking the Dictaphone (s. 2(1)(b)).[10] If section 2(1) does not apply, **Ghosh** will be applied. The honest and reasonable person would probably not

[10] Refer back to the discussion of section 2(1)(b) above re honest belief in consent.

regard Jonathan's conduct as dishonest, and even if they did, Jonathan is unlikely to have realised that his conduct was objectively dishonest. Thus, the mens rea elements of theft are probably not satisfied.

Nadine's ideas

In relation to Nadine's ideas, Jonathan may have a defence to theft. Jonathan has appropriated the ideas by using them in his article. This is enough to amount to an assumption of a right of the owner: section 3(1); *Morris*. Although Jonathan does not appear to have consent to use the ideas, consent is irrelevant to appropriation: *Gomez*. The ideas were Nadine's and may 'belong' to her in a sense; however, ideas do not amount to property because information is not property for the purposes of theft: Oxford v Moss [1979] Crim LR 119. Jonathan is not guilty.[11]

[11] Although you may wish to explore the mens rea in respect of Nadine's idea, if you are pushed for time, you might choose not to do so here since the actus reus of theft is clearly not present.

£30,000 gift

By taking the £30,000, Jonathan may have committed theft. He appropriates it by assuming the right of possession: section 3(1); *Morris*. According to *Hinks*, it is possible to appropriate a valid gift. Under section 4(1), property includes money. Although title passes on receipt of a valid gift, the prosecution may rely upon *Hinks* to argue that Jonathan is guilty if he dishonestly accepts the gift. Jonathan intends to permanently deprive H.H.J. Monaghan of the money as he intends to keep it. However, he might argue that he honestly believed he had a right in law to keep the money as it was a gift (s. 2(1)(a)). If so, he is not dishonest. If section 2(1) does not apply, *Ghosh* will be applied. If the jury thinks that the honest and reasonable man would regard keeping the £30,000 as dishonest, and that Jonathan knew this, he will be guilty of theft. As H.H.J. Monaghan is vulnerable and suggestible, Jonathan may be objectively dishonest for taking the money. He probably realises this and will be guilty.

✓ Make your answer stand out

- It is important that you structure your answer clearly. Plan your answer before you begin to write so that you know in advance whether you are going to conclude that Jonathan is likely to be guilty of the theft of each item or not. This helps you to focus and avoid waffle and a muddled answer.

- Use any key quotes from cases that are relevant. It is worth learning key quotes from cases such as *Gomez, Hinks, Lloyd, Ghosh* along with the name of the relevant judge so that you can cite them where relevant.

- Where the facts are vague, allowing for different possibilities, you should apply the law to each variable. For instance, the facts do not expressly state whether or not Jonathan honestly believed that Professor Williams would have consented to him taking the textbook – you should apply the law to both variables.

- You should incorporate some academic opinion where possible. As this question involves the theft of a gift, you could include reference to Shute, S., Appropriation and the Law of Theft (2002) Crim LR 445.

! Don't be tempted to . . .

- Speculate about matters which are not relevant to the specific problem scenario.

- Forget to discuss the negative aspect of dishonesty under section 2(1) of the Theft Act 1968 before applying *Ghosh*. Even where section 2(1) is unlikely to apply, you should state this (albeit briefly) in order to demonstrate to the examiner that you fully understand the law relating to dishonesty.

- Forget that section 2(1) is assessed on a purely subjective basis. Do not be tempted to apply an objective test to the negative aspect of dishonesty as you will lose marks for this.

📖 Question 4

'The Law Commission recently commented that it found the criticisms of the present law [on dishonesty] "compelling". It was suggested that *Ghosh* was not so much a definition as a way of coping with the absence of a definition'. (Ormerod and Williams, *Smith's Law of Theft* (2007), OUP, p. 115)

To what extent do you agree that the test for dishonesty in *Ghosh* is in need of reform?

Answer plan

➡ Define theft and state where it comes from.

➡ Explain the law relating to dishonesty using both the negative aspect under section 2(1) of the Theft Act 1968 and the positive aspect from *Ghosh*.

➡ Consider the judgment of Lord Lane CJ in the Court of Appeal in *Ghosh*.

➡ Set out the criticisms which have been made of the *Ghosh* test by academics.

➡ Put forward any arguments in favour of the current law on dishonesty.

➡ Conclude by providing your own informed opinion on the law and address the quote by commenting as to whether you agree with it or not.

Diagram plan

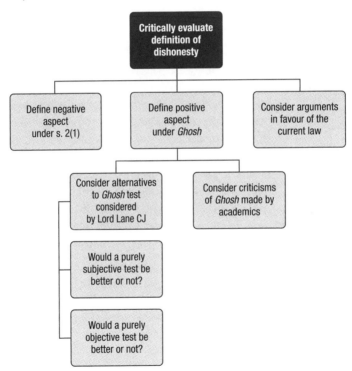

A printable version of this diagram plan is available from www.pearsoned.co.uk/lawexpressqa

Answer

This question requires a critical evaluation of the law relating to dishonesty. The quote suggests that there is validity in the criticisms of the current law and that the *Ghosh* [1982] 2 All ER 689 test is not a satisfactory way of dealing with the absence of a statutory definition of dishonesty. The *Ghosh* test has been subject to much criticism, but no suitable alternative has been found.[1]

[1] This paragraph addresses the concerns of the quote directly and demonstrates both that you have read the question and that you intend to engage with the points made within it.

Theft is defined under section 1(1) of the Theft Act 1968. Dishonesty is one of the mens rea elements of theft. The actus reus elements of theft are widely interpreted; this means that liability for theft hinges on the prosecution's ability to prove that the defendant was dishonest.[2] The question of dishonesty is one of fact, and thus is left to the jury to determine.

[2] This sentence demonstrates that you appreciate the importance of the role of dishonesty in a defendant's liability for theft.

There is no definition of dishonesty in the Theft Act 1968. However, the Act does provide three scenarios in which a defendant is not dishonest. This is the negative aspect of dishonesty.[3] Under section 2(1), a defendant is not dishonest if: (a) he honestly believes that he had a right in law to the property; (b) he honestly believed that he had or would have had the owner's consent had the owner known about the circumstances; or (c) he honestly believed that the owner could not be found even if all reasonable steps were taken to try to find him. It should be noted that reasonable steps do not actually have to be taken. This negative, partial definition of dishonesty is subjectively assessed.[4] Where section 2(1) applies, no consideration need be given to *Ghosh*. However, where none of the scenarios under section 2(1) apply, then the *Ghosh* test is considered.

[3] Deal first with section 2(1), Theft Act 1968 rather than jumping straight to the *Ghosh* test. Section 2(1) is considered first in practice because if any of the scenarios within section 2(1)(a)–(c) applies, *Ghosh* need not be considered.

[4] Acknowledge that section 2(1) is very different from the *Ghosh* test in the sense that it provides a negative, partial definition of dishonesty which is subjectively assessed, whereas *Ghosh* provides a positive, part-objective and part-subjective test.

The positive aspect of dishonesty comes from *Ghosh*. The *Ghosh* test has two limbs. The first, objective limb came from *Feely* [1973] QB 530 and requires the jury to consider whether the honest and reasonable person would regard what the defendant did as dishonest. If this is answered in the affirmative, the second, subjective limb requires the jury to question whether the defendant himself realised that the honest and reasonable man would regard what the defendant did as dishonest. This is called the subjective limb, but it contains an objective element and calls for the defendant's recognition of his objective dishonesty.[5] Only if both the objective and the subjective questions are answered in the affirmative, can the defendant be found to be dishonest.

[5] This sentence demonstrates that you understand the second limb of the test as Lord Lane CJ intended it, although it should be noted that academic commentary has debated this second limb (see Campbell [1994] CLJ 349).

The ***Ghosh*** test has been severely criticised by academics, most notably by Professor Griew[6] ([1985] Crim LR 341) and the arguments against the test are indeed compelling.[7] The dishonesty element in theft has become increasingly important in the assessment of a defendant's liability, especially since appropriation has been very widely interpreted by the courts (***Hinks*** [2001] 2 AC 241). However, Lord Lane CJ demonstrated in ***Ghosh***, that the test does provide a compromise between the unsatisfactory alternatives of a purely subjective or a purely objective approach.

As Lord Lane CJ suggests in ***Ghosh***, if dishonesty is meant to categorise a state of mind, then a purely objective test of dishonesty would not be suitable because the knowledge and belief of the defendant are at the root of the problem. His Lordship provides the example[8] of a man who comes to England from a country where public transport is free and travels by bus without paying. His mind is clearly honest, although his conduct, objectively speaking, is dishonest. Thus, an objective test of dishonesty would convict this man and Lord Lane CJ takes the view that this is not what Parliament could have intended. His Lordship notes that section 2(1) is drafted in subjective terms and relates to the belief of the defendant rather than his conduct and concludes that this subjective partial definition could not be made to work with an objective test.

Consideration should also be given to the suitability of a subjective test. Lord Lane CJ criticises the objection that a subjective test would 'abandon all standards but that of the accused himself, and to bring about a state of affairs in which "Robin Hood would be no robber"'. The objection suggests that on a subjective approach a defendant could argue that he himself did not believe his conduct to be dishonest, and thus that he is not dishonest. This is known as the 'Robin Hood defence'.[9] However, His Lordship states that this objection 'misunderstands the nature of the subjective test' which incorporates an objective element such that the defendant is judging his knowledge or belief of the objective standard of dishonesty. Thus, His Lordship was satisfied that the ***Ghosh*** test would not provide the 'Robin Hood defence'.

While the ***Ghosh*** test has been applauded for adding clarity to the law (see Smith, 'Commentary' [1982] Crim LR 608), it has also been strongly criticised. Griew argues that there is no ordinary standard of

[6] Professor Griew is probably the most famous critic of the *Ghosh* test, so you should (at the very least) refer to his articles and opinion.

[7] You should address aspects of the quote directly throughout your answer to ensure that you are engaging with the question.

[8] This is a famous example and you should discuss it here.

[9] You should also consider the alternative 'Robin Hood defence' argument.

honesty; he calls this the 'fiction of community norms'. What one person regards as honest another might regard as dishonest. Similarly, what might be regarded as honest in one part of the country might be deemed dishonest in another. Thus, the standard of honesty has too many variables. The test also assumes that jurors are themselves honest.

Griew further argues that leaving the question of dishonesty to the jury leads to inconsistent verdicts and uncertainty in the law, as well as longer and more expensive trials as defendants are more likely to plead not guilty and take their chances with a jury. Griew suggests that dishonesty is a question of law which should not be left to the jury. Spencer argues that the test is too complicated for juries and that it provides a defence of mistake where a defendant can argue that he did not realise that honest and reasonable people would regard his conduct as dishonest ((1982) CLJ 222). Campbell argues that the second limb of the test is not necessary where the jury are directed to consider all the circumstances under the first limb ([1994] 43 CLJ 349).[10]

[10] You should try to refer to a number of different academics' opinions. The greater number of academics' opinions you incorporate into your answer, the better your mark will be.

In conclusion, the **Ghosh** test is by no means perfect, but despite its critics, the test has survived. The criticisms of it may very well be compelling: views of jurors as to what is honest differ, the test may fail to offer consistency, the law might be uncertain in this respect and inaccessible as a defendant does not know if his conduct will be deemed dishonest until after the jury's verdict. The law must be flexible enough to adapt to changing views in society, but should also provide consistency and certainty. However, the alternatives suggested so far are less than satisfactory, and it seems that the **Ghosh** test is currently the best definition that we have, albeit not a perfect one.[11]

[11] Refer back to the quote in your conclusion and offer your own opinion in respect of the Ghosh debate.

✓ **Make your answer stand out**

- Refer to academic opinion as much as possible in order to demonstrate that you have engaged with the academic debate.
- You should read the articles referred to in the answer and get to grips with the arguments being made by different academics: Smith, J., Commentary on R v Ghosh [1982] Crim LR 608; Griew, E., Dishonesty, the objections to Feely and Ghosh [1985] Crim LR 341; Spencer, J., Dishonesty: what the jury thinks the defendant thought the jury would have thought (1982) CLJ 222; and Campbell, K., The test of dishonesty in Ghosh [1994] 43 CLJ 349.

- You should also refer to other academic opinion. For instance, consider the solution proposed by D.W. Elliott in Dishonesty in theft: a dispensable concept [1982] Crim LR 395.
- You should refer to any judicial opinion that might be relevant, such as Lord Lane CJ in *Ghosh*.
- You could refer to Law Commission publications, such as *Fraud* (Report No. 276, 2002) and *Legislating the Criminal Code: Fraud and Deception*, Consultation Paper No. 155 (1999).
- You should demonstrate your knowledge of how the *Ghosh* test of dishonesty is applied to fraud, but section 2(1) of the Theft Act 1968 is not. Consider the implications of this.

! Don't be tempted to . . .

- Use the first person (the word 'I'), although you are asked to give your opinion in this question. You should adopt a more formal style of writing when writing academic answers. You could take guidance on writing style from good textbooks and academic journals.
- Forget that section 2(1) is based upon the honest belief of the defendant, and thus is subjectively assessed.
- Misstate the *Ghosh* test. Do not be tempted to shorten the test – you must set it out in full.
- Recite the facts of *Ghosh*. This question is asking you about the academic debate surrounding the test and the facts of the case are not relevant to this.

www.pearsoned.co.uk/lawexpressqa

 Go online to access more revision support including additional essay and problem questions with diagram plans, You be the marker questions, and download all diagrams from the book.

Other property offences

8

How this topic may come up in exams

Other property offences, such as burglary, aggravated burglary, robbery, handling stolen goods and criminal damage are often examined by way of problem questions. Such questions might examine just one or two property offences, while others might require exploration of a mixture of property offences including theft and fraud.

Burglary and robbery are often assessed as part of the same problem question, as they are closely related, both being found under the Theft Act 1968. When answering a question on burglary you should also be aware of the possible existence of the offence of aggravated burglary appearing in the question.

Attack the question

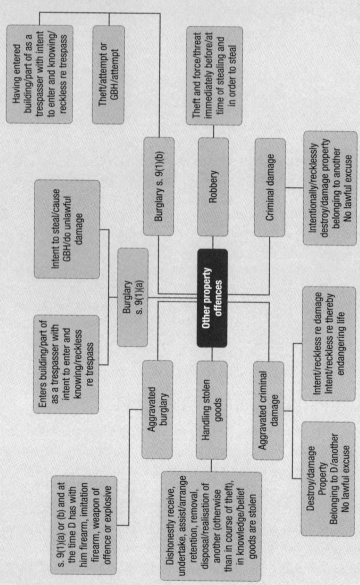

A printable version of this diagram is available from www.pearsoned.co.uk/lawexpressqa

permanent because Angelo smashes the glass cabinet, thus actus reus is satisfied. The cabinet is personal property (s. 10(1)) a it belongs to another (s. 10(2)). Angelo will have no defence of law excuse here. Angelo also has the requisite mens rea of crimi damage because he intends to damage the glass, or at the very le he is reckless as to the damage because the damage is a necessa by-product of his purpose in stealing the gem. Thus, Angelo will guilty of criminal damage under section 1(1) of the Criminal Dama Act 1971.

Angelo might also be guilty of aggravated burglary under section of the Theft Act 1968. This offence requires proof of a burglary wh at the time of the burglary the defendant has with him a firear imitation firearm, weapon of offence or explosive. When Angelo fir enters the study and commits burglary under section 9(1)(a), has the knife with him. The knife can be classed as a 'weapon offence', which includes any article intended for use for causir injury to or incapacitating a person (s. 10(1)). Angelo has the knif with him in order to injure somebody if necessary, thus he has th requisite intention (**Kelly** (1993) 97 Cr App R 24). Where aggravate burglary is charged in respect of a burglary under section 9(1)(a), th time at which the defendant must be proved to have the weapon offence with him is upon entry.[9] Here, Angelo does have the knif with him on entry, thus he may be convicted of aggravated burglary

Angelo might also be guilty of aggravated burglary when he steal the gem because he commits a section 9(1)(b) burglary at this stage and has the knife with him. According to **O'Leary** (1986) 82 Cr Ap R 341, it is necessary to prove that the defendant had the weapon with him at the time of the ulterior offence, but it is not necessary to prove that he had it with him on entry. Thus it would have to be established that Angelo had the knife with him when he stole the gem. If this is proved, he will be guilty of a further aggravated burglary.

Pushes Glen

Under section 8 of the Theft Act 1968, Angelo will be guilty of rob- bery if it can be established that immediately before or at the time of stealing, and in order to steal, Angelo used force on Glen or put or

[?] Question 1

Angelo decides to break into a stately home in order to steal a valuable gem which is housed in a glass cabinet in the study. Angelo enters the house through the kitchen window. Whilst in the kitchen he sees a steak knife on a sideboard in the dining room. He leans through the kitchen hatch and picks up the steak knife, planning to use it if necessary.

He then makes his way to the study and sees the glass cabinet with the valuable gem. He smashes the glass and steals the gem.

On his way out of the property, Angelo is approached by Glen, a security guard who heard the glass breaking and came to investigate the disturbance. Angelo panics, dropping the gem. He runs towards the exit, pushing Glen as he passes him.

Discuss Angelo's criminal liability.

Diagram plan

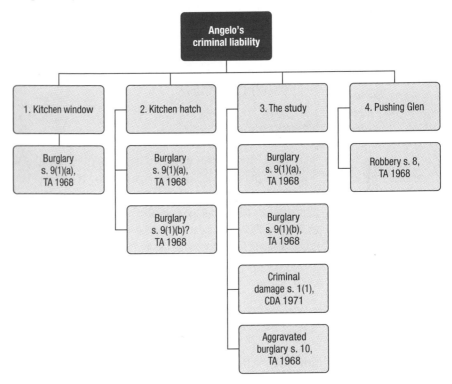

A printable version of this diagram plan is available from www.pearsoned.co.uk/lawexpressqa

Answer plan

→ Distinguish the offences of burglary under section 9(1)(a) and (b) of the Theft Act 1968.

→ Discuss Angelo's liability for burglary under section 9(1)(a) when he enters the house through the kitchen window.

→ Explore Angelo's liability for burglary under section 9(1)(a) when he leans through the kitchen hatch and section 9(1)(b) and/or theft when he picks up the steak knife.

→ Discuss Angelo's liability for burglary under section 9(1)(a) and (b) in respect of the study and criminal damage when he breaks the glass cabinet.

→ Consider whether Angelo is guilty of aggravated burglary under section 10.

→ Consider whether Angelo is guilty of robbery when he pushes past the security guard.

Answer

Angelo could be guilty of burglary under section 9(1)(a) and (b) of the Theft Act 1968, theft, criminal damage under section 1(1) of the Criminal Damage Act 1971, aggravated burglary under section 10 of the Theft Act 1968 and robbery under section 8 of the Theft Act 1968.[1] There are two offences of burglary under section 9(1)(a) and (b) of the Theft Act 1968.[2]

[1] Listing the relevant offences at the start demonstrates that you have properly considered and understood the question before commencing your answer.

[2] This demonstrates that you are aware that there are two distinct offences of burglary.

Kitchen window[3]

Angelo is guilty of burglary under section 9(1)(a) when he enters the house through the kitchen window. Under section 9(1)(a), a defendant commits burglary if he enters a building or part of a building as a trespasser with the intention to steal, inflict GBH or do unlawful damage (s. 9(2)). It is clear that Angelo enters a building when he climbs through the window and he does so without permission, and thus as a trespasser. Angelo has the requisite mens rea for burglary under section 9(1)(a) because he knows that he is trespassing[4] and he does so with the intention to steal the gem. Thus, at this stage, he is guilty of burglary under section 9(1)(a).

[3] Ensure that your structure is clear and logical. Go through the scenario chronologically.

[4] Do not forget to set out and apply the mens rea relating to the trespass.

Kitchen hatch

When Angelo leans through the kitchen hatch he is guilty of burglary under section 9(1)(a),[5] because he enters a part of a building as a

[5] Where the defendant is guilty under both sections 9(1)(a) and (b), deal with section 9(1)(a) first.

trespasser (*Walkington* [197... [1973] QB 100, entry must ... in *Brown* [1985] Crim LR ... 'effective'. In *Ryan* [1996] ... window constituted sufficie... effective. Angelo is still a ... passing. However, it is al... ulterior intention upon en... element is satisfied. In ... the gem.

Section 9(1)(b) requires ... building as a trespasse... inflicts or attempts to ... constitutes theft or ... burglary under sectio... priates it and it is cle... dishonest if the hon... knife as dishonest ... However, it is uncle... owner of the knife ... use it as a weap... glary under secti... site ulterior inter... (b) if theft of the ...

[6] As this question encompasses a number of offences, you will probably not have time to go through all of the elements of theft in detail. However, mentioning the elements demonstrates that you are aware of them.

[7] Highlight the fact that the prosecution will have difficulty proving this element to show your understanding of the law.

[8] As this section of your answer covered two potential offences, use a sentence at the end to briefly conclude.

Study

When he ent... tion 9(1)(a) ... building as ... Upon entry ... ulterior int... guilty of b... room, he ...

At this s... tion 1(1... offence... anothe... trivial (

[9] Demonstrate that you understand the distinctio... between an aggravated ... section 9(1)(a) and an ... aggravated section 9(1)(b... by drawing on the importa... of the meaning of 'at the ... time'.

sought to put Glen in fear of being then and there subjected to force. Angelo pushes Glen, thus the use of force is clear. However, this use of force does not take place immediately before stealing, and it must be questioned whether it takes place at the time of stealing because Angelo drops the gem before using force. If the theft is not continuing and the force is not used 'at the time' of stealing, there is no robbery. It is also questionable whether he uses force 'in order to steal'; instead it appears that Angelo uses force in order to effect an escape.[10] Thus, Angelo is not likely to be guilty of robbery.

[10] This sentence demonstrates a good understanding of the law on robbery.

✓ Make your answer stand out

- You should demonstrate to the examiner that you are aware of the differences between the offence of burglary under section 9(1)(a) and that under section 9(1)(b) of the Theft Act 1968.

- Make sure that you apply the law to the facts of the problem scenario throughout. An examiner does not simply want you to recite everything you know about the relevant offences, but they want to know why these offences are relevant.

- Use a separate paragraph for each offence that you discuss so as to avoid confusing the examiner and in order to maintain your focus.

- Ensure that you correctly apply the offence of aggravated burglary and accurately identify the burglary that the aggravated offence applies to.

! Don't be tempted to . . .

- Simply recite the relevant sections from the Theft Act 1968 or the Criminal Damage Act 1971 verbatim. The examiner wants to know that you understand the law and can apply it well, rather than that you can memorise the words of the sections.

- Confuse the elements of burglary under section 9(1)(a) and (b), Theft Act 1968.

- Spend too much time discussing the elements of theft at the expense of other property offences. The instruction line of this question does not restrict your answer to theft, and thus requires a wider exploration of property offences.

Question 2

'Determining whether there has been an entry has proved more difficult than might be envisaged . . . The Act gives no express guidance and it seems to have been assumed in Parliament that the common law rules would apply. The courts have, however, adopted inconsistent approaches . . .' (Ormerod, D. and Williams, D., *Smith's Law of Theft*, 9th edn (2007) Oxford: Oxford University Press, p. 249).

Critically evaluate the law relating to entry in burglary.

Answer plan

→ Outline the old common law meaning of entry.

→ Discuss the approach taken more recently by the courts.

→ Consider academic opinion on the meaning of entry.

Diagram plan

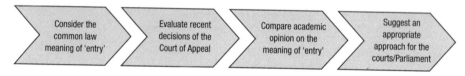

A printable version of this diagram plan is available from www.pearsoned.co.uk/lawexpressqa

Answer

Burglary requires the defendant to enter a building or part of a building as a trespasser (s. 9(1)(a) and (b), Theft Act 1968). However, the word 'entry' has not been defined under the Act. This has proved more of a problem than perhaps might have been expected and the courts have adopted inconsistent approaches. As a result, the law is confused. Under the common law, the insertion of any part of the body (however small) into the building was sufficient (*Smith and Hogan Criminal Law*, 13th edn, p. 953). According to **Davis** (1823) Russ & Ry 499, the insertion of the forepart of the forefinger was sufficient.[1] The Theft Act 1968 does not assist on the meaning of entry as it provides no definition of 'entry'. Parliament assumed that the old common law would apply (*Smith and Hogan Criminal Law*,

[1] Mention the facts of the case very briefly just to provide an example of the way in which the old common law rule was applied.

pp. 953–4). However, it seems the task of interpreting 'entry' has fallen to the courts which have adopted inconsistent approaches.

In **Collins** [1973] QB 100, Edmund Davies LJ stated that the crucial issue was where exactly the defendant was at the time that the victim invited him in.[2] Applying the common law rule, if any part of D's body had been inserted into the building before she invited him in, he had entered the building as a trespasser. However, if no part of his body had been inserted into the building before she invited him in, he would have entered lawfully. Instead, Edmund Davies LJ stated that the defendant's entry must be 'effective and substantial'. No further guidance was given. 'Effective' might mean that the defendant must be able to carry out his ulterior intent, but this interpretation would conflict with the common law rule which merely requires the insertion of part of the body. 'Substantial' might mean that most of the defendant's body must be inserted through the window. This would also conflict with the common law rule which only requires the insertion of any part of the body, *howsoever small*.[3]

In **Brown** [1985] Crim LR 212, the Court of Appeal still failed to apply the common law rule. Professor Griew comments that: 'The court might in **Brown** have supported **Collins** by adopting the same simple rule. It did not do so; and its judgment is explicable only on the basis that the rule has not survived. If that is right, we are left in need of further authority, preferably in firm terms that will make for uniformity of decision' (*The Theft Acts 1968 and 1978* (1986), p. 91). Instead, the court modified the test in **Collins** and held that entry need not be 'substantial', but had to be 'effective'. It was unclear whether this meant that while the defendant need not insert most of his body into the building, he must be able to carry out his ulterior intent.[4] In **Ryan** [1996] Crim LR 320, the defendant became stuck and unable to steal anything. Nevertheless, the Court of Appeal held that his entry was effective. This renders the word 'effective' meaningless.

As the law stands, entry has to be effective but not substantial, yet the defendant does not have to be able to carry out the ulterior offence. Ormerod argues that we should revert to the common law position: 'It is unsatisfactory that such a crucial *actus reus* element of a serious offence should be left for a jury to determine; the best course would be to accept the continued existence of

[2] Rather than recite the facts of the case in detail, you should focus on the key issue in the case.

[3] Offer your own analysis of the meaning of these words.

[4] Compare the different decisions of the courts to highlight the inconsistencies in approach in each case.

[5] You should acknowledge the criticisms of the old common law approach.

[6] Refer back to the question at this point in your answer in order to maintain the focus of the answer.

[7] Compare various academic views to show your wider knowledge.

[8] You would not be expected to remember long quotes verbatim, but you should be able to at least paraphrase the academic view.

the common law rule' (*Smith and Hogan Criminal Law*, p. 954). Although this is a much wider approach,[5] it is a simple one which provides clarity and accessibility. The current law is unsatisfactory because it is confusing on the meaning of 'entry': the cases are inconsistent.[6]

It is also unclear whether the insertion of other objects, such as a child under 10 or an animal, into a building is sufficient to constitute entry. A child will not be convicted if he is under 10 years old as he will have a defence of infancy. The adult who causes the child to enter might be guilty of burglary under the doctrine of innocent agency (**Michael** (1840) 9 C & P 356); however, there is no recent authority directly on this point. There is conflicting academic opinion about the application of the doctrine of innocent agency to burglary.[7] Professor Williams states that: 'At common law one could enter through an innocent agent, e.g. through a small child (under the age of responsibility) who was put into the premises to steal. There is little social need for this construction of the offence, since few people would feel alarmed by the entry of a small child . . . However, the courts will probably continue the old rule if the question arises' (*Textbook of Criminal Law* (1983), p. 840).[8] Ormerod comments that 'This is probably not burglary under the 1968 Act' (*Smith and Hogan Criminal Law*, p. 955). Griew acknowledges that there is no authority on the point but argues that the doctrine of innocent agency should apply to burglary (*The Theft Acts 1968 and 1978* (1986), p. 92).

It is difficult to distinguish the insertion of an inanimate object, such as a pole or hook or even a bomb thrown or a bullet shot through a window, into a building for the purpose of the commission of an ulterior offence. Ormerod (2011) states that the courts may not be willing to preserve the old technical rules regarding instruments because they lead to 'outlandish results' (p. 954). Ormerod also argues that this does not constitute entry in the simple language of ordinary men in which the Act was said to be written (p. 954). Ormerod suggests perhaps the defendant must be at least present at the scene – 'on the job' (p. 954). Perhaps there is arguably a distinction between the defendant causing an instrument to enter a building (e.g. by throwing something), and where an instrument represents an extension of the defendant's body (e.g. a pole). Ormerod comments that there have not been problems in practice due to the sensible

CPS charging guidance that where there are factual difficulties, the CPS should consider charging a different offence (e.g. theft) (p. 955).

There is no clear and settled meaning of entry, and as such, the law is not accessible and is ambiguous.[9] It is arguable that this runs contrary to the rule of law which requires that 'The law must be open and adequately publicised. If it is to guide people they must be able to find out what it is' (Raz, J., 'The Rule of Law and its virtue' [1977] 93 LQR 195). While Parliament could intervene here, it is submitted that a simpler, and preferable, approach would be for the courts to follow the common law rule.[10] It is true that the common law rule adopted a very wide approach to entry, but it was at least clear and accessible.

[9] Link your conclusion back to the title to show that you have maintained focus throughout.

[10] Suggest an approach that the courts and/or Parliament could take in order to remove the confusion which currently exists.

✔ Make your answer stand out

- You should explore the criticisms of the old common law approach in more detail. This approach is obviously much wider than the approach taken by the courts. Consider why this might not be preferable.

- You could also consider other cases on entry as a trespasser, including: *Walkington* [1979] 1 WLR 1169 (going behind a moveable counter amounts to entry of a part of a building) and *Jones and Smith* [1976] 1 WLR 672 (going into father's house with the intention of taking the TV exceeds the implied permission of D's entry).

- You could incorporate further academic opinion into your answer, particularly relating to burglary via the insertion of animate or inanimate objects into a building.

- You might also expand upon the requirement of clarity and accessibility under the rule of law and the particular implications of violating the rule of law in relation to the criminal law.

! Don't be tempted to . . .

- Merely recite the facts of the three main cases on 'entry'. You really need to analyse the inconsistent approaches, rather than set out the facts.

- Explore the other elements of burglary in detail. The examiner here is looking for your evaluation of the meaning of 'entry' and reference to academic critique in relation to that element.

❓ Question 3

Gerald is an anti-capitalist protester. He attends an unofficial protest in the City of London and joins a march towards the Bank of England. On his way through the City, Gerald smashes several shop windows. A fellow protestor smashes the window of a sandwich shop and steals two bottles of soft drink. He hands a bottle to Gerald and says, 'Here, drink this'. Gerald does not see where the drink comes from, but he takes it and drinks it anyway. He then throws the empty glass bottle through the front windscreen of a taxi which is driving at 30 mph. The taxi swerves to try to avoid the bottle and crashes into a metal railing. The passenger and driver are both injured. On arriving at the Bank of England, Gerald takes out a spray can and begins to draw his 'tag' on the walls of the Bank. He then throws a petrol bomb towards an empty police van, setting the van on fire.

Discuss whether Gerald is criminally liable for any property offences.

Answer plan

→ Consider the offences of criminal damage, aggravated criminal damage and arson under the Criminal Damage Act 1971 and handling stolen goods under section 22 of the Theft Act 1968.

→ Discuss Gerald's liability for criminal damage under section 1(1) for smashing the windows.

→ Examine Gerald's liability for handling stolen goods under section 22 of the Theft Act 1968 in respect of the soft drink.

→ Explore Gerald's liability for aggravated criminal damage under section 1(2) when he throws the bottle through the windscreen of the taxi.

→ Discuss Gerald's liability for criminal damage to the Bank under section 1(1) of the Criminal Damage Act 1971 with respect to Gerald drawing on the walls.

→ Consider Gerald's liability for criminal damage by fire under section 1(1) and (3) when he sets the police van on fire.

Diagram plan

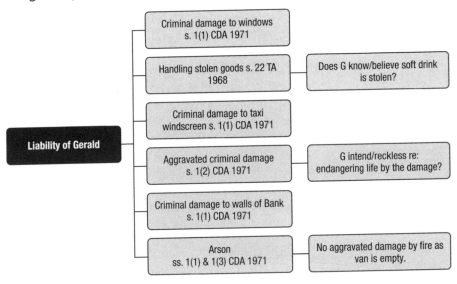

A printable version of this diagram plan is available from www.pearsoned.co.uk/lawexpressqa

Answer

This question requires consideration of the property offences of which Gerald might be convicted. Gerald could be guilty of simple criminal damage under section 1(1) of the Criminal Damage Act 1971, handling stolen goods under section 22 of the Theft Act 1968, aggravated criminal damage under section 1(2) of the Criminal Damage Act 1971, and criminal damage by fire (arson) under section 1(1) and (3) of the Criminal Damage Act 1971. Gerald's liability for these offences will be explored in chronological order.[1]

[1] Set out your intended structure in your introduction so that you let the examiner know exactly how you are going to approach the question.

Smashing the windows

Gerald may be guilty of criminal damage to the windows under section 1(1) of the Criminal Damage Act 1971. Simple criminal damage is found under section 1(1) of the Criminal Damage Act 1971 and requires proof that the defendant intentionally or recklessly destroyed or damaged property belonging to another without lawful excuse. The damage need not be permanent (*Gayford v Chouler* [1898] 1 QB 316), but must be more than trivial (**A (a juvenile) v R** [1978] Crim LR 689). What constitutes damage is a matter of fact and degree (**Roe v Kingerlee** [1986] Crim LR 735). As the damage to the windows is permanent, it will definitely constitute damage. The windows are personal property (s. 10(1), Criminal Damage Act 1971) and they belong to another person. Gerald has no defence of lawful excuse here as he cannot argue that he honestly believed that he had (or would have had) the consent of the owner under section 5(2)(a) of the Criminal Damage Act 1971 and he did not honestly believe that the property was in need of immediate protection under section 5(2)(b) of the Criminal Damage Act 1971.[2] Consequently, the actus reus of simple criminal damage is satisfied. The mens rea of simple criminal damage requires proof that Gerald intended or was reckless as to causing such damage. It is quite clear that Gerald intended to cause the damage here.[3]

[2] Although the defence of lawful excuse does not apply here, this sentence demonstrates that you understand when the defence under section 5(2) is available.

[3] Do not forget to state and apply the mens rea elements of the offence.

The soft drink

In respect of the soft drink, Gerald may be convicted of handling stolen goods under section 22 of the Theft Act 1968. The actus reus is satisfied as Gerald receives the goods (soft drink) which is in fact stolen property.[4] The mens rea requires proof that Gerald did so dishonestly, knowing or believing the goods to be stolen. Gerald might know that the soft drink is stolen; at the very least, he suspects that it is. More than mere suspicion is required to establish a belief (**Hall** (1985) 81 Cr App R 260) and the defendant's belief is subjectively assessed. If Gerald did believe the soft drink to be stolen, the next question to ask is whether he was dishonest. It is unlikely that the negative aspect of dishonesty under section 2(1) of the Theft Act 1968 applies,[5] so **Ghosh** [1982] 2 All ER 689 must be applied. If the honest and reasonable person would find Gerald's conduct dishonest, and Gerald realised this, then he is dishonest.

[4] You should not write out verbatim the wording of section 22 of the Theft Act 1968 because it is a lengthy section and this is a waste of time. Simply apply the relevant part of it to the scenario.

[5] As section 2(1) of the Theft Act 1968 is unlikely to apply, there is no need to provide any detail about the provision. Including this brief sentence is sufficient to demonstrate your knowledge.

Taxi windscreen

When he throws the glass bottle through the front windscreen of the moving taxi, Gerald commits simple criminal damage of the window and the taxi (if any damage is caused to the taxi upon crashing) under section 1(1) of the Criminal Damage Act 1971. The windscreen (and the taxi) are permanently damaged and are both personal property (s. 10(1), Criminal Damage Act 1971) which belong to the taxi driver

(s. 10(2), Criminal Damage Act 1971). Gerald has no lawful excuse for damaging the windscreen and taxi and it is likely that he intends to do so, thus the offence of simple criminal damage is established. Even if he does not intend to smash the windscreen or cause damage to the taxi, he is at the very least reckless in this regard. Recklessness is subjectively assessed under **G** [2003] UKHL 50, and requires Gerald to have considered the risk that his conduct might cause damage, but to have taken that risk anyway. The risk is certainly an unjustifiable one.[6]

[6] Set out and apply the current subjective test of recklessness where appropriate. There is no need to apply the old law under *MPC* v *Caldwell* [1982] 1 AC 341 in a problem scenario.

It is also necessary to consider whether Gerald might also be guilty of aggravated criminal damage under section 1(2) of the Criminal Damage Act 1971. This offence contains an extra mens rea require-ment. In order to successfully convict Gerald of aggravated criminal damage, the prosecution must also prove that Gerald thereby[7] intended to or was reckless as to endangering the life of another. The fact that Gerald threw the bottle directly at the front windscreen of a car moving at considerable speed, which would be likely to crash as a result, is evidence from which it could be inferred that he thereby intended to endanger life. However, at the very least he must have been reckless as to whether life would be endangered. Thus, Gerald is likely to be convicted of aggravated criminal damage under section 1(2).

[7] The inclusion of this word 'thereby' is crucial and demonstrates that you understand the law. There must be an intention or recklessness *by* the damage or destruction to endanger life.

Paint on Bank

Gerald could be convicted of criminal damage when he sprays paint on the walls of the Bank of England. It has been held that painting on a pavement in water soluble paint is sufficient to constitute dam-age (*Hardman* v *Chief Constable of Avon & Somerset* [1986] Crim LR 330), thus spraying paint on the walls will constitute dam-age.[8] The wall is personal property under section 10(1) of the Criminal Damage Act 1971, it belongs to another under section 10(2) of the Criminal Damage Act 1971, and Gerald has no lawful excuse for damaging the walls, thus the actus reus of criminal damage is satis-fied.[9] The mens rea of simple criminal damage requires proof that Gerald intended or was reckless as to causing such damage. It is quite clear that Gerald intended to cause the damage here.

[8] If you know of a case with similar facts to the one in the question, apply the principle derived from that case in your answer.

[9] These elements are not really in issue here. If you are pushed for time (or space), you should try to state why they are satisfied and cite appropriate legal authority as succinctly as possible.

Setting police van on fire

Gerald is guilty of simple criminal damage by fire (arson) when he sets the empty police van on fire. Simple criminal damage by fire is

[10] Where criminal damage is committed by fire, the offence is charged contrary to both section 1(1) (or s. 1(2) if dealing with aggravated criminal damage) and section 1(3), Criminal Damage Act 1971.

an offence under sections 1(1) and (3) of the Criminal Damage Act 1971.[10] Burning the police van will amount to destruction of property by fire. The van is personal property (s. 10(1), Criminal Damage Act 1971) and it belongs to another under section 10(2) of the Criminal Damage Act 1971. Gerald has no lawful excuse for damaging the police van.

The mens rea of criminal damage by fire is simply an intention or recklessness as to the damage. Gerald clearly intends to damage the police van here, so he is likely to be convicted of simple criminal damage by fire. He is unlikely to be convicted of aggravated damage by fire as the police van is said to be empty at the time.

✓ Make your answer stand out

- Think carefully about your structure where you have more than one defendant. You should adopt a structure which is clear and logical. It may be better to deal with events chronologically; alternatively, it may make more sense to deal with each defendant in turn.

- Refer to relevant judicial comment. For instance, you could cite Boreham J in *Hall* (1985) on the definition of 'belief' for the purposes of handling stolen goods.

- Ensure that you apply the law to the problem question every time you cite a legal principle.

- Ensure that you always identify and apply the specific mens rea of all relevant offences.

! Don't be tempted to . . .

- Waste valuable time in the exam by reciting large chunks of statute. Instead, you should at times paraphrase the relevant section you wish to refer to and apply the law to the scenario.

- Misstate the tests on lawful excuse in criminal damage under section 5(2) of the Criminal Damage Act 1971. Ensure that you are familiar with the subjective/objective nature of the tests so that you apply the law accurately.

- Forget to spend time discussing the mens rea of offences. Having explored and applied the actus reus elements, students often then forget to do the same for the mens rea. If you do this, you are really only providing part of an answer and this will gravely affect your performance in the exam.

Offences under the Fraud Act 2006

9

How this topic may come up in exams

Fraud could be examined by way of an essay or in a problem question. Essay questions on fraud may ask you to compare the law under the Fraud Act 2006 with the old deception offences which the Act replaced. You may be asked for a critical evaluation of the law and to consider whether the scope of the Act is problematic. You should prepare by reading the academic opinion surrounding fraud. Problem scenarios might ask you to discuss fraud only or you might be required to identify a number of different property offences in a mixed problem question.

Attack the question

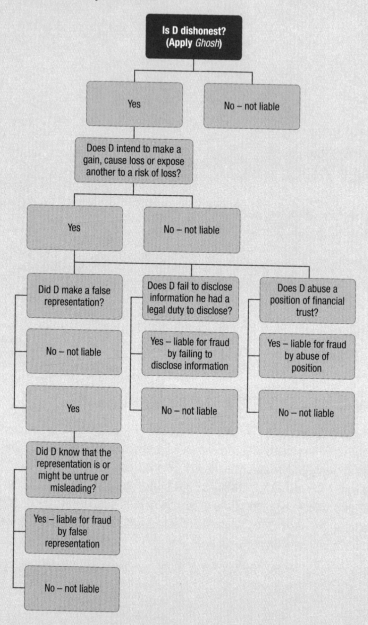

A printable version of this diagram is available from www.pearsoned.co.uk/lawexpressqa

❓ Question 1

Rita fills out an application form for a mortgage for herself and her husband, Joseph. Page 4 of the mortgage application form asks applicants whether they have any outstanding loans or credit card debts. Rita suspects that Joseph may have taken out a loan but, out of fear of causing an argument, she ticks the box marked 'no'. In fact, Joseph took out a loan for £20,000 last year.

Later that day, Rita decides to go shopping. As she knows the PIN number for Joseph's debit card, she takes his card and uses it to withdraw money from a cash machine. She does not think that Joseph will mind, as he has given her his card to use in the past.

Rita wants to buy herself an expensive pair of designer shoes, but does not want Joseph to know, so does not use his debit card. Instead, she decides to use the funds from the Abbey View Country Club. As Treasurer of the club, she has easy access to the club's funds.

Discuss Rita's criminal liability for the offence of fraud.

Answer plan

➡ Refer to the offence of fraud under section 1 of the Fraud Act 2006 and the three ways it can be committed.

➡ Discuss whether Rita is liable for fraud in relation to the mortgage application. This may be a false representation and a failure to disclose information about the loan.

➡ Discuss whether Rita is liable for fraud for using Joseph's debit card to withdraw money. The issue of dishonesty will be relevant here.

➡ Consider whether Rita is guilty of fraud by abusing a position of trust in respect of the Country Club funds.

Diagram plan

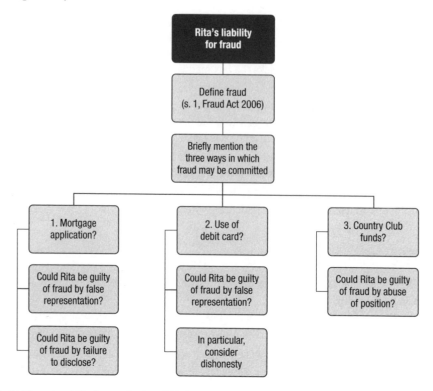

A printable version of this diagram plan is available from www.pearsoned.co.uk/lawexpressqa

Answer

Rita could be criminally liable for fraud in relation to the mortgage application, her use of Joseph's debit card and in respect of the Country Club's funds. Fraud is an offence under section 1 of the Fraud Act 2006.[1] It may be committed in one of three ways: by false representation (s. 2), by failing to disclose information (s. 3) or by abuse of position (s. 4).[2] Although sections 2–4 provide for three distinct methods of committing fraud, each of these types of fraud contains some common elements.[3] Dishonesty is a mens rea element common to each fraud. As the term 'dishonesty' is not defined under the Fraud Act 2006, the courts will look to the meaning of the term within the context of theft. The negative aspect of dishonesty under section 2(1) of the Theft Act 1968 does not apply to fraud.

[1] Be clear to show that you are aware that there is only one offence of fraud under section 1 of the Fraud Act 2006.

[2] This demonstrates that you are aware that there is just the one offence of fraud which may be committed in three ways.

[3] Make a brief mention of the common elements at the start of your answer in order to demonstrate to the examiner that you are aware of the relationship between the different ways in which fraud can be committed. However, do not write out everything you know about these just yet.

[4] Adopt a clear and logical structure. Use headings in order to ensure that you focus on one incident at a time.

[5] Identify the relevant method of fraud before exploring the elements of fraud.

However, the positive aspect under **Ghosh** [1982] 2 All ER 689 will be applied. Another common element in the mens rea is the requirement that the defendant intend to gain for himself or another, or to cause loss to another or to expose another to a risk of loss.

Mortgage application[4]

In respect of the mortgage application, Rita may be guilty of fraud by false representation under section 2.[5] The actus reus of this offence requires that Rita makes a false representation, which she does when she ticks the box marked 'no'. Under section 2(3), a representation includes a representation as to fact, which this is. This is a false representation under section 2(2)(a) because she is applying for a joint mortgage and Joseph has taken out a loan for £20,000.

The mens rea requires that Rita knows that the representation is or might be untrue or misleading under section 2(2)(b). As Rita suspects that Joseph might have taken out a loan, she knows that the representation might be untrue. The offence of fraud also requires proof of dishonesty. The **Ghosh** test must be applied here. Applying the first objective limb of **Ghosh**, the honest and reasonable person would regard declaring that she and Joseph have no loans when she suspects that Joseph may have taken out a loan as dishonest. The second limb is subjective and requires consideration of whether Rita realised that the honest and reasonable person would regard this as dishonest. If she did, then she will be dishonest. The final mens rea element which needs to be established is that Rita intended to make a gain for herself or another or cause loss to another or to expose another to a risk of loss (s. 2(1)(b)). Under section 5(2)(a), gain and loss extend only to gain or loss of money or other property. Property includes real or personal property, things in action and other intangible property (s. 5(2)(b)). By completing the application form for a mortgage, Rita intends to gain a thing in action, *property*.

[6] Set out any possible alternative offences which Rita might be charged with.

Alternatively, Rita might be charged with fraud by failing to disclose information under section 3.[6] By ticking the box marked 'no', she is not only making a false representation, but is also failing to disclose the loan that Joseph has taken out. The actus reus of this offence requires that the defendant fail to disclose information which he has a legal obligation to disclose. The mens rea elements require that Rita is dishonest and has an intention to make a gain or cause loss.

Thus, Rita is likely to be guilty of fraud by false representation and may also be guilty of fraud by failing to disclose information.

Debit card withdrawal

By using Joseph's card to withdraw money from a cash machine, Rita may be guilty of fraud by false representation under section 2. She makes a false representation of fact to the cash machine that she has the authority to use the card in question. Under section 5(2), a representation is made if it 'is submitted in any form to any system or device designed to receive, convey or respond to communications (with or without human intervention)'.[7] Thus, using the card in the cash machine and entering Joseph's PIN number will be sufficient. The representation is false because it is 'untrue' or at the very least 'misleading' (see s. 2(2)(a)).

[7] Use a short quote from the relevant section if you can remember it.

The mens rea requires that Rita knows that the representation is or might be false under section 2(2)(b). Rita knows that the representation that she is making to the machine is false. It is irrelevant that Joseph would have consented to her use of the card as the false representation is made to the machine, not to Joseph. Rita clearly has an intention to gain property, namely money, for herself. Section 2(1) of the Theft Act 1968 does not apply to the Fraud Act 2006, so the fact that Rita honestly believed that Joseph would have consented to her use of the card is not relevant. Thus, the *Ghosh* test of dishonesty must be applied. The honest and reasonable person would find the use of another person's debit card dishonest. However, as dishonesty is a question of fact for the jury to determine, the jury might take into account factors such as the relationship between Rita and Joseph, the likelihood of Joseph consenting to Rita's use of the card and whether the account was a joint one or not. As the fraud is practised against the cash machine, and by extension the bank, Joseph's consent is arguably irrelevant. If Rita's conduct is objectively dishonest, then she will be convicted of fraud by false representation if she realised this.

[8] This sentence demonstrates a wider understanding of the law relating to fraud. It shows the examiner that you have not merely learnt the provisions of the Fraud Act 2006, but that you are also aware of what is missing from the Act.

Country Club funds

In respect of the Country Club funds, Rita might be convicted of fraud by abuse of position under section 4. Unfortunately, neither of the terms 'abuse' and 'position' were defined under the Fraud Act 2006.[8] Nevertheless, it is likely that this offence will apply here because, as Treasurer of the club, Rita surely 'occupies a position in which [s]he is expected to safeguard, or not to act against, the financial interests of another person'[9] under section 4(1)(a). The offence requires that she abuse that position under section 4(1)(b). Rita does so by using the funds of the Country Club for her personal purchases.

[9] This is another good extract from a section to learn.

The mens rea of this offence requires proof that Rita has been dishonest in abusing her position (s. 4(1)(b)) and again the *Ghosh* test of dishonesty will be applied. The honest and reasonable person would certainly regard Rita's conduct as dishonest and Rita is very likely to realise this. Rita clearly intends, by means of the abuse of her position, to make a gain for herself (s. 4(1)(c)). The property she intends to gain are the shoes, which amounts to personal property under section 5(2)(b). Therefore, Rita is likely to be guilty of fraud by abuse of position in respect of the Country Club funds.[10]

[10] Conclude in relation to each incident of fraud as you go along. There is no need to write a long conclusion detailing Rita's liability for each scenario again at the end.

✓ **Make your answer stand out**

- Deal with each incident of fraud as it occurs in order to maintain a logical structure.
- Ensure that you consider whether Rita might be guilty of fraud via any of the three methods for each scenario.
- Set out the relevant sections from the Fraud Act 2006 where appropriate.
- Refer to academic opinion to make your answer really stand out. You could make reference to leading articles on fraud such as Professor Ormerod, The Fraud Act 2006 – criminalising lying? [2007] Crim LR 193.
- Refer to other sources, such as the Explanatory Notes to the Fraud Act 2006 and Farrell, S., Yeo, N. and Landenberg, G., *Blackstone's Guide to the Fraud Act 2006* (2007), Oxford: Oxford University Press, both of which provide examples of the application of the Fraud Act 2006.

❗ **Don't be tempted to . . .**

- Merely write out everything you know about each of the types of fraud without applying the law.
- Make the mistake of applying section 2(1) of the Theft Act 1968 to the meaning of dishonesty, but do set out and apply both limbs of the *Ghosh* test.
- Gloss over the elements which are common to each type of fraud, namely dishonesty and an intention to gain or cause loss. Even though these are common to each type of fraud, you must apply the law relating to these elements in each different scenario.

Question 2

The old deception offences were problematic and in need of reform. The Fraud Act 2006 has removed many of the problems with the former law, but it has been criticised for being far too wide in scope. To what extent do you agree that the offence of fraud is too broad?

Answer plan

→ Outline the elements of fraud and the three ways it can be committed.

→ Discuss criticisms of the deception offences and the rationale behind the Fraud Act 2006.

→ Examine whether the Act resolved the problems with the old law.

→ Analyse the scope of the Fraud Act 2006.

Diagram plan

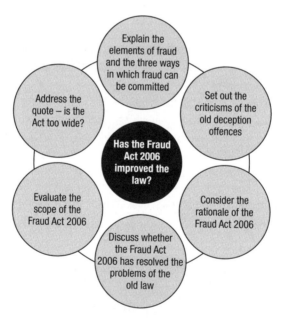

Explain the elements of fraud and the three ways in which fraud can be committed

Set out the criticisms of the old deception offences

Consider the rationale of the Fraud Act 2006

Discuss whether the Fraud Act 2006 has resolved the problems of the old law

Evaluate the scope of the Fraud Act 2006

Address the quote – is the Act too wide?

Has the Fraud Act 2006 improved the law?

A printable version of this diagram plan is available from www.pearsoned.co.uk/lawexpressqa

Answer

This question requires discussion of the effect of the Fraud Act 2006 and the scope of the offence of fraud. The Act came into force on

15 January 2007 and created a general offence of fraud which can be committed in three ways (s. 1): by false representation (s. 2); by failing to disclose information (s. 3); or by abuse of position (s. 4). This single offence replaced the old deception offences which had been problematic for a number of reasons. In doing so, the Act eliminated many of the problems with the former law. However, the Act has been the subject of much academic criticism.

One important criticism of the old law was that there were too many complicated offences of deception. Professor Ormerod describes the deception offence as 'notoriously technical' and 'over-particularised' ('The Fraud Act 2006 – criminalising lying' [2007] Crim LR 193).[1] These offences were very specific and narrowly defined. The actus reus of the deception offences required proof that deception had been caused and that either property, services, a pecuniary advantage or a money transfer had been obtained. The offences were heavily dependent upon proof of actus reus elements. Many defendants who should have been convicted secured acquittals due to technicalities, such as being charged with the wrong offence. Thus, the deception offences had a detrimental effect on the effectiveness of the criminal justice system.

The old offence of obtaining property by deception (s. 15, Theft Act 1968) was inadequate in dealing with cases in which the defendant had obtained a money transfer by deception. Problems arose in the case of **Preddy** [1996] AC 815. The House of Lords held that where a person transferred money from one bank account to another, he could not be convicted of obtaining property by deception as the debit leaving one bank account did not amount to the same property belonging to another as the credit which entered the other bank account. A new offence of obtaining a money transfer by deception under section 15A of the Theft Act 1968 was created.[2]

The old offences required proof of causation. This created a further difficulty for the prosecution. If the causative link between the obtaining and the deception was not proved, no conviction could result. It was also unclear whether an omission was sufficient under the old deception offences or whether a conviction was dependent upon an act (**Firth** (1989) 91 Cr App R 217). It is now clear under the Fraud Act 2006 that an offence of fraud may be committed by an omission to disclose information which one has a legal duty to disclose (s. 3) and by abuse of position (s. 4).[3]

[1] Incorporate academic opinion into your answer. You should refer directly to this leading academic article on fraud as this demonstrates that you have read widely in your revision.

[2] Cite Preddy and explain the problems highlighted by this case in order to demonstrate your knowledge of the technical problems with the old deception offences.

[3] This sentence compares the position under the new Fraud Act 2006.

The old deception offences were also criticised for failing to meet the requirements of an offence of fraud in today's technological and internet focused age. The offences did not allow for a deception to be practised against a machine. It was only possible to practice a deception against a person (***Davies* v *Flackett*** [1974] RTR 8). Thus, the deception offences were inadequate to deal with fraud via a machine. The Fraud Act 2006 deals with this by providing that a false representation may be made if it 'is submitted in any form to any system or device designed to receive, convey or respond to communications (with or without human intervention)' (s. 2(5)).

A further criticism of the old deception offences was that they were difficult for juries to understand. As the tribunal of fact, jurors must be able to understand the elements of the offences, otherwise there is a risk of an unfair trial and the integrity of the criminal justice system is compromised.

The Fraud Act 2006 eliminated these problems by creating one single offence of fraud. The offence is not heavily focused on actus reus elements. For instance, instead of requiring proof of anything having been obtained (an actus reus element), fraud requires proof of an intention to make gain for himself or another, or to cause loss or expose another to a risk of loss (a mens rea element). There is no longer any requirement of proof that the obtaining caused a deception to be practised. Instead, fraud simply requires a form of conduct to be proved, such as the making of a false representation, a failure to disclose information, or abuse of position. The offence of fraud focuses on the mens rea, which simply requires dishonesty and the intention to gain or cause loss.

While the provisions of the Theft Act 1968 have been heavily criticised by many academics, such as Professor Ormerod and the judiciary (see Lord Goff's opinions in ***Preddy***), the new Fraud Act 2006 had also been subject to criticism. One criticism of the Fraud Act 2006 is that it has created an offence in which the actus reus is too wide, to the extent that liability is too heavily dependent upon proof of dishonesty.[4] The Act relies upon the ***Ghosh*** ([1982] 2 All ER 689) test of dishonesty which is used in theft cases and which has itself been the subject of much discomfort within the criminal law (see the criticisms made by Professor Griew in [1985] Crim LR 341 and Professor Spencer in (1982) CLJ 222). It has been claimed

[4] This sentence draws the answer back to the criticisms of the Fraud Act 2006 and thus the title of the question.

that the test assumes a fictional standard of honesty and leaves too much in the hands of the jury, leading to inconsistent verdicts.

Although the objective of the Fraud Act 2006 was to expand the scope of fraud in order to ensure the successful prosecution of fraudsters, the Fraud Act 2006 has gone too far. The offence of fraud is so widely drafted that it overlaps with the offence of theft and catches behaviour which should not really be regarded as fraud. It creates criminal liability where a matter could be dealt with by civil law (e.g. providing bad references) or internal procedure, or where no civil court would deem the matter actionable (e.g. trade puffs).

✓ Make your answer stand out

■ Refer to other academic opinion, such as: Withey, C., The Fraud Act 2006 – some early observations and comparisons with the former law (2007) 71 JCL 220; Allgrove B. and Sellers, S., The Fraud Act 2006: is breach of confidence now a crime? (2009) 4 JIPLP 278; Monaghan, C., To prosecute or not to prosecute? A reconsideration of the overzealous prosecution of parents under the Fraud Act 2006 (2010) 74 *Journal of Criminal Law* 259.

■ You should explore further examples of the types of conduct which the Fraud Act 2006 criminalises unnecessarily.

■ You should also refer to the Law Commission Report, *Fraud* (Law Commission, No. 276, 2002) and the Explanatory Notes to the Fraud Act 2006.

■ You could further explore the criticisms of the old law and elaborate on the problems caused by the case of *Preddy*.

! Don't be tempted to . . .

■ Describe all of the old deception offences from the Theft Acts 1968 and 1978 in detail as these are now redundant.

■ Simply write everything you know about the Fraud Act 2006 as you will not be addressing the question which asks you to critically evaluate whether the Fraud Act 2006 has improved the law relating to fraud.

■ Forget to address the quote directly in your answer.

www.pearsoned.co.uk/lawexpressqa

 Go online to access more revision support including additional essay and problem questions with diagram plans, You be the marker questions, and download all diagrams from the book.

Defences

How this topic may come up in exams

General defences could be examined by way of essay questions on individual defences or on a mixture of the defences, or by a problem question. Essay questions might require you to critically evaluate a particular general defence, such as intoxication or self-defence. Alternatively, an essay question might take a more general approach and ask you to consider a certain category of defences, such as those concerned with the capacity of the defendant (e.g. insanity and automatism). Problem scenarios could require you to identify and apply the law relating to one or more general defences.

Attack the question

Insanity

- Is D suffering from a defect of reason caused by a disease of the mind?

- Defence if D does not know the nature and quality of his act or that his act was wrong.

Automatism

- Did D suffer a total loss of control?

- Caused by an external factor?

- No defence if automatism was self-induced.

Intoxication

- Defence if involuntary intox and unable to form mens rea.

- If voluntary intox, was the offence specific or basic intent?

- Defence if specific intent and unable to form mens rea.

- No defence if basic intent.

Self-defence

- Did D honestly believe the use of force was necessary in defence?

- Was the amount of force used reasonable?

Duress by threats

- Was D impelled to act due to a reasonable belief in a threat of death or serious injury to D or another?

- Would a sober person of reasonable firmness, sharing D's characteristics, have responded in the same way?

A printable version of this diagram is available from www.pearsoned.co.uk/lawexpressqa

❓ Question 1

Florian decides to have a party at his house. He hires some strobe lights and some powerful speakers and invites his friends, including Lisa, round. Lisa, who is.35 years old, suffers from epilepsy. While she had frequent seizures as a child, in her adult years she has only had one or two seizures. However, after a few hours of dancing, Lisa complains about feeling 'a bit funny'. She suffers an epileptic seizure, during which she lashes out at Florian who is trying to help her. She strikes Florian several times in the head, causing severe bruising. Lisa is charged with assault occasioning actual bodily harm contrary to section 47 of the Offences Against the Person Act 1861.

Advise Lisa as to her criminal liability. Would your answer be any different if:

(a) instead of being epileptic, Lisa is diabetic and she failed to take her insulin before attacking Florian?

(b) or if Lisa had taken her insulin, but suffered the attack because she failed to eat sufficiently after taking the insulin?

Answer plan

➡ Discuss the defence of insanity in relation to Lisa's epileptic seizure.

➡ Consider the defence of insanity in respect of the hyperglycaemic attack.

➡ Consider the defence of automatism in relation to the hypoglycaemia.

➡ Examine whether Lisa's automatism was self-induced and the effect of this.

Diagram plan

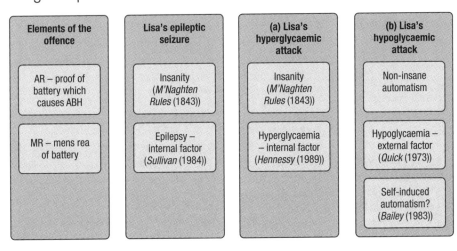

Elements of the offence	Lisa's epileptic seizure	(a) Lisa's hyperglycaemic attack	(b) Lisa's hypoglycaemic attack
AR – proof of battery which causes ABH	Insanity (M'Naghten Rules (1843))	Insanity (M'Naghten Rules (1843))	Non-insane automatism
MR – mens rea of battery	Epilepsy – internal factor (Sullivan (1984))	Hyperglycaemia – internal factor (Hennessy (1989))	Hypoglycaemia – external factor (Quick (1973))
			Self-induced automatism? (Bailey (1983))

A printable version of this diagram plan is available from www.pearsoned.co.uk/lawexpressqa

Answer

This question requires consideration of the defences of automatism and insanity. However, before exploring these it is necessary to discuss the elements of the offence charged. The prosecution will be able to establish that Lisa has the actus reus of assault occasioning actual bodily harm contrary to section 47 of the Offences Against the Person Act 1861.[1] The offence may be committed by either an assault or a battery which causes actual bodily harm. In this case, Lisa inflicts unlawful force on Florian, which is the actus reus of a battery (see **Collins v Wilcock** [1984] 1 WLR 1172). Lisa is clearly both the factual and legal cause of Florian's injuries. Actual bodily harm is widely defined in **Miller** [1954] 2 WLR 138 so as to include 'any hurt or injury calculated to interfere with health or comfort' (per Lynskey J). Florian suffers severe bruising, which is most likely to be sufficient for actual bodily harm. The prosecution will also need to establish the mens rea of assault occasioning actual bodily harm, namely that Lisa had the requisite mens rea for battery – intention or recklessness in relation to the infliction of unlawful force.[2] It is unclear here whether Lisa has the necessary mens rea as there is no evidence as to whether she was aware of her actions.

As stated above, two defences might be available to Lisa. These are insanity (also known as insane automatism) and automatism (also known as non-insane automatism). Non-insane automatism is a preferable defence, due to the fact that a successful plea results in a complete acquittal and the burden of proof is on the prosecution.[3] By contrast, a successful plea of insanity results in a verdict of not guilty by reason of insanity (s. 1, Criminal Procedure (Insanity) Act 1964) and the burden of proving the elements of insanity is on the defence. However, although Lisa would prefer to rely upon the defence of non-insane automatism in the first given scenario, this would be unlikely to succeed due to the fact that the factor which caused Lisa's attack was an internal factor (her epilepsy) rather than an external factor which is required for non-insane automatism.[4] This means that Lisa will be left with the defence of insanity as an available alternative.

Insanity is governed by the M'Naghten rules (**M'Naghten** (1843) 10 Cl & F 200), which were set down by the House of Lords. These rules state that every man is presumed sane, but he may rebut that

---

[1] As the question asks you about Lisa's liability, you will need to briefly discuss whether the elements of the offence charged are satisfied.

[2] Do not forget that the mens rea of assault occasioning ABH is the mens rea of an assault or a battery. No additional mens rea is required: *Savage; Parmenter* [1992] 1 AC 699.

[3] This shows that you know more than just the elements of the defences, but that you can advise a client as to the implications of the defences and which would be preferable.

[4] If this defence obviously does not apply here, then rule it out concisely explaining why and move on to the more appropriate defence.

presumption by proving, on a balance of probabilities, that at the time of the offence he was suffering from a defect of reason caused by a disease of the mind, and that he did not know the nature and quality of his act or that he did not know that the act he was doing was wrong. A defect of reason involves proof that Lisa was deprived of her power of reasoning and not mere absentmindedness (*Clarke* [1972] 1 All ER 219). The defect of reason must be caused by a disease of the mind, which must affect the ordinary mental faculties of reason, memory and understanding (per Devlin J in *Kemp* [1957] 1 QB 399).[5] Lisa suffers from epilepsy and this is deemed to be a disease of the mind, which is an internal factor (*Bratty v AG for Northern Ireland* [1963] AC 386 and *Sullivan* [1984] AC 156). Thus, in this scenario, the only defence available to Lisa would be the defence of insanity.[6]

[5] You should learn the key parts of leading judgments so that you can cite them in your answer.

[6] Set out your conclusion as to the most likely defence along with your reasoning.

Lisa would also be required to prove either that she did not know the nature and quality of her act or that she did not know that the act was wrong. The first of these two alternatives is a denial of the mens rea of the offence – Lisa must prove that she did not know the physical nature of the act she was doing (*Codere* (1917) 12 Cr App R 21). Alternatively, Lisa must prove that she did not know that the act was legally wrong. There is little evidence of either of these elements on the facts, but one is necessary for the plea of insanity to be successful.[7]

[7] If there is no evidence on a particular point, then say so. Do not ignore these elements as they are a necessary part of the defence.

Looking at the alternative set of facts in part (a), Lisa suffers from diabetes and has had a hyper-glycaemic attack. According to the case of *Hennessy* [1989] 1 WLR 287, a defendant who commits an offence during a hyperglycaemic attack may only plead insanity. Lord Lane CJ held that 'hyperglycaemia . . . caused by an inherent defect, and not corrected by insulin is a disease, and if . . . it does cause a malfunction of the mind, then the case may fall with *M'Naghten* rules'. Thus, as hyperglycaemia is caused by the condition of diabetes itself, an internal factor, the defence of insanity is the only option available to Lisa here. Again, she would have to prove that she did not know the nature and quality of her act or that she did not know that the act was wrong.

In part (b), the attack is due to the fact that Lisa had taken her insulin but had failed to eat sufficiently after doing so. In this case, Lisa would not be forced to plead insanity, but she would instead be advised to try to plead non-insane automatism on the basis that the insulin (an external factor) caused the reaction. Non-insane automatism has been defined by Lord Denning as 'an act which is done by the muscles without any control by the mind, such as a spasm, a reflex action or a convulsion; or an act done by a person who is not conscious of what he is doing, such as an act done whilst suffering from concussion or whilst sleepwalking' (**Bratty v Attorney-General for Northern Ireland**).[8] This defence involves a total loss of voluntary control due to an external factor. A defendant who commits an offence during a hypoglycaemic attack may rely on the defence of non-insane automatism (**Quick and Paddison** [1973] QB 910 and **Bingham** [1991] Crim LR 433). However, in this particular scenario, Lisa has failed to eat sufficiently after taking her insulin. If she is deemed to be reckless in doing so (i.e. it is necessary to question whether or not she knew that by failing to eat properly she was running the risk of unpredictable or aggressive conduct),[9] then her non-insane automatism may be said to be self-induced (**Bailey** [1983] 1 WLR 760). If there is evidence that Lisa's automotive state was self-induced and that she was at fault, then she will have no defence to a basic intent offence such as assault occasioning actual bodily harm because the necessary recklessness for the mens rea of that offence will have been established.[10]

[8] This is a very widely cited quote that you should ensure that you are fully aware of and prepared to refer to.

[9] Explain what recklessness would mean here in plain language.

[10] This demonstrates that you can distinguish between specific and basic intent offences in context and apply the law accurately.

✓ Make your answer stand out

- Where a problem scenario gives you alternative sets of facts ensure that you address all alternatives and that you do so in a logical, structured and clear way so that the examiner can follow your answer easily.

- Where a question requires consideration of a number of defences, you should deal with the most appropriate defences in the most detail and rule out any inappropriate ones concisely.

- Ensure that you use authorities to support every principle of law that you rely upon.

- Make reference to relevant quotes from judgments where appropriate to show the depth of your knowledge.

- You could refer to academic opinion on the point of whether insanity is an appropriate defence in relation to epilepsy or not. For instance, see Mackay, R.D. and Reuber, M., Epilepsy and the defence of insanity – time for a change [2007] Crim LR 782.

Don't be tempted to . . .

- Forget to address the elements of the offence he/she has been charged with as well as the defences, where a question on defences asks you to consider the liability of the defendant. A defendant's liability is obviously dependent upon both the elements of the offence being established as well as the success of any defences.

- Simply set out everything you know about the defences. You must ensure that you apply the law to the particular facts of the question.

- Make the mistake of failing to answer the parts which give you alternative facts. Ensure that you manage your time well so that you are able to deal with all parts that require answering. You will lose valuable marks by not addressing the alternative scenarios.

Question 2

'It remains deeply unsatisfactory for the law [on insanity] to remain so ill-defined as to leave exposed to the risk of such a verdict a person with a mental condition of what may be a trivial nature and who poses no real future risk to society.' (Ormerod, D., *Smith and Hogan Criminal Law* (2008), Oxford: Oxford University Press, p. 283.)

Discuss with reference to case law.

Answer plan

→ Consider the M'Naghten rules.

→ Consider examples of a 'disease of the mind'.

→ What are the implications of a successful plea of insanity?

→ Discuss automatism and diminished responsibility as alternatives.

→ Conclude with the Law Commission review of insanity.

Diagram plan

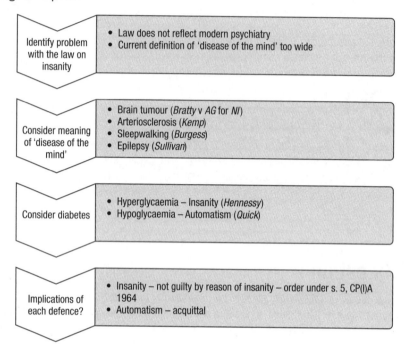

| Identify problem with the law on insanity | • Law does not reflect modern psychiatry
• Current definition of 'disease of the mind' too wide |

| Consider meaning of 'disease of the mind' | • Brain tumour (*Bratty* v *AG for NI*)
• Arteriosclerosis (*Kemp*)
• Sleepwalking (*Burgess*)
• Epilepsy (*Sullivan*) |

| Consider diabetes | • Hyperglycaemia – Insanity (*Hennessy*)
• Hypoglycaemia – Automatism (*Quick*) |

| Implications of each defence? | • Insanity – not guilty by reason of insanity – order under s. 5, CP(I)A 1964
• Automatism – acquittal |

A printable version of this diagram plan is available from www.pearsoned.co.uk/lawexpressqa

Answer

The law on insanity has been subject to much criticism and there have been many calls for reform. The law is outdated and fails to reflect modern psychiatric views of mental disorders.[1] As the Law Commission has recognised, the main problem is the fact that 'the key concept of "disease of the mind" has no agreed psychiatric meaning. As interpreted by the courts, it has even come to include conditions that are not mental disorders, such as epilepsy and diabetes' (Law Commission (2010), *Unfitness to Plead and the Insanity Defence*, see www.lawcom.gov.uk/insanity.htm).[2] As the title suggests, the rules on insanity are ill defined and 'deeply unsatisfactory' in today's society.

The law on insanity is governed by the *M'Naghten* rules, in which the House of Lords stated that there is a general presumption that every man is sane, such that if he wishes to raise insanity as a

[1] Identify the key problem with the law at the very start in your own words.

[2] Citing the Law Commission in your opening paragraph demonstrates that you are aware that this is an area which is currently being considered by the Commission. You should paraphrase this rather than remember the quote verbatim.

defence, he must rebut that presumption by proving insanity on a balance of probabilities. Thus the burden of proving the defence is on the defendant. The defendant must prove that at the time of the offence he was suffering from a defect of reason caused by a disease of the mind, and that he did not know the nature and quality of his act or that he did not know that the act he was doing was wrong.

The first element, 'a defect of reason' involves proof that the defendant was deprived of his power of reasoning and not merely absentminded (*Clarke* [1972] 1 All ER 219). The defect of reason must be caused by a disease of the mind. The term 'disease of the mind' is not a medical one but a legal one.[3] The types of conditions which are covered by the term are wide in scope, ranging from a brain tumour to sleepwalking. According to Devlin J in *Kemp* [1957] 1 QB 399, a disease of the mind must affect the 'mind' (i.e. the ordinary mental faculties of reason, memory and understanding) rather than just the 'brain' in the physical sense. A closer reference to case law illustrates the types of conditions which have been deemed to constitute a 'disease of the mind'. In the case of *Kemp*, arteriosclerosis was held to constitute a disease of the mind, and it is likely that a brain tumour would amount to a disease of the mind after Lord Denning suggested as much in *Bratty v AG for Northern Ireland* [1963] AC 386 (although it should be noted that this obiter comment conflicts with the decision in *Charlson* (1955) 39 Cr App R 37[4]). More controversially, epilepsy has been deemed to constitute a disease of the mind (see *Bratty v AG for Northern Ireland* and *Sullivan* [1984] AC 156). In *Bratty v AG for Northern Ireland*, Lord Denning defined a disease of the mind as 'any mental disorder which has manifested itself in violence and is prone to recur'. This term has been further extended to sleepwalking in the case of *Burgess* [1991] 2 QB 92. These cases demonstrate that a defendant who commits a criminal offence during an epileptic seizure or while sleepwalking is deemed to be legally 'insane'. Mackay and Reuber take the view that it is 'surely no longer acceptable to use the label "insanity" for any case of epileptic automatism' ('Epilepsy and the defence of insanity – time for a change' [2007] Crim LR 782).[5] These cases are highly controversial and 'deeply unsatisfactory', and as the title suggests, they expose individuals with relatively trivial conditions who pose no real future risk to society to the risk of a verdict of not guilty by reason of insanity.[6]

[3] Once again, reiterate the fact that the problem with the law is the fact that the rules have been developed by lawyers rather than experts in psychiatry.

[4] Ensure that you are aware of which comments are *obiter dicta* and which statements are binding *ratio decidendi*. Drawing such a distinction demonstrates the detailed level of your knowledge.

[5] Incorporate some academic opinion into your answer. This means that you will need to read more than just your textbook and module guide.

[6] Refer back to the title at appropriate points during your answer to maintain both your focus and that of the examiner.

An area of confusion in the law on insanity is the way in which the law deals with defendants with diabetes. According to the case of **Hennessy** [1989] 1 WLR 287, a defendant who commits an offence during a hyperglycaemic attack may plead insanity. However, a defendant who commits an offence during a hypoglycaemic attack may plead the more favourable defence of automatism. A successful plea of insanity leads to a verdict of not guilty by reason of insanity and the disposal options available to a judge are a hospital order, a supervision and treatment order or an absolute discharge (s. 5, Criminal Procedure (Insanity) Act 1964). A plea of insanity is not favoured by defendants who fear being labelled as 'insane' and would prefer a successful plea to lead to acquittal rather than a hospital or supervision and treatment order. By contrast, a successful plea of automatism leads to no such label and a complete acquittal. On first glance it seems odd that the fate of a defendant with diabetes whose condition is linked to his commission of an offence will depend upon whether at the time of the offence he was suffering from hyperglycaemia or hypoglycaemia. The distinction made by the law is grounded in the direct causes of these different states. Hyperglycaemia (high blood sugar level) is caused by a lack of insulin. In **Hennessy**, Lord Lane CJ held that 'hyperglycaemia . . . caused by an inherent defect, and not corrected by insulin is a disease, and if . . . it does cause a malfunction of the mind, then the case may fall

[7] Draw on judicial comment where you can in order to support your arguments.

within the **M'Naghten** rules'.[7] Thus, as hyperglycaemia is caused by the condition of diabetes itself, an internal factor, the defence of insanity is the only available option. However, hypoglycaemia (low blood sugar level) is caused by excess insulin in the body. A defendant who commits an offence during a hypoglycaemic attack may rely on the defence of automatism because the cause of hypoglycaemia is an external factor, namely the insulin which has been administered to the defendant (see **Quick and Paddison** [1973] QB 910 and **Bingham** [1991] Crim LR 433). Although these conditions are caused by different factors, the distinction made seems improper and inappropriate.

[8] It is prudent to give some consideration to alternative defences that might be available, but do not spend too much time on this.

It is clear from the cases mentioned that the term 'disease of the mind' has been given a wide interpretation to the extent that it now encompasses many trivial conditions which should not fall within the remit of insanity. Unfortunately, the law has developed so that such defendants are left with no suitable alternative defence.[8] Automatism

⁹ Refer back to the title directly at the end of your answer. The Law Commission is currently reviewing the law relating to insanity with a view to making recommendations on reform.

has been ruled out in the above cases as this defence is deemed to apply where the automaton state is caused by an external factor. The only alternative which might apply to some of the above defendants is the defence of diminished responsibility, but this is not a general defence (it only applies to murder) and it is a partial defence (reducing liability rather than absolving a defendant of liability). The law is in a 'deeply unsatisfactory' state and reforms are necessary.[9]

✓ Make your answer stand out

- You should refer to further academic opinion by the leading academics in this field. In particular, you should read Mackay, R.D., *Mental Condition Defences in Criminal Law* (1998), Oxford: Oxford University Press; Mackay, R.D., Fact and fiction about the insanity defence [1990] Crim LR 247; Mackay, R.D. and Kearns, G., More fact(s) about the insanity defence [1999] Crim LR 714; and Mackay, R.D., Mitchell, B. and Howe, L., Yet more facts about the insanity defence [2006] Crim LR 399.

- You could also refer to the proposals for reform made by the Butler Committee in 1975. Read the 'Report of the Committee on Mentally Abnormal Offenders' (The Butler Report), Cmnd. 6244, 1975.

- You might also make reference to the terminology used in the Mental Health Act 2007 in respect of the meaning of 'mental disorder'.

- You should also refer to the recent Law Commission Scoping Paper on 'Insanity and Automatism' (available at http://lawcommission.justice.gov.uk/docs/insanity_scoping. pdf).

! Don't be tempted to . . .

- Set out the facts of all the cases that you refer to. Your knowledge of the principles of law from each case and your analysis of the law are far more important and will earn you higher marks.

- Spend too much time considering the other elements of insanity. This question is about the meaning of 'disease of the mind', so you should focus on that rather than merely set out your knowledge of the other elements of insanity.

- Forget to address the quote directly in your answer.

❓ Question 3

Raymond works for an investment bank. As a result of the recession, the bank decides to make several compulsory redundancies and Raymond loses his job. After being told that he is being made redundant, Raymond goes to the nearest pub to drown his sorrows. After drinking several pints of beer with a bottle of whisky, Raymond begins flirting with the barmaid. As she walks past him when collecting empty glasses, Raymond slaps her bottom. The landlord of the pub witnesses the event and throws Raymond out of the pub.

On his way home, Raymond passes the bank. He picks up a newspaper seller stand and throws it at the bank window. The window shatters. When he arrives home, Raymond realises that he has lost his house keys. He breaks into a house, believing it to be his own home. However, he actually breaks into his next door neighbour's house.

The following week, Raymond finds that he is struggling to get to sleep. He decides to take a dose of sleeping pills which had been prescribed to his wife. When Raymond goes to bed he repeatedly beats his wife over the head with a vase, killing her. Raymond has no recollection of this.

Discuss Raymond's possible defences to charges of sexual assault, criminal damage and murder.

Answer plan

➜ Consider the fact that Raymond was voluntarily intoxicated and the *DPP* v *Majewski* [1977] AC 443 rules.

➜ Can Raymond rely on his intoxication in respect of the sexual assault?

➜ Can Raymond rely on his intoxication in respect of the basic intent offence of criminal damage?

➜ Consider Raymond's intoxicated mistake in breaking into the house.

➜ Discuss whether Raymond's intoxication in respect of the murder is voluntary or not.

➜ Discuss whether Raymond may rely on his intoxication in respect of the murder.

Diagram plan

Sexual assault
• Voluntary intoxication (*Majewski*)   • Basic intent offence (*Heard*)   • No defence

Damage to window
• Voluntary intoxication (*Majewski*)   • Basic intent offence   • No defence

Breaking into house
• Intoxicated mistake (*Jaggard* v *Dickinson*)

Murder/manslaughter
• Involuntary intoxication?   • Apply *Hardie*? Was D reckless?   • Guilty of basic intent offence of manslaughter   • Intoxication may negate intention for specific intent offence of murder

A printable version of this diagram plan is available from www.pearsoned.co.uk/lawexpressqa

Answer

This question requires consideration of whether Raymond has any defences to the charges of sexual assault, criminal damage and murder. Raymond is intoxicated throughout the scenario. For policy reasons, intoxication is not a defence per se, but in certain circumstances evidence of intoxication may be used to negate the mens rea of an offence.[1] The effect of raising evidence of intoxication will be explored in respect of each charge.

[1] You should recognise the fact that intoxication itself is no defence, but that intoxication is really evidence of mistake or a denial of the mens rea elements of an offence.

Sexual assault of the barmaid

The first potential offence that Raymond may be charged with is sexual assault under section 3 of the Sexual Offences Act 2003. It is important to note that where the defendant does have the necessary intention for the offence, the fact that he is intoxicated will provide no defence because a drunken intent is still an intent:[2] *Sheehan and Moore* [1975] 1 WLR 739. So, if there is any evidence that

[2] Before you discuss the rules relating to voluntary intoxication, you should address the principle that an intoxicated intent is sufficient mens rea.

Raymond intended the sexual assault, he will be guilty of the offence irrespective of any intoxication. However, it is not clear in this scenario whether Raymond had the necessary intention, thus it is necessary to explore his intoxication.

There are two types of intoxication: voluntary intoxication and involuntary intoxication. At this stage in the scenario, Raymond is voluntarily intoxicated.[3] The rules which apply to voluntary intoxication are set out by the House of Lords in **DPP v Majewski** [1977] AC 443. In this case it was held that voluntary intoxication is no defence to crimes of basic intent, although it may be evidence which goes towards negating the mens rea in a specific intent offence. A specific intent offence is one which requires proof of intention as the mens rea element of the offence. A basic intent offence is one which requires proof of a lesser form of mens rea, such as recklessness. Lord Elwyn-Jones held that voluntarily becoming intoxicated is a reckless course of conduct to take.[4] Thus, a voluntarily intoxicated defendant is automatically reckless and therefore he has the mens rea for every basic intent crime. However, this distinction between specific and basic intent offences has been criticised for being illogical and confusing. At first glance, it is difficult to categorise sexual assault as a specific or basic intent offence. The Court of Appeal has held that sexual assault is a basic intent offence, despite the fact that intentional touching is a requisite element of the offence: see **Heard** [2007] EWCA Crim 125.[5] On this interpretation, Raymond's voluntary intoxication will not negate the mens rea of sexual assault, thus it will provide no defence to the charge of sexual assault.

[3] Ensure that you distinguish between voluntary and involuntary intoxication and state which applies to this part of the question.

[4] Refer to specific judges names from leading judgments in your answer to a problem question to show that you have actually read the case in question.

[5] Where there is a more recent case dealing with the specific issue in the question, you must ensure that you refer to this.

Breaking the window of the bank

In respect of breaking the window of the bank, Raymond will be charged with criminal damage under section 1(1) of the Criminal Damage Act 1971. If Raymond does have the necessary intention for the offence, the fact that he is intoxicated will provide no defence because a drunken intent is still an intent: **Sheehan and Moore**. If there is evidence proving beyond reasonable doubt that Raymond intended the criminal damage, he will be guilty. Further to this, any evidence that Raymond's intoxication was 'Dutch courage' to give him the confidence to commit the offence will provide no defence to the charge: **Attorney General for Northern Ireland v Gallagher** [1963] AC 349.

Criminal damage is a basic intent offence because the mens rea requires proof of either intention or recklessness as to causing damage, thus Raymond will not be able to rely on evidence of his voluntary intoxication in his defence. In light of Lord Elwyn-Jones' opinion in *Majewski*, evidence of voluntary intoxication is evidence of recklessness, thus in this scenario Raymond's intoxication provides evidence of the mens rea required for criminal damage.

Breaking into the wrong house

In respect of the act of breaking into the wrong house, Raymond will again be charged with criminal damage. He may attempt to plead lawful excuse under section 5(2) of the Criminal Damage Act 1971 if he honestly believed that he had consent to damage the property. In this case, as he honestly believed it to be the house he shared with his wife, he may have honestly believed that he had her consent to damage the property in order to gain entry. Despite the fact that he made a mistake due to his intoxication, he may still rely upon lawful excuse as a defence: *Jaggard v Dickinson* [1981] QB 527. Bizarrely, in such situations, the *Majewski* rule does not apply. Ormerod acknowledges the anomalous result here: 'Where the defendant did not intend any damage to property (but was reckless) he may be held liable because he was drunk; but where he did intend damage to property but thought the owner would consent he is not liable, however drunk he may have been' (*Smith and Hogan Criminal Law* (2011), pp. 323–4).[6]

[6] If you can incorporate some academic opinion into your answer to a problem question you should do so.

Killing his wife

Raymond may be charged with murder for killing his wife. At this stage, Raymond's intoxication is due to the sleeping pills that he has taken. It is necessary to ascertain whether Raymond is voluntarily or involuntarily intoxicated. Raymond will argue that his intoxication was involuntary due to the fact that he took prescription drugs which should have a sedative effect on him and that he was unaware of the effect the tablets would have on him.[7] Involuntary intoxication may provide a defence to any offence provided that the defendant did not have the requisite mens rea for the offence (i.e. an intention to kill or cause GBH in this case). However, in this case Raymond took tablets which were prescribed to his wife.[8] The facts here are similar to

[7] This sentence sets out the argument that the defendant will seek to put forward in his defence and explain the rationale behind it.

[8] This sentence sets out the counter-argument (which the prosecution will seek to rely on).

those in **Hardie** [1985] 1 WLR 64, in which the Court of Appeal held that consideration must be given to whether the defendant's conduct in taking the non-dangerous drug was reckless. If his conduct was not reckless, he could rely on evidence of his involuntary intoxication to negate his mens rea for murder. Consideration should be given to the fact that the drug Raymond took is lawful in prescribed quantities and that he was unaware of the effect the drug would have on him, as well as the fact that the normal effect of taking the drug is sedative. In these circumstances, Raymond's intoxication is likely to be treated as involuntary. Thus, it may provide evidence to negate the mens rea of murder and any lesser charge of manslaughter.

[9] Briefly summarise the conclusions you reached in respect of each offence.

In conclusion,[9] Raymond's voluntary intoxication is likely to provide no defence to the sexual assault and the criminal damage of the window of the bank. However, he may rely on evidence of his intoxication in defence of criminal damage to the house and murder.

✓ Make your answer stand out

- You should include references to academic opinion to make your answer stand out.
- You could also refer to judicial comment in *Majewski, Heard* or *Hardie.*
- Ensure that you apply the law to the specific facts of the problem scenario each time you set out a legal principle.
- You could also refer to the Law Commission Report, *Intoxication and Criminal Liability* (Law Com. No. 314, 2009), which makes a number of recommendations on reforming the law.

! Don't be tempted to . . .

- Confuse the rules relating to voluntary intoxication from *Majewski* with those relating to involuntary intoxication.
- Recite the facts of *Majewski.* Although *Majewski* is the leading case on voluntary intoxication, the principle of law derived from this case is of more relevance in an answer than the specific facts of the case.
- Forget to ensure that you revise the effect that intoxication has on specific defences, such as mistaken belief in lawful excuse (*Jaggard* v *Dickinson*), mistaken belief in self-defence (*O'Connor* [1991] Crim LR 135; *O'Grady* [1987] QB 995), etc.

✒ Question 4

'If a man of his own volition takes a substance which causes him to cast off the restraints of reason and conscience, no wrong is done to him by holding him answerable criminally for any injury he may do while in that condition. His course of conduct in reducing himself by drugs and drink to that condition . . . supplies the evidence of mens rea . . .' (Lord Elwyn-Jones, *DPP* v *Majewski* [1977] AC 443).

To what extent is the law on voluntary intoxication in a satisfactory state?

Answer plan

➡ Analyse criticisms of Majewski.

➡ Consider the distinction between specific and basic intent.

Diagram plan

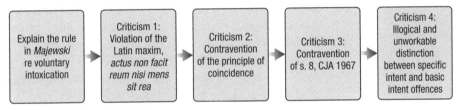

| Explain the rule in *Majewski* re voluntary intoxication | Criticism 1: Violation of the Latin maxim, *actus non facit reum nisi mens sit rea* | Criticism 2: Contravention of the principle of coincidence | Criticism 3: Contravention of s. 8, CJA 1967 | Criticism 4: Illogical and unworkable distinction between specific intent and basic intent offences |

A printable version of this diagram plan is available from www.pearsoned.co.uk/lawexpressqa

Answer

The courts frown upon defendants using evidence of their intoxication as a defence. The courts must not be seen to be condoning drunken behaviour which culminates in the commission of an offence by permitting defendants to escape liability due to intoxication.[1] Therefore, intoxication is said to be no defence *per se*; however, evidence of intoxication may be sufficient to deny the mens rea of an offence. The quote refers to the rule in **DPP v Majewski** [1977] AC 443, the leading authority on voluntary intoxication from the House of Lords. According to Lord Elywn-Jones in **Majewski**, voluntary intoxication is no defence to crimes of basic intent, but it may be a partial defence to crimes of specific intent if the defendant lacks the requisite intention for the offence.[2] A specific intent offence

[1] This sentence provides a justification for the statement in the first line.

[2] You should explain the quote in the title (and therefore the rule in *Majewski*) in your own words to demonstrate that you fully understand the rule.

is one which requires proof of intention as the mens rea element of the offence. By contrast, the mens rea of a basic intent offence may be satisfied by proof of a lesser form of mens rea, such as recklessness.[3] As the quote above demonstrates, Lord Elwyn-Jones took the view that voluntarily becoming intoxicated is a reckless course of conduct to take. Thus, a voluntarily intoxicated defendant is automatically reckless and therefore he has the mens rea for every basic intent crime. This means that a defendant will be guilty of a basic intent offence if he then performs the actus reus of a basic intent crime. However, where the defendant does have the necessary intention for the offence, the fact that he is intoxicated will provide no defence because a drunken intent is still an intent: **Sheehan and Moore** [1975] 1 WLR 739.

The decision of **Majewski** has been criticised for a number of reasons, and thus it may be argued that the law is not in a satisfactory state.[4] As stated above, **Majewski** was a decision dictated by policy reasons as the courts did not want to be seen to be condoning drunken behaviour which could be harmful to society. The criticisms of **Majewski** are 'aimed at the decision of the House [of Lords] to compromise fundamental principles of criminal law for reasons of policy' (Monaghan, N., *Criminal Law Directions* (2012), p. 310). The main criticisms are that the rule in **Majewski** violates fundamental principles of criminal law such as the Latin maxim *actus non facit reum nisi mens sit rea* ('an act does not make a man guilty of a crime, unless his mind be also guilty,' per Lord Hailsham in **Haughton v Smith** [1975] AC 476), the principle of coincidence of actus reus and mens rea and section 8 of the Criminal Justice Act 1967 and justifies compromising these principles for policy reasons.[5]

The principle that 'an act does not make a man guilty of a crime, unless his mind be also guilty' is compromised because **Majewski** does not require proof of the defendant's state of mind, which is instead presumed to be guilty. Where, at the time of the offence, the defendant is completely unaware of what he is doing due to his intoxicated state (although he is not suffering a disease of the mind), he is nonetheless guilty of any relevant basic intent offence (Monaghan (2012), p. 310).

The rule in **Majewski** also ignores the principle that the actus reus and the mens rea of an offence must coincide in order for the

[3] Demonstrate your understanding of the distinction between specific intent and basic intent offences.

[4] This sentence addresses the second part of the title directly and ensures that you (and the examiner) remain focused on the point in issue.

[5] Summarise the criticisms by listing them before explaining them in further detail below.

defendant to be guilty of an offence. Lord Elwyn-Jones regards a defendant who becomes intoxicated as reckless. This mens rea is formed as the defendant becomes intoxicated and before the actus reus of the offence is performed. Subjective recklessness requires that a defendant recognises the risk of a consequence (the actus reus) occurring but goes on to take that risk anyway. However, '[t]he 'recklessness' of the defendant which is presumed under *Majewski* is not related to the defendant's actus reus as it arises prior to his performance of the actus reus' (Monaghan, p. 311).

The effect of the rule in *Majewski* is that where a defendant voluntarily becomes intoxicated, there is a presumption that he is reckless. Ormerod refers to this as a 'form of "prior fault"' (Ormerod, D., *Smith and Hogan Criminal Law* (2011), p. 315).[6] It can be argued that this presumption of mens rea contravenes section 8 of the Criminal Justice Act 1967, which requires a jury to decide whether the defendant foresaw the result of his actions (i.e. was subjectively reckless) by reference to all the evidence.

[6] Refer to academic opinion to demonstrate that you have read beyond your module guide/lecture notes.

The use of the distinction between specific intent and basic intent offences has also been criticised for being confusing and unclear. Ormerod comments that '[i]n view of the rule in *Majewski*, the nature of "specific intent" is a matter of great importance but a careful scrutiny of the authorities, particularly *Majewski* itself, fails to reveal any consistent principle by which specific and basic are to be distinguished' (p. 317). Thus, it would appear that the distinction between basic and specific intent offences lacks any logical rationale.

These principles have been compromised in the interest of policy considerations. However, the policy aims that the rule was designed to tackle remain problematic in cases where there is no lesser basic intent offence of which to convict the defendant (e.g. theft is a specific intent offence to which voluntary intoxication could be a defence, but there is no lesser offence that the defendant could be convicted of).[7]

[7] Illustrate your point here with an example.

It is interesting to note that new offences created today are more frequently avoiding the traditional intention/recklessness approach to the mental element of the offence.[8] This has been seen with the Sexual Offences Act 2003, under which offences such as rape and sexual assault no longer include the word recklessness. The Serious

[8] This paragraph demonstrates your wider knowledge of criminal law.

Crime Act 2007 also prefers intention and belief over recklessness. Consequently, it must be questioned to what extent the basic/ specific intent offence distinction is still useful. In **Heard** [2007] EWCA Crim 125, the Court of Appeal stated that the use of the terms 'specific intent' and 'basic intent' might not be suitable for every offence. This case involved an allegation of sexual assault which requires intentional touching, yet the court held that basic intent was required and thus the defendant's intoxication could not negate the mens rea. The approach taken was that 'specific intent' offences require proof of purpose or consequence. This case conflicts with the approach taken in **Majewski** and appears to add to the confusion already created by the House of Lords.

[9] Refer back to the question in your conclusion and use this final paragraph to briefly summarise your findings.

In conclusion, the law on voluntary intoxication is not in a satisfactory state[9] as it compromises fundamental principles of criminal law in the name of policy and provides an illogical and confusing manner of distinguishing offences which is becoming increasingly inappropriate for modern day offences. The law is in need of significant reform in this area.

 Make your answer stand out

- Refer to further academic opinion, such as Gough, S., Surviving without *Majewski* [2000] Crim LR 719 and Simester, A., Intoxication is never a defence [2009] Crim LR 3.

- Refer to the recent recommendations for reform in the Law Commission Report, *Intoxication and Criminal Liability* (Law Com. No. 314, 2009) and the Draft Criminal Law (Intoxication) Bill. These recommendations seek to clarify the terminology used.

- You could expand your discussion of the case of *Heard*.

- You could also refer in more detail to judicial comment on the distinction between specific intent and basic intent offences.

! Don't be tempted to . . .

- Merely set out everything that you know about voluntary and involuntary intoxication. This question is specifically asking you to critically analyse the rule relating to voluntary intoxication.
- Recite the facts of cases in detail. If you do think that certain facts of a case are particularly relevant to the point you are making then you should refer to them briefly. For example, see the (very brief) reference to the facts of *Heard* in the answer above.
- Forget to address the quote directly in your answer.

? Question 5

Define self-defence and assess its availability as a legal argument in the following situation.

After a night out, Leo is walking home late at night when he hears the sound of a person running behind him. He turns to see a man in a hooded top running towards him. Leo perceives the man to be threatening and he decides to stand and fight the man. Leo takes up a karate stance and repeatedly kicks the person unconscious as soon as he approaches. However, the man turns out to have been Duncan, an acquaintance of Leo's, who was out for an evening run. Duncan suffers a serious head injury as a result. Would it make a difference to your answer if Leo was drunk at the time?

Answer plan

→ Briefly give the definition of self-defence with authorities.

→ Discuss the likelihood of a plea of self-defence being successful.

→ Assess whether Leo's pre-emptive strike precludes the defence.

→ Consider the effect of Leo's mistaken belief in self-defence.

→ Examine the implication of the drunken mistake.

Diagram plan

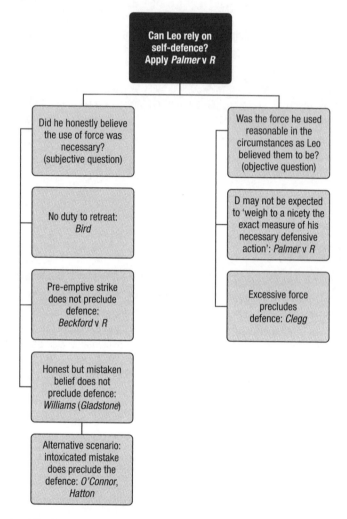

A printable version of this diagram plan is available from www.pearsoned.co.uk/lawexpressqa

Answer

[1] Explain briefly what self-defence is before then elaborating on this and setting out the tests from the authorities.

Self-defence is a common law defence which permits a defendant to use reasonable force to protect himself if he honestly believes that the use of force is necessary.[1] It is a general defence to any offence and if pleaded successfully it leads to a complete acquittal. Some principles of law related to the defence have recently been put on a statutory footing by section 76 of the Criminal Justice and Immigration Act 2008. The objective of this section is to clarify the law relating to self-defence: section 76(9).[2] In the leading authority of *Majewski* [1971] AC 814, the Privy Council confirmed the two limbs necessary for a successful plea of self-defence. The first limb is a subjective question which asks whether the defendant honestly believed that the use of force was necessary. The second limb is objective and asks whether the amount of force used was reasonable. This test was later reiterated in *Oatridge* (1992) 94 Cr App R 367, in which Mustill LJ held that three questions must be asked: (i) was the defendant under actual or threatened attack by the victim? (ii) did the defendant act to defend himself? (iii) was his response commensurate with the degree of danger created by the attack? This case also requires both a subjective belief that force was necessary in self-defence, along with an objective assessment of the level of force used, which must be proportionate to the perceived attack.[3] This is really the same as the test in *Majewski*, albeit expressed differently (as (i) is phrased objectively). While the defendant bears an evidential burden in respect of self-defence (i.e. the defendant must raise some evidence of self-defence in order to make the issue a live one), the prosecution bear the legal burden of disproving self-defence beyond reasonable doubt: *Lobell* [1957] 1 QB 547.

As Leo caused serious injuries to Duncan, he is likely to be charged with wounding or inflicting GBH under section 20 of the Offences Against the Person Act (OAPA) 1861, or wounding or causing GBH with intent under section 18 of the OAPA 1861. In order to ascertain Leo's chances of successfully pleading self-defence to these charges, it is necessary to apply these two limbs from *Majewski* to the problem scenario. In respect of the first limb, it must be questioned whether Leo honestly believed that force was necessary to defend himself. A defendant may not rely on self-defence if he acts out of revenge or for any other reason than the defence of himself. In this scenario, Leo acts because he perceives the man running towards him to be threatening. Thus, he is acting out of an honest belief that it is necessary to act to defend himself.[4] However, it is clear that he has made a mistake because the man running towards him posed

[2] This demonstrates to the examiner that you are aware of recent legislation and its purpose.

[3] Summarise the two main limbs of self-defence and identify which limb is subjective and which is objective.

[4] Identify the facts in the scenario that relate to the first limb and ensure that you apply the law to the facts.

no such threat. Nevertheless, Leo's mistake does not preclude him from relying upon self-defence provided that his belief that force was necessary was honestly held: **Williams (Gladstone)** [1987] 3 All ER 411 (confirmed in s. 76(4), Criminal Justice and Immigration Act 2008). Thus, Leo will be judged according to the circumstances as he honestly believed them to be. As he honestly believed that the man posed a threat to him and that he was defending himself, the first limb is satisfied.[5]

[5] After stating this further principle re mistake, ensure that you also apply the law to the facts and conclude in relation to the first limb.

The danger to the defendant must be sufficiently imminent according to **Devlin v Armstrong** [1971] NI 13. It appears in this scenario that the danger is sufficiently imminent to Leo as Duncan is running towards him. Consideration should be given to the fact that Leo kicked Duncan first and before any violence from Duncan. Such a pre-emptive strike does not preclude Leo from relying upon self-defence: see **Beckford v R** [1988] AC 130, in which Lord Griffiths held that a man 'does not have to wait for his assailant to strike the first blow'.[6] There is also no duty on a defendant to retreat: **Bird** [1985] 2 All ER 513. Thus, there is no duty on Leo to retreat and the fact that he adopted a karate stance does not preclude the defence.

[6] Try to memorise a few key quotes from leading judgments.

The second limb of the test from **Majewski** requires consideration of whether the amount of force actually used by the defendant was reasonable. This is objectively assessed and is a question for the jury to determine. Another way of asking this question is: was the response commensurate with the attack? (**Oatridge**). Where a defendant uses excessive or disproportionate force, his defence of self-defence will not be successful: **Clegg** [1995] 1 AC 482 (see s. 76(6), Criminal Justice and Immigration Act 2008).[7] Although this limb carries an objective test, there is a subjective element to the question because the defendant must use reasonable force in the circumstances as he believed them to be: **Owino** [1996] 2 Cr App R 128 (also reiterated under s. 76(3) of the Criminal Justice and Immigration Act 2008). In this scenario, Leo repeatedly kicks the man until he falls unconscious. Although the facts do not state where on the man's body Leo was aiming the blows with his feet, the use of the word 'repeatedly' and the fact that the man falls unconscious would lead one to infer that Leo has not used reasonable force.[8] Some leeway is given to defendants who act in 'the heat of the

[7] Where appropriate, make reference to the provisions of the Criminal Justice and Immigration Act 2008, which purports to clarify the law. This adds further support to your arguments.

[8] Identify key words within the facts of the scenario and use them to support your answer.

moment'. In **Majewski**, the Privy Council recognised the fact that a defendant may not be expected to 'weigh to a nicety the exact measure of his necessary defensive action' (placed onto a statutory footing by s. 76(7) of the Criminal Justice and Immigration Act 2008). Thus, in this scenario, the fact that Leo may have been taken a bit by surprise may be taken into account here, although it must be conceded that the facts suggest that Leo in fact had time to stand and face Duncan, and thus that he may not have been acting in 'the heat of the moment'. This will, of course, ultimately be a matter for the jury to decide upon.

[9] Do not forget to deal with the alternative scenario at the end of your answer, otherwise you will lose valuable marks.

If Leo was drunk at the time of the incident, the answer would be different.[9] This is because, although an honest but mistaken belief does not preclude self-defence (**Williams (Gladstone)**), a mistake which is made due to intoxication will preclude the defence. This was stated *obiter* in **O'Grady** [1987] QB 995 and confirmed by the Court of Appeal in **O'Connor** [1991] Crim LR 135 and more recently in **Hatton** [2005] EWCA Crim 2951. This has also been clarified by section 76(5) of the Criminal Justice and Immigration Act 2008. Thus, if Leo's mistake in perceiving Duncan to be a threat was made due to his intoxicated state, he will not be able to rely upon the defence of self-defence.

✓ Make your answer stand out

- Problem scenarios on self-defence can be quite difficult to structure due to the fact that there are several important principles of law from key authorities which need to be addressed and applied. So, ensure that you adopt a clear structure and are aware which principle relates to the subjective limb and which to the objective limb.

- Whenever you set out a legal principle, ensure that you state the relevant authority and apply the principle to the facts of the problem scenario.

- Identify brief quotes from key judgments which you can rely upon to support your arguments.

- Be aware of which cases have been put onto a statutory footing by section 76 of the Criminal Justice and Immigration Act 2008 and refer to both the case and provision together to demonstrate your knowledge of this.

> **!** **Don't be tempted to . . .**
>
> ■ Merely provide a textbook recitation of the law on self-defence. The examiner does not want to read a narrative of the law but is looking to see whether you can identify relevant principles of law and apply these appropriately to the facts in the question.
>
> ■ Confuse the subjective and the objective limbs of the test and ensure that you distinguish clearly between these.
>
> ■ Provide the facts of the cases unless these are directly relevant to the question. If they are, you should then only set out material facts briefly.

Question 6

Critically evaluate the extent to which section 76 of the Criminal Justice and Immigration Act 2008 clarifies and improves the law on self-defence.

Answer plan

→ Refer to the common law on self-defence.

→ Discuss section 76 of the Criminal Justice and Immigration Act 2008.

→ Consider the background to section 76, CJIA 2008.

→ Compare and contrast academic critique on the enactment of section 76.

Diagram plan

| Explore the common law defence of self-defence | Explain the background to and aims of s. 76, CJIA 2008 | Set out the principles under s. 76, CJIA 2008 | Consider academic opinion relating to s. 76 |

A printable version of this diagram plan is available from www.pearsoned.co.uk/lawexpressqa

Answer

The law on self-defence was recently codified by the enactment of section 76 of the Criminal Justice and Immigration Act 2008 ('CJIA 2008'). The aim of this provision was to provide much sought after clarification of the law on self-defence and the prevention of crime

[1] Set out the aim of the reforms at the very start of your answer. There is no need to go into very much detail in your introduction as this is something you will come back to later in your answer.

[2] Cite academic opinion to support your answer as well as to demonstrate that you have read widely.

[3] You should use the leading authority on self-defence to set out the test under the common law.

(s. 76(9)), in particular the use of the defence by householders who attack burglars.[1] The section does not purport to change the law, but simply to provide clarity as to its application. However, section 76 has received less than glowing comments from academics. It has been described as 'pointless' (Professor Dennis (Editorial) 'A pointless exercise' [2008] Crim LR 507) and 'patchy in its coverage' (Padfield, 'The Criminal Justice and Immigration Act 2008' (2008) Archbold News 5).[2] Thus, it must be questioned whether this provision was at all necessary to clarify the common law position.

Self-defence is defined by common law. It is a defence which may be pleaded by a defendant who uses reasonable force in order to protect himself from an attack which he honestly believes he will be subjected to. Thus, the defence is both subjectively and objectively assessed. According to the leading authority of *Majewski* [1971] AC 814, the Privy Council confirmed that self-defence requires proof that the defendant honestly believed that the use of force was necessary (the subjective limb) as well as proof that the amount of force used by the defendant in his own defence was reasonable (the objective limb).[3] Self-defence is a complete defence which leads to acquittal if pleaded successfully. The defendant bears an evidential burden in respect of self-defence. The prosecution bears the legal burden of disproving self-defence beyond reasonable doubt: *Lobell* [1957] 1 QB 547.

Common law also provides that a defendant's mistake does not preclude him from relying upon self-defence provided that his belief that force was necessary was honestly held: *Williams (Gladstone)* [1987] 3 All ER 411. The defendant is judged according to the circumstances as he honestly believed them to be. This principle has since been confirmed by section 76(4), CJIA 2008. However, a mistake which is made due to intoxication will preclude the defence: *O'Grady* [1987] QB 995, *O'Connor* [1991] Crim LR 135 and *Hatton* [2005] EWCA Crim 2951. This has since been clarified by section 76(5), CJIA 2008. According to *Clegg* [1995] 1 AC 482, the use of excessive or disproportionate force precludes the defence. This has since been given statutory effect in section 76(6), CJIA 2008. The 'reasonable force' limb of self-defence also contains a subjective element because the defendant must use reasonable force in the circumstances as he believed them to be: *Owino* [1996] 2 Cr App R 128. This has also since been confirmed by section 76(3),

CJIA 2008. Under the common law, the defendant has been given a degree of leeway in the amount of force used. The Privy Council in *Majewski* recognised the fact that a defendant may not be expected to 'weigh to a nicety the exact measure of his necessary defensive action'. This has also been codified by section 76(7), CJIA 2008.

[4] Explain what led to the enactment of section 76, CJIA 2008.

[5] Provide an example of a significant case which provided some of the impetus behind the enactment of section 76, CJIA 2008.

Section 76 was enacted largely as a result of media pressure on Parliament to clarify the law on self-defence.[4] This media pressure arose due to high profile cases, such as the case of *Martin (Anthony)* [2002] 2 WLR 1, in which the defendant shot two burglars who had broken into his property.[5] The case raised questions about the use of self-defence by householders who attack intruders: how much force may householders use in dealing with an intruder? Is a householder permitted to use pre-emptive action? Clarification of the law purported to come in the form of section 76, CJIA 2008, but (as stated above) this section did not reform the law on self-defence. In fact, just one section was devoted to clarifying the law on self-defence. This section actually fails to answer the questions posed by the media and merely restates the common law principles on self-defence. To this extent, it is difficult to see how section 76 clarifies the law for members of the public.[6]

[6] This sentence provides some criticism of the section and relates back to the title.

Further criticism of the section is that it fails to codify all of the principles of law relating to self-defence. Padfield states that the section is 'patchy in its coverage of the complexities of the "defence"' (at p. 8). Dennis comments that '. . . the more critical practitioner might well ask what is the point of setting out a partial codification of these principles' (2008 at p. 5). Dennis lists several principles of law that the section fails to codify, including all the purposes for which force may lawfully be used, the meaning of the word 'force', acts preparatory to the use of force or pre-emptive conduct, the use of force against a police officer, the fact that there is no duty to retreat, etc. The following principles of self-defence are enshrined in common law: the danger to the defendant must be sufficiently imminent (*Devlin* v *Armstrong* [1971] NI 13), a pre-emptive strike does not preclude the defendant from relying upon self-defence (*Beckford* v *R* [1988] AC 130), and there is no duty on a defendant to retreat: *Bird* [1985] 2 All ER 513. No mention of these is made in the CJIA 2008.[7]

[7] You must provide evidence to support the criticism of section 76, CJIA 2008 that you make in this paragraph.

Section 76 was not intended to change the law on self-defence or reinvent it in any way. Its purpose was merely to 'improve the understanding of the practical application' of the defence (Explanatory Notes to the CJIA 2008, para. 532). Despite this aim, Dennis comments that 'Practitioners will learn nothing new from this provision' (2008 at p. 5). Dennis also points out a problem created by the Act by its reference to 'an honest and instinctive action being "strong evidence" that the reaction was reasonable'. He questions the significance of something being 'strong evidence' and whether this creates a 'presumption of reasonableness' (at p. 507).[8] Ormerod states 'it might be doubted whether the section has done much to clarify anything' (case commentary to **Drane (Paul)** [2009] Crim LR 202). In fact, he goes so far as to state that the enactment of the section was a 'waste of valuable parliamentary time which could have been spent on more pressing issues of criminal justice' (at p. 203).

[8] Use academic commentary to provide a further criticism of section 76, CJIA 2008.

In conclusion, while section 76 purports to have 'clarified' the law on self-defence, it appears that it has added very little to the law. The codification of the law on self-defence is a half-hearted attempt which failed to incorporate all the key principles of common law which have developed over the years. As such, the section does not improve the law and may in fact have served to complicate the law by creating new problems for the courts to decipher.[9]

[9] Refer back to the title in your conclusion in order to demonstrate your focus on the title.

✓ Make your answer stand out

- Incorporate more academic criticism of section 76, CJIA 2008 into your answer.
- Consider the compatibility of section 76(6) on the proportionality of the defendant's response with Article 2 of the ECHR. In particular, see Ormerod [2009] Crim LR 202 at 203.
- Explore the defences under section 3(1), Criminal Law Act 1967 (prevention of crime and protection of another).
- Discuss the extent to which section 76(8), CJIA 2008 permits the characteristics of the defendant to be taken into account. Compare the common law position in *Martin (Anthony)*.

> **!** **Don't be tempted to . . .**
>
> ■ Merely set out verbatim the wording of section 76, CJIA 2008. You need to explain the effect of the section and consider whether it has clarified and improved the law.
>
> ■ Set out the facts of the cases, as these are not directly relevant to the question and you will waste valuable time.
>
> ■ Simply provide an emotive narrative of your views on how much force a householder should be permitted to use in attacking an intruder or in defence of his property.

? Question 7

Answer **BOTH** parts.

Discuss which defences, if any, are available to the parties in the following scenarios:

(a) Mike and Dave are members of a criminal gang known for its violent methods. Mike tells Dave that he must shoot the leader of a rival gang. Dave, who has a particularly low IQ, initially refuses to carry out the shooting. Mike then threatens Dave that he will kidnap and torture Dave's wife and children unless Dave shoots the rival gang leader. Dave agrees to shoot the rival gang leader and does so.

AND

(b) Bob confides in a work colleague, Ernie. Bob tells Ernie that he is homosexual and that he is petrified that their boss, who is openly homophobic, might find out and fire him. Ernie, who is heavily in debt, threatens to reveal Bob's secret to their boss unless Bob gives him £1,000 by the end of the week. Bob is terrified that Ernie will carry out his threat, so the following day he drinks half a bottle of vodka to steady his nerves and then robs a post office. He gives £1,000 to Ernie.

Answer plan

→ Outline the test for duress from *Graham* (1982) 74 Cr App R 235 and *Hasan* [2005] UKHL 22.

→ Consider the effect that Dave's voluntary association with a criminal gang has on a plea of duress.

→ Examine the availability of duress as a defence to murder (if the shooting is fatal).

→ Consider the fact that there must be a threat of death or serious violence and the effect that the other threats directed at Bob will have on a plea of duress.

→ Address Bob's intoxication ('Dutch courage').

Diagram plan

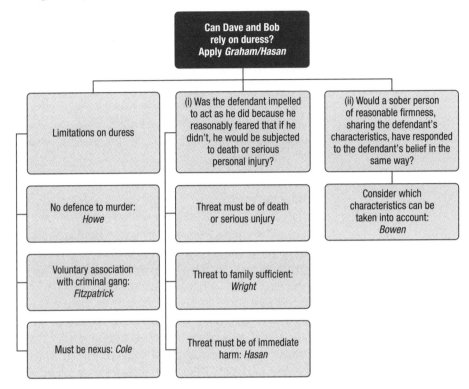

A printable version of this diagram plan is available from www.pearsoned.co.uk/lawexpressqa

[1] At the very start you should briefly identify the main issues before exploring the question in more detail.

Answer

This question requires consideration of whether Dave and Bob will be able to rely on the defence of duress in respect of the offences that they have committed. A further issue is the effect of Bob's intoxication.[1]

[2] Where a question is divided into parts, deal with each part separately, using headings to highlight the division in your answer.

Part (a)[2]

[3] You should state the result of a successful plea of the defence as this is obviously an important factor which influences your advice to a defendant.

Duress by threats is a complete defence available where the defendant commits a criminal offence because his will is overborne by threats of death or serious violence. A successful plea of duress will result in a complete acquittal.[3] The test for duress is now set out in the Court of Appeal decision in *Graham* (1982) 74 Cr App R 235 and

[4] Before applying the law to the facts, you should set out the two limbs of the test and cite supporting authorities.

the House of Lords authority of **Hasan** [2005] UKHL 22. The test requires consideration of two main questions:[4] the first asks whether the defendant was impelled to act as he did because he reasonably feared that, if he didn't, he would be subjected to death or serious personal injury? This is the subjective limb which contains an objective element. The second question asks whether a sober person of reasonable firmness, sharing the defendant's characteristics, would have responded to the defendant's belief in the same way. This is the objective limb which contains a subjective element (the reasonable man may share certain characteristics of the defendant: **Bowen** [1996] 2 Cr App R 157.

Dave will seek to plead duress as a defence in respect of the shooting. However, there are some limitations on the defence and it is not clear on the facts in the scenario what offence Dave has been charged with. It is also unclear whether the shooting of the rival gang leader leads to the death of that gang leader.[5] If Dave is charged with murder, he will not be able to rely upon the defence of duress because duress is no defence to murder: **Howe** [1987] AC 417. Even if the gang leader does not die, duress may not be a defence to Dave if he is charged with attempted murder: **Gotts** [1992] 2 AC 412. Duress will be a defence if Dave is charged with an offence such as wounding or inflicting GBH under section 20, Offences Against the Person Act (OAPA) 1861, or wounding or causing GBH with intent under section 18, OAPA 1861.

[5] If the facts are unclear or some important information is omitted from the facts, then say so. This demonstrates your awareness of which issues are important.

Applying the subjective question to the facts in part (a), the threat here was of violence to Dave's family. This is a sufficient threat for the purposes of duress because according to the case of **Wright** [2000] Crim LR 510, the threat of death or serious injury need not be directed at the defendant himself, but may be directed at his immediate family or someone close to him.[6] This has also been confirmed in **Hasan**. Thus, the threats towards Dave's family are sufficient. The law also requires that the threats be of immediate harm so that the defendant cannot take evasive action. According to **Hasan**, the harm must reasonably be expected to follow immediately or almost immediately. It is not clear here how immediate the harm is on the facts. Any delay between the threat and Dave carrying out the shooting will rule out the defence of duress.

[6] Apply the law by explaining why the threat is sufficient in this case.

[7] Adopt an appropriate structure, dealing with the subjective limb in one paragraph and then the objective limb in a separate paragraph.

The second question which must be addressed is the objective limb of duress.[7] This asks whether a sober person of reasonable firmness, sharing the defendant's characteristics, would have responded to the defendant's belief in the same way. According to *Graham*, the defendant's age and sex can be taken into account. In *Bowen*, this was extended to include other characteristics, such as pregnancy, serious physical disability, recognised mental illness or a psychiatric condition. The facts indicate that Dave has a particularly low IQ. This is not a relevant factor and may not be taken into account, unless Dave's IQ is so low that he may be deemed to be suffering from a mental illness. Whether this is the case is unclear on the facts. Duress may be successful here if the jury are satisfied that a reasonable man would have acted in the same way. However, if there is any psychiatric evidence that Dave is suffering from some mental illness or impairment, this could be taken into account in respect of whether it renders him more susceptible to pressure and threats.

A further issue requiring consideration is the fact that Dave has voluntarily associated with a gang known to use violent methods. According to the House of Lords, Dave's defence of duress will fail where he has voluntarily associated himself with a criminal gang: [8] *Hasan*.[8] Dave has exposed himself to the risk of being forced to commit a crime by associating with a criminal gang: see *Fitzpatrick* [1977] NILR 20 and *Sharp* [1987] QB 853.

[8] Do not forget to deal with any facts which may limit the defence, such as voluntary associations with criminal gangs.

Part (b)

Bob will be charged with robbery and will seek to plead duress as a defence. As stated above, the test for duress is set out in *Graham* and *Hasan*. The test requires consideration of two questions: (i) was the defendant impelled to act as he did because he reasonably feared that if he didn't he would be subjected to death or serious personal injury? (ii) would a sober person of reasonable firmness, sharing the defendant's characteristics, have responded to the defendant's belief in the same way? It is worth pointing out at this stage that the defence of duress requires a threat of death or serious injury. However, on the facts, Ernie has threatened to reveal Bob's sexuality and has made no threats of death or serious injury, thus the defence of duress is not available here: *Baker and Wilkins* [1997] Crim LR 497.[9] In *Valderrama-Vega* [1985] Crim LR 220, the Court of Appeal held that threats to disclose homosexual orientation alone are insufficient for the defence of duress. In addition to this, on the

[9] If on the facts it is clear that the defence is not available, then you should state this early on after setting out the test for duress.

facts it is clear that Ernie did not actually tell Bob to rob the post office, but merely told him to give him £1,000. Thus, there is an insufficient nexus between the threat and the offence of robbery and the defence of duress is not available: see *Cole* [1994] Crim LR 582.

Bob's intoxication is unlikely to provide any defence to a charge of robbery. Although the intoxication is voluntary and under the rule in *DPP* v *Majewski* [1977] AC 443 evidence of voluntary intoxication may negate the mens rea in a specific intent offence. Here Bob's intoxication is 'Dutch courage'. Intoxication as a result of 'Dutch courage' is no defence in law: see *Attorney General for Northern Ireland* v *Gallagher* [1963] AC 349. Although the intoxication is voluntary here, a drunken intent is still an intent: *Sheehan and Moore* [1975] 1 WLR 739 and there is clear evidence of intention on the facts. Bob still had the mens rea for robbery at the time and thus he will be guilty: *Kingston* [1995] 2 AC 355.

 Make your answer stand out

- Use a range of different authorities to support the principles you rely upon.
- There are many principles of law and authorities which you may rely upon in respect of duress, thus it is important that you ensure that you structure your answer in a logical and coherent way.
- Add reference to judicial comment to your answer. For instance, you could refer to Lord Bingham's opinion in *Hasan*.
- You could also try to incorporate some academic opinion in your answer, particularly in relation to the leading House of Lords' decision in *Hasan*.

! Don't be tempted to . . .

- Merely cite *Hasan* as an authority on duress because it is the most recent leading authority. *Hasan* draws upon previous case law, thus you should demonstrate your knowledge of other earlier cases too.
- Forget to apply every principle of law which you cite. The examiner is not just looking for your knowledge of legal principles, but also for your ability to apply the law appropriately to the facts of a question.

11

Inchoate offences

How this topic may come up in exams

Inchoate offences might be examined by essay questions or problem questions. Problem questions on inchoate offences lend themselves easily to simultaneous examination of accessorial liability; you may find these two topics mixed in a problem question. Problem questions will require you to have knowledge of other offences, such as burglary, theft and offences against the person. Essay questions might require you to critically evaluate a particular element of an inchoate offence, such as the actus reus of attempt, or it might require consideration of wider issues, such as the overlap between the Serious Crime Act 2007 and accessorial liability.

■ Attack the question

Encouraging or assisting crime	Conspiracy	Attempt
ss. 44–46 Serious Crime Act 2007	s. 1(1) Criminal Law Act 1977	s. 1(1) Criminal Attempts Act 1981
AR – doing an act capable of assisting or encouraging an offence	AR – agreement to commit an offence	AR – more than merely preparatory acts
MR – intention or belief re encouragement or assistance (depending on offence charged)	MR – intention to carry out course of conduct and to commit full offence	MR – intention to commit full offence

A printable version of this diagram is available from www.pearsoned.co.uk/lawexpressqa

❓ Question 1

Shaun and Grant are career criminals. Grant owes Shaun a favour and Shaun asks Grant for a considerable sum of money because he is in debt to a dangerous criminal gang. Shaun asks Grant if he will commit a robbery of a security van which delivers cash to the local banks as the vans carry large amounts of cash, and share the money with him. Shaun tells Grant that he has been monitoring the movements of a particular security van for the past few months and he believes that this van could be an easy target, due to the fact that the security guards who drive the van do not follow security procedures properly. He also promises Grant that he will obtain all the security details that Grant will need in exchange for a third of the cash seized.

Shaun obtains security information for Grant regarding the arrival time of the van, the number of security guards with the van and the positioning of the guards during a delivery of cash. Grant then decides that he will commit the robbery and persuades his friend Kane to help. Grant and Kane meet to discuss how best to approach the crime and together they come up with a plan to commit the robbery while armed and using disguises.

One week before the planned robbery, Shaun decides to commit the robbery of the security van himself so that he can keep all of the money seized. Shaun arrives at the bank and hides in a street round the corner to wait for the van. However, when the van shows up, Shaun runs away. The following week, following the original plan, Grant and Kane arrive at the scene of the planned robbery. When the van turns up, Grant and Kane approach the van shouting threats of violence, but a security guard activates an alarm and Grant and Kane make their escape.

Discuss the criminal liability of Shaun, Grant and Kane.

Answer plan

→ Refer to Shaun encouraging and assisting Grant to commit a robbery.

→ Discuss the conspiracy between Grant and Kane and any liability of Grant under the Serious Crime Act (SCA) 2007 for encouraging Kane to commit the robbery.

→ Consider whether Shaun may be liable for attempted robbery.

→ Consider whether Grant and Kane may be liable for attempted robbery.

Diagram plan

1. Shaun encourages and assists Grant to commit robbery	• Encouraging or assisting crime – Serious Crime Act 2007

2. Grant encourages Kane to commit robbery	• Encouraging crime – Serious Crime Act 2007

3. Grant and Kane conspire to commit robbery	• Conspiracy – s. 1, Criminal Law Act 1977

4. Shaun not guilty of attempted robbery	• Not more than merely preparatory under s. 1, Criminal Attempts Act 1981 • *Campbell* (1991) 93 Cr App R 350 and *Geddes* [1996] Crim LR 894

5. Grant and Kane commit attempted robbery	• Attempted robbery – s. 1, Criminal Attempts Act 1981 • *Jones* [1990] 1 WLR 1057

A printable version of this diagram plan is available from www.pearsoned.co.uk/lawexpressqa

Answer

This scenario involves inchoate liability and requires consideration of the encouragement and assistance of robbery by Shaun, conspiracy to commit robbery between Grant and Kane, and attempts to commit robbery by Shaun initially and then by Grant and Kane.[1]

[1] Keep your introduction short and to the point. Identify the topic and the potential offences which require discussion.

The first offence is committed by Shaun when he asks Grant to commit the robbery. This constitutes encouragement to commit robbery under sections 44–46 of the Serious Crime Act 2007. When Shaun provides security details on the van he also assists a crime under sections 44–46. The actus reus of these offences is similar. Under sections 44 and 45, it must be proved that Shaun did an act capable of encouraging or assisting the commission of an offence. Section 46 applies where a defendant does an act capable of encouraging or assisting the commission of one or more of a number of offences (here there could be a robbery or theft). In this case,

Shaun asking Grant to commit the offence and stating that he can provide security details might constitute encouragement. The word 'encouraging' is not defined in the Act, but it is thought that the old common law meaning of incitement will apply.[2] In *Race Relations Board* v *Applin* [1973] 1 QB 815, Lord Denning defined incitement widely, as 'to spur on by advice, encouragement or persuasion'. Shaun's words will most likely constitute encouragement to commit robbery. By providing security details relating to the van, Shaun has done an act capable of assisting robbery. Thus, the actus reus elements of these offences are satisfied.

[2] This sentence demonstrates wider knowledge of the law (including the old common law offence of incitement which the offences under the SCA 2007 replaced) and, in the absence of any authorities on the point, the way in which the courts are likely to apply the law.

Shaun could be convicted under section 44 if it can be proved that he intentionally encouraged or assisted the commission of the robbery. This offence requires proof of various mens rea elements.[3] The first is an intention to do the acts of encouragement or assistance. This is clearly present here – it cannot be said that Shaun does not intend to provide advice or security details to Grant. It must also be proved that Shaun intended to encourage or assist commission of an offence. On the facts, it seems clear that Shaun's purpose in providing advice and the security details is to encourage or assist the doing of an act capable of amounting to the commission of an offence: section 47(2). Shaun must also believe that, or be reckless as to whether, Grant will have the mens rea for robbery: section 47(5)(a). Here, in light of the fact that they are career criminals, Shaun probably believes that Grant has the mens rea for robbery. Shaun must also believe that, or be reckless as to whether, if the act is done, it will be done in the circumstances or with the consequences required for robbery: section 47(5)(b). It is likely that Shaun does believe that the circumstances and/or consequences of the offences will be present. Thus, the mens rea of section 44 is satisfied and Shaun could be guilty of intentionally encouraging or assisting the commission of robbery under section 44.

[3] Do not forget to apply the mens rea elements of the offences and to distinguish between sections 44 and 45, SCA 2007.

If the prosecution have any difficulty proving the intention under section 44, the mens rea under section 45 will be satisfied in any event.[4] The mens rea under section 45 is a belief that the offence will be committed and a belief that his act will encourage or assist the commission of the offence. It is unlikely that the prosecution will need to charge Shaun with the offence under section 46 of encouraging or assisting offences believing that one of more offences will

[4] In this scenario, this offence need only be dealt with briefly as the more serious offence under section 44, SCA 2007 applies.

be committed, as this offence is really intended to cover situations where the defendant does not know (or has no belief as to) which offence will be committed.[5] By contrast here, it can be said that Shaun does know the offence which will be committed, namely robbery.

[5] If one of the offences does not apply, state this and briefly explain why.

It could also be said that Grant is guilty of encouraging Kane to commit the robbery under section 44 of the SCA 2007. Grant performs the actus reus of doing an act capable of encouraging or assisting the commission of an offence by persuading Kane to help. He also has the mens rea because he intends to persuade Kane to commit a robbery and he believes that, or is reckless as to whether, Kane will have the mens rea for robbery and that the act will be done in the circumstances or with the consequences required for robbery.

There is a conspiracy between Kane and Grant to commit robbery. Conspiracy is a statutory offence under section 1(1) of the Criminal Law Act 1977. Conspiracy requires proof that there was an agreement between two or more persons to pursue a course of conduct which amounts to a criminal offence: section 1(1)(a). There is an agreement between Grant and Kane to steal money from the security van using the threat of force and this would amount to a robbery. Thus the actus reus of conspiracy is present. The mens rea requires proof that Grant and Kane intended that the agreement be carried out and that the robbery be committed: *Yip Chiu-Cheung v R* [1995] 1 AC 111.[6] There is evidence on the facts that at the time of the agreement they did intend that the agreement be carried out because they decided to get guns and disguises and they then did so.[7] The final mens rea requirement under section 1(2) is that the defendant intended or knew the facts or circumstances which constitute the actus reus of the robbery. This is unlikely to be an issue. Grant and Kane will be convicted of conspiracy to commit robbery.

[6] Do not forget to address the mens rea of conspiracy after setting out and applying the actus reus elements.

[7] Make direct reference to relevant facts in the problem scenario in order to support your argument.

When Shaun turns up to carry out the robbery a week earlier than planned, he may be guilty of attempted robbery under section 1(1) of the Criminal Attempts Act (CAA) 1981.[8] He clearly has the mens rea of an attempt as he intends to commit the full offence of robbery, by stealing money from the security guards, and immediately before or at the time of stealing to use or threaten force in order to do so (s. 8, Theft Act 1968). The actus reus of an attempt requires that the defendant takes steps that are more than merely preparatory

[8] Do not forget that attempts are charged contrary to the CAA 1981 and not under the statute which prescribes the full substantive offence (such as the Theft Act 1968).

towards the commission of the offence. In **Campbell** (1991) 93 Cr App R 350, the defendant was not guilty of attempted robbery after he walked backwards and forwards outside the post office he planned to rob. It could be argued that by simply arriving at the scene of the crime, Shaun has not done enough to be guilty of an attempt.[9] Similarly, in **Geddes** [1996] Crim LR 894, the defendant's conviction for an attempted false imprisonment of a school pupil was quashed because he had not had any contact with a pupil. Rather, he had merely got himself in a position to commit the offence. On this basis, Shaun is unlikely to be convicted of attempted burglary. Although he has the mens rea of attempted robbery because he intends to commit a robbery, he does not have the actus reus as arriving at the scene and hiding is likely to constitute mere preparation.

[9] When applying the actus reus of an attempt, use factually similar cases to support your conclusion.

However, Grant and Kane get a little further and actually approach the van shouting threats of violence before the alarm is activated and they run off. By actually approaching the guards and threatening them, they have probably done acts more than merely preparatory. This is similar to the case of **Jones** [1990] 1 WLR 1057 in which pointing the gun at a person took the situation beyond mere preparation and into an attempt. They clearly have the intention to commit a robbery and will probably be convicted of an attempted robbery under section 1(1) of the CAA 1981.

✓ Make your answer stand out

- Ensure that you adopt a clear and logical structure when answering a problem question on inchoate offences. A chronological approach is usually most appropriate.

- Use authorities to support your argument as to whether the defendant has satisfied the actus reus of an attempt.

- Choose factually similar cases which reflect the steps taken by the defendant in the problem scenario. There are six key authorities which you should seek to apply where relevant: *Campbell*, *Geddes* and *Jones* (cited above), *Gullefer* [1990] 1 WLR 1063, *Boyle and Boyle* (1987) 84 Cr App R 270 and *Tosti* [1997] Crim LR 746.

- Ensure that you are familiar with the distinction between the offences under sections 44–46 of the SCA 2007.

> ## ! Don't be tempted to . . .
>
> - Use terms such as conspiracy and attempt in the abstract. A defendant may not be guilty of 'conspiracy' or 'attempt', but may be guilty of 'conspiracy to steal' or 'attempted robbery'.
> - Forget that offences of conspiracy are charged contrary to the Criminal Law Act 1977 and attempts are charged contrary to the CAA 1981. Inchoate offences are not charged contrary to the legislative provision in which the full substantive offence is found (e.g. attempted robbery is charged contrary to the CAA 1981 and not the Theft Act 1968).
> - State the mens rea of inchoate offences incorrectly. The mens rea of conspiracy and the offences under the SCA 2007 is confusing and you must demonstrate a good knowledge of these elements.

? Question 2

Patty is an employee at Greens Ltd, a garden supplies wholesaler. Her boss, Frank, is a bully and terrorises his staff with threats to withhold their pay and cancel their annual leave unless they achieve unrealistic sales targets. Patty often comes home from work in tears and tells her husband, Brian, about the awful things that Frank has said that day. Brian becomes angry with Frank and he decides to discuss with Patty a plan to kill Frank. Patty and Brian agree to use weed-killer to poison Frank by placing it in his coffee. Patty does not want to be actively involved in placing the weed-killer in Frank's coffee, so Patty and Brian consult Patty's colleague, Andreas, about their plan. Andreas, who also hates Frank, thinks that the plan is a good idea and agrees to poison Frank.

The following morning at work, Andreas goes to the warehouse at Greens Ltd and takes a packet of weed-killer off the shelf. He places a small quantity of the weed-killer into Frank's jar of coffee. However, Andreas doesn't place enough weed-killer in the coffee for the poison to have any effect on Frank. Later that day, having seen Frank still alive after drinking his coffee, Andreas decides to stab Frank to death. He arms himself with a knife and goes up to Frank's office. Approaching Frank's chair from behind, Andreas reaches out to stab Frank, but stops when he realises that Frank is already dead.

Discuss the criminal liability of Patty, Brian and Frank.

Answer plan

→ Consider whether Patty and Brian can be guilty of conspiracy to kill (as husband and wife).
→ Examine the conspiracy to kill Frank between Brian and Andreas and Patty and Andreas.
→ Consider whether Andreas may be guilty of the attempted murder of Frank.
→ Discuss impossibility and attempts.

Diagram plan

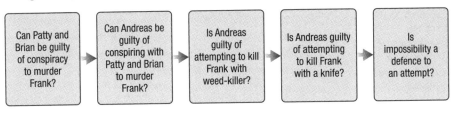

A printable version of this diagram plan is available from www.pearsoned.co.uk/lawexpressqa

Answer

This question requires consideration of the liability of Patty, Brian and Andreas for inchoate offences in respect of Frank. There is initially a conspiracy to murder Frank and it will be necessary to explore who may be liable in respect of this conspiracy. Consideration of Andreas's liability for attempted murder will also require discussion, as will the issue of whether impossibility is a defence to an attempt.[1]

[1] Demonstrate that you have identified the key issues from the start by setting out briefly what you intend to address in your answer.

The first offence to consider is conspiracy to murder. Patty and Brian initially agree to kill Frank using weed-killer. Conspiracy is a statutory offence under section 1(1) of the Criminal Law Act 1977. According to section 1(1)(a), the actus reus of conspiracy requires proof that two or more people agreed to pursue a course of conduct which amounts to a criminal offence. However, under section 2(2)(a) of the Criminal Law Act, a husband and wife cannot be guilty of conspiracy to commit a crime[2] if they come to an agreement together about pursuing a course of conduct which amounts to an offence. However, Patty and Andreas may conspire to kill Frank, and Brian and Andreas may conspire to kill Frank; indeed they have the actus reus of such conspiracies.[3]

[2] Do not forget to check the facts of the question to see if any of the limitations to conspiracy apply.

[3] Ensure that you apply this principle to the facts of the question after setting out the legal limitation.

The mens rea of conspiracy will be established if it is proved that Patty, Brian and Andreas intended to enter into the agreements and that they intended the agreement to be carried out and the substantive offence committed: *Yip Chiu-Cheung* v *R* [1995] 1 AC 11. This is likely to be satisfied on the facts. However, there is no requirement that the defendant intend to play an active part in carrying out the agreement: *Siracusa* (1990) 90 Cr App R 340. According to O'Connor LJ in *Siracusa*, Patty could demonstrate an intention to play a part in carrying out the agreement by failing to stop the course of conduct. Thus, Patty will still be liable for conspiring with Andreas to kill Frank, even though she does not want to play an active part in putting the weed-killer in Frank's coffee.[4] There is a further mens rea requirement under section 1(2) which is that the defendant intends or knows of the facts or circumstances which constitute the actus reus of the killing. This is unlikely to be in issue here. Thus, Patty, Brian and Andreas are guilty of conspiring to kill Frank.

[4] Addressing the fact that Patty does not want to administer the poison by referring to *Siracusa* demonstrates a high level of detailed knowledge of conspiracy.

The next offence to take place is Andreas's attempt to kill Frank the following morning when he places the weed-killer in Frank's coffee jar. An attempt is a statutory offence under section 1(1) of the Criminal Attempts Act (CAA) 1981. The mens rea of an attempt is intention to commit the full offence and the actus reus requires the defendant to take steps which are more than merely preparatory towards the commission of the offence.[5] On these facts, if Andreas is to be charged with attempted murder, it must be proved that Andreas intended to commit the full offence of murder, i.e. that he intended to kill Frank: see *Whybrow* (1951) 35 Cr App R 141.[6] An intention to cause GBH is not sufficient. The Court of Appeal has also confirmed that intention under the CAA 1981 has the same meaning as it does under the common law: see *Pearman* (1985) 80 Cr App R 259. Thus, on a charge of attempted murder, the court might apply the meaning given to oblique intent in *Nedrick* (1986) 83 Crp App R 267: see *Walker and Hayles* (1990) 90 Cr App R 226. In this scenario, there is clear evidence that Andreas intends to kill Frank when he places the weed-killer in Frank's coffee.

[5] When introducing a new offence, set out the source of law from which it derives and then define the actus reus and mens rea elements of the offence. This improves the structure of your answer.

[6] As there is a specific authority on the mens rea of attempted murder, you should refer to this directly to demonstrate your knowledge to the examiner.

The actus reus of an attempt involves taking steps that are more than merely preparatory towards the commission of the offence. Whether a defendant has taken such steps is a question of fact for the jury to decide: section 4(3) of the CAA 1981.[7] This must be determined on a case-by-case basis. To take the approach used by the Court of Appeal in *Jones* [1990] 1 WLR 1057, the events should be broken down and examined in turn.[8] On the facts, Andreas's conduct in going to the warehouse and picking up the weed-killer is merely preparatory. The key question is whether, when he places the weed-killer in the coffee jar, Andreas has taken steps which are more than merely preparatory. The approach adopted by the Court of Appeal in *Geddes* [1996] Crim LR 894, is that the question to be asked is whether the defendant 'has done an act which shows that he has actually tried to commit the offence in question or has he merely put himself in a position or equipped himself to do so?'[9] Here, Andreas has not gone as far as he

[7] Show your knowledge of the relevant provisions of the legislation as well as of the practical aspects of prosecution.

[8] This sentence demonstrates a good understanding of the approach taken by the Court of Appeal which can be applied to the facts of the problem scenario.

[9] If you can remember a relevant part of the judgment to cite, then do so as this will back up your argument.

could have gone by actually making the coffee for Frank and handing it to him. However, he has done more than merely put himself in a position to commit the murder as he has placed the coffee in the jar and has left the jar for Frank to use. Thus, the jury may very well decide on the evidence that Andreas is guilty of attempted murder here. The fact that Andreas has used inadequate means to try to kill Frank by placing too little of the weed-killer in the jar is irrelevant because impossibility through inadequate means is no defence to an attempt.[10]

> [10] Do not forget to deal with this issue of impossibility due to inadequate means. Thus Andreas is likely to be guilty of attempted murder at this stage.

After this unsuccessful attempt to kill Frank, Andreas tries to do so again later that day. At this stage he could be charged with another offence of attempted murder under section 1(1) of the CAA 1981. The mens rea of attempted murder is present because Andreas clearly intends to kill Frank: **Whybrow**. The actus reus is also present because Andreas has taken steps that are more than merely preparatory by actually reaching out to stab Frank with the intention of killing him. According to the Court of Appeal in **Jones**, pointing a gun at the victim with the intention to kill him would be sufficient for attempted murder. The fact that Frank is already dead at this stage will provide Andreas with no defence because under section 1(2) of the CAA 1981, impossibility is no defence to an attempt: see also **Shivpuri** [1987] AC 1.[11]

> [11] You should deal with any factual impossibility briefly citing the correct statutory provision. Do not confuse the old common law approach with that under the statute.

In conclusion, although husband and wife cannot be guilty of a conspiracy alone, they will both be guilty of conspiracy to murder Frank contrary to section 1(1) of the Criminal Law Act 1977, along with Andreas. Andrea will also be guilty of two separate counts of attempted murder contrary to section 1(1) of the CAA 1981, to which impossibility will be no defence.

✓ Make your answer stand out

- You could address the conflict between the House of Lords' opinion in *Anderson* [1986] AC 27 and the preferred Court of Appeal decision in *Siracusa* on the mens rea of conspiracy.
- You could also explain how O'Connor LJ in *Siracusa* dealt with Lord Bridge's comments in *Anderson*.
- Refer to judicial comment or particular approaches taken by the courts in order to support your arguments. For instance, in *Jones*, the Court of Appeal broke down the events in the case. The same approach could be applied to a problem scenario.
- You could refer to academic opinion in support of your answer.

! Don't be tempted to . . .

■ Confuse the position under the common law with that under the statute when dealing with whether impossibility is a defence to an attempt. As the defendant is charged with the offence of attempted murder under section 1(1) of the CAA 1981, the statutory rules on impossibility set out under section 1(2) of the same Act will apply rather than the common law position.

■ Misstate the mens rea for attempted murder. Students often confuse the mens rea of attempted murder (intention to kill) with the mens rea for the full offence of murder (intention to kill or cause GBH). It may seem bizarre, but the mens rea for attempted murder is higher than the mens rea for the full offence of murder.

🖎 Question 3

'At common law the courts distinguished between acts that were merely preparatory . . . which could not be an attempt, and proximate acts, which could . . . Occasionally the judges construed the notion of a proximate act so narrowly that obvious rascals who had gone very far towards committing the intended offence were acquitted.' (Williams 1983, pp. 410–11)

Critically evaluate the actus reus of an attempt.

Answer plan

➜ Consider the actus reus of an attempt (common law and Criminal Attempts Act 1981).

➜ Discuss the rationale for criminalising attempts.

➜ Examine academic commentary on the scope of attempts.

Diagram plan

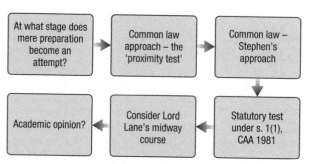

A printable version of this diagram plan is available from www.pearsoned.co.uk/lawexpressqa

Answer

It has proved difficult to define with any precision and clarity a general test for the actus reus element of an attempt. The key question is: at what stage do acts intended to result in the commission of an offence go from being merely preparatory to an attempt in law?[1] At common law, the courts found it difficult to precisely articulate a definition of an attempt. The preferred approach, cited in many authorities was known as the 'proximity test'. However, the proximity test was narrowly construed by judges in some cases, resulting in unjustified acquittals.[2] After the Law Commission made recommendations for reform, the task fell to Parliament to provide a statutory definition of an attempt under section 1(1) of the Criminal Attempts Act 1981 (CAA 1981). However, the statute failed to provide any clarification on the actus reus of an attempt.

Under the old common law, acts which were merely preparatory were not regarded as attempts, whereas proximate acts were. The proximity test was first elucidated in *Eagleton* (1855) Dears CC 515, in which Parke B stated that 'Acts remotely leading to the commission of the offence are not to be considered as attempts to commit it, but acts immediately connected with it are . . .'.[3] Baron Parke elaborated by explaining that if 'any further step on the part of the defendant had been necessary [the act of the defendant] would not have been sufficiently proximate'. This was referred to as the 'last act' test. This was a restrictive approach which meant that defendants who had got 'very far' in their conduct towards the commission of the offence but had not quite reached the last act would be acquitted. The approach in *Eagleton* was approved in the case of *Robinson* [1915] 2 KB 342, in which it was held that acts 'remotely connected with the commission of the full offence' were not an attempt, while acts 'immediately connected with it' were. The proximity test was then also applied in *Comer v Bloomfield* (1971) 55 Cr App R 305 and by the House of Lords in *DPP v Stonehouse* [1977] 2 All ER 909. Lord Diplock in *DPP v Stonehouse* stated that the defendant must have 'crossed the Rubicon and burnt his boats' (i.e. gone so far that he would be unable to change his mind and retreat from his actions).

While the above authorities took the 'last act' approach, a second line of authorities took a different approach which was based on

---

[1] This sentence explains exactly what the problem with the law has been.

[2] Make reference to the question in your introduction as this shows that you are focusing on the issue in the question rather than writing everything you know about the topic.

[3] Set out the test using the words from the judgment if you can.

[4] This sentence demonstrates your awareness of the second line of authorities and demonstrates that you have read around the subject.

Stephen's *Digest of the Criminal Law* (1894).[4] This second approach was that 'An attempt to commit a crime is an act done with intent to commit that crime, and forming part of a series of acts which would constitute its actual commission if it were not interrupted.' This approach was approved in **Hope v Brown** [1954] 1 WLR 250 and **Davey v Lee** [1968] 1 QB 366.

Attempts are charged contrary to section 1(1), CAA 1981, according to which the actus reus of an attempt is satisfied when the defendant takes steps which are more than merely preparatory towards the commission of an offence. Although the judge will make an initial assessment as to whether there is sufficient evidence that the defendant did do an act which is more than merely preparatory, this is ultimately a question of fact to be decided by the jury: section 4(3), CAA 1981. According to Glanville Williams: 'There was nothing new in this [test]. It was simply an affirmation of the common law. This section does not try to tell us what such an act is, even by a very general formula' (1991, p. 416).[5] The Act provides no further guidance as to what constitutes mere preparation and when a defendant has taken steps that go beyond merely preparing to commit an offence. Thus, whether the actus reus of an attempt is satisfied must be determined on a case-by-case basis.

[5] Refer to leading academic opinion on the issue to support your argument that the CAA 1981 was an unhelpful reform.

[6] Make reference to the Law Commission recommendations to show your knowledge of the background to the reforms.

In accordance with recommendations made by the Law Commission,[6] the Act avoids using the word 'proximate' in defining an attempt. Lord Lane has stated that the 'words of the Act seek to steer a midway course' between the two approaches under the old common law (*Gullefer* [1990] 1 WLR 1063 at 1066). Lord Lane took the view that the attempt begins when the defendant 'embarks on the crime proper' or 'actual commission of the offence'. Smith argues that this approach 'would be as restrictive as demanding the defendant's "last act"' and that this midway course 'hardly advances the matter in any constructive fashion' (1991). Although on the face of it the wording of section 1(1) may not be as restrictive as the 'proximity test' under the old common law, the case law post-1981 appears to have taken a narrow approach to the interpretation of the section.[7] In *Campbell* (1991) 93 Cr App R 350, the defendant's conviction quashed on the basis that 'A number of acts remained undone' (Watkins LJ)[8] despite the fact that the defendant was arrested outside a post office equipped to commit robbery. The restrictive scope of the Act is confirmed by Williams who argues that requiring

[7] Provide your interpretation of or opinion on the approach under the CAA 1981.

[8] Support your argument by reference to a specific case.

proximity is the same as requiring more than mere preparation: 'A proximate act was one that went beyond mere preparation, and an act that went beyond mere preparation was proximate.'

Smith criticises section 1(1) for leaving the courts to 'construe "more than merely preparatory" virtually unaided' and argues that the Court of Appeal should 'provide the lower courts with a collection of illustrations' on the matter.[9] Similarly, Dennis argues that the test was 'imprecise' and that it was 'undesirable to give no further guidance to either judge or jury on its application' and that this would 'carry risks of perverse and inconsistent verdicts' (1982). The Law Commission rejected the 'substantial step' test adopted in the US through fear that it would widen the law too much and because it was not capable of further elucidation (Law Commission 1980). However, Williams argues that 'this is not true of the substantial step test' and states that 'the commission's objection is impressively true of its own test . . . which is to be left without any statutory examples' (1991, p. 422).

[9] After highlighting the criticisms of the CAA 1981, make suggestions as to how the law might have been improved. Use of academic opinion is appropriate to support your argument.

In conclusion, defining the actus reus of an attempt has been problematic and it would appear that Parliament's efforts to 'rationalise' the law with legislation has provided no general test which may be capable of uniform application. Thus, whether the actus reus of an attempt is satisfied must be determined on a case-by-case basis.

✓ Make your answer stand out

- Refer to further academic opinion, such as Rogers, J., The codification of attempts and the case of 'preparation' [2008] Crim LR 937.

- You should refer to the Law Commission Consultation Paper, *Conspiracy and Attempts* (2007), in which the Law Commission recommend the abolition of the CAA 1981 and an approach to attempts based on the last act principle as well as a further offence of criminal preparation.

- Cite relevant authorities to support your arguments and consider key passages from judgments.

- You could also incorporate a discussion on the rationale behind the criminalisation of attempts into your answer. Refer to Wilson, W., Criminal attempts, in *Central Issues in Criminal Theory* (2002); Ashworth, A., Inchoate offences, in *Principles of Criminal Law* (2006), Oxford: Oxford University Press.

> **! Don't be tempted to . . .**
>
> - Merely recite the facts of the cases on attempts as these are ancillary to the question.
> - There is no need to explore the mens rea element of an attempt or the issue of impossibility. You should instead focus on the actus reus of an attempt as the question requires you to.

🔊 Question 4

'It is doubtful whether these tortuously complex offences [of encouragement and assistance under the Serious Crime Act 2007] were necessary. The law of incitement . . . was well settled. It seemed to present little difficulty in practice . . .' (Ormerod 2011, p. 461).

To what extent do you agree with the above quote? Is the Serious Crime Act 2007 a positive and necessary addition to the inchoate offences?

Answer plan

→ Discuss the background to the reforms and incitement.

→ Consider the necessity of the new offences under sections 44–46, SCA 2007.

→ Examine academic opinions on the reforms.

Diagram plan

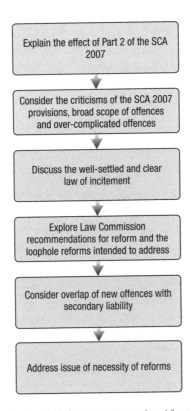

```
┌─────────────────────────────────────┐
│  Explain the effect of Part 2 of the SCA │
│  2007                                  │
└─────────────────────────────────────┘
                  ↓
┌─────────────────────────────────────┐
│  Consider the criticisms of the SCA 2007 │
│  provisions, broad scope of offences  │
│  and over-complicated offences        │
└─────────────────────────────────────┘
                  ↓
┌─────────────────────────────────────┐
│  Discuss the well-settled and clear   │
│  law of incitement                    │
└─────────────────────────────────────┘
                  ↓
┌─────────────────────────────────────┐
│  Explore Law Commission               │
│  recommendations for reform and the   │
│  loophole reforms intended to address │
└─────────────────────────────────────┘
                  ↓
┌─────────────────────────────────────┐
│  Consider overlap of new offences with │
│  secondary liability                  │
└─────────────────────────────────────┘
                  ↓
┌─────────────────────────────────────┐
│  Address issue of necessity of reforms │
└─────────────────────────────────────┘
```

A printable version of this diagram plan is available from www.pearsoned.co.uk/lawexpressqa

Answer

[1] Address the quote in the question in the first paragraph. You must ensure you address the question rather than state everything you know about the law.

[2] Make brief mention of the reasons for the reform at the start but be sure to address this more fully later in your answer.

The quote by Professor Ormerod questions the need for the reforms to the law on inchoate offences as introduced by sections 44–46 of the Serious Crime Act 2007 (SCA 2007).[1] These provisions abolished the old common law offence of incitement and replaced this offence with three offences of encouraging or assisting crime. Whilst the rationale put forward in support of these reforms was the need to plug a loophole which existed under the old law,[2] academics have questioned whether such extensive and complicated provisions were really necessary in order to achieve this seemingly simple objective. The merits of the reforms under the SCA 2007 and the criticisms levelled at these provisions will be explored.

227

Part 2, SCA 2007 came into force on 1 October 2008. Section 59 abolished the common law offence of incitement and sections 44–46 created three new offences of encouraging or assisting an offence. The most serious of these offences is found under section 44 and is the offence of intentionally encouraging or assisting an offence. The offence under section 45 requires a lesser form of mens rea as no intention is needed, rather a defendant may be convicted of an offence of encouraging or assisting an offence if he believes that it will be committed. Finally, the offence under section 46 is encouraging or assisting offences, believing one or more of those offences will be committed (but the defendant has no belief as to which).

The offences under Part 2 of the SCA 2007 are widely drafted and enlarge scope of liability unnecessarily.[3] The actus reus of the offences under sections 44–46 is broader, due to the inclusion of liability for assisting the commission of a substantive offence which does not then occur. The wide mens rea of the offences has also widened the scope of liability. Section 47(5) deals with the mens rea that must be proved where the offence encouraged or assisted has a fault element or requires proof of circumstances or consequences. This complicated provision further enlarges the scope of liability. Liability is extended to a defendant who is reckless as to the fault requirement of the offence encouraged or assisted, or as to the requirement of particular circumstances or consequences of that offence. Under the SCA 2007, even if a defendant believes that the person encouraged or assisted to commit an offence does not have the mens rea for that offence, he is guilty under the SCA 2007 if he himself had the mens rea for the offence that he encouraged or assisted. The mens rea provisions are complicated and leave the mental element of encouraging or assisting crime unnecessarily unclear.[4]

These offences replaced the old common law offence of incitement. Incitement was defined in *Race Relations Board v Applin* [1973] 1 QB 815 as 'to urge or spur on by advice, encouragement, and persuasion', but that incitement also included threatening or bringing pressure to bear on a person. Incitement could be express or implied (see *Invicta Plastics Ltd v Clare* [1976] RTR 251) and could be addressed to the world at large (as in *Most* (1881) 7 QBD 244). However, the incitement had to be communicated to the incitee (*Ransford* (1874) 13 Cox CC 9) and the act incited had to amount to a criminal offence if performed by the incitee (*Whitehouse*

[3] This sentence sets out a key criticism of the new offences and addresses the question directly. This demonstrates that your answer is focused rather than a recitation of your notes on inchoate offences.

[4] Summarise your point in the final line of the paragraph in order to reiterate your point.

[1977] 3 All ER 737). The mens rea of the common law offence of incitement required that the defendant intend that the offence be committed by the incitee and that the defendant knew or believed that the incitee would act with the mens rea for the offence incited (*DPP v Armstrong* [2000] Crim LR 379). The old common law has been described as 'the simple and well-established common law offence of incitement' (Ormerod and Forston (2009)). The law on incitement presented no great problems to the courts and the only real criticism levelled at the old law was the loophole which the SCA 2007 aimed to plug. Thus, the extent to which such extensive reforms were really necessary is rightly questioned.

The reforms made by the SCA 2007 were the result of recommendations made by the Law Commission in a Report published in 2006, which was entitled *Inchoate Liability for Assisting and Encouraging Crime* (Law Com. No. 300).[5] However, as Ormerod and Forston point out, 'These offences differ significantly from the Law Commission's Report . . . on which they were based' (at 390). The Law Commission criticised the old common law of incitement and proposed the abolition of this offence (at para. 8.16). The Law Commission was concerned that the old law left a loophole in the law under which defendants who have assisted an offence which did not actually take place would escape liability (at para. 3.2).[6] The reforms under the SCA 2007 were intended to cover this loophole.

As suggested in the title, it is highly questionable whether such extensive reforms were necessary in order to plug such a small loophole. As Ormerod and Forston argue, 'Even if it were to be accepted that a new facilitation offence was desirable, if not necessary, we suggest that this might have been achieved with a simple provision comprising no more than a few lines of statute' (2009, at p. 397).[7]

With the creation of a new offence of facilitation of an inchoate offence, the SCA 2007 will not only have an extensive impact on the area of inchoate liability, but will also impact upon accessorial liability. The offences under the SCA 2007 now overlap significantly with accessorial liability[8] because the SCA 2007 does not insist upon the offence assisted or encouraged being an inchoate offence, but it also encompasses encouraging or assisting an offence which is committed. At the time of enactment, the Law Commission also considered secondary liability and its recommendations were published in the Report, *Participating in Crime* (2007b). It is surprising that Parliament enacted

[5] When discussing reforms of the law, ensure that you address the Law Commission recommendations which preceded the reforms as these usually provide the rationale for the reforms.

[6] Do not forget to discuss the loophole that the reforms were intended to address.

[7] Cite academic opinion in support of your argument and in order to demonstrate that you have read widely around the topic.

[8] This sentence sets out a further criticism of the reforms under the SCA 2007 which you could develop further to demonstrate a wider knowledge of other areas of criminal law and how they fit together.

the SCA 2007 dealing with such a narrow loophole without also considering the wider issue of secondary liability. Parliament's failure to consider both inchoate and secondary liability together has led to a significant overlap, and consequentially, confusion in the criminal law.

[9] Use the conclusion to address the question again, drawing your arguments together in support of your view.

In conclusion, it is not clear why the over-complicated reforms under Part 2, SCA 2007 were necessary,[9] especially since the old common law offence of incitement was well settled. The loophole which the SCA 2007 provisions were designed to plug could easily have been addressed by a simpler amending provision. It would have arguably been more sensible for Parliament to have waited and reformed both inchoate offences and secondary liability together, thus avoiding the present overlap and confusion.[10]

[10] This sentence suggests a more sensible approach that Parliament could have taken and adds further support to your criticisms of the reforms.

✓ **Make your answer stand out**

- You should refer to academic opinion, such as Ormerod, D. and Forston, R., Serious Crime Act 2007: the Part 2 offences [2009] Crim LR 389; Bohlander, M., The conflict between the Serious Crime Act 2007 and section 1(4)(b) Criminal Attempts Act 1981 – a missed repeal? [2010] Crim LR 483; and Forston, R., *Blackstone's Guide to the Serious Crime Act 2007* (2008), Oxford: Oxford University Press.

- You could make greater reference to the Law Commission Reports, *Inchoate Liability for Assisting and Encouraging Crime* (Law Com. No. 300, 2006) and *Participating in Crime* (Law Com. No. 305, 2007).

- You could address the recommendations for reform made in respect of accessorial liability.

- Demonstrate your level of knowledge and ability to think critically by providing your own opinion of the SCA 2007. You must ensure that you support your opinion with critical evaluation of the addition of these inchoate offences.

! **Don't be tempted to . . .**

- Merely set out everything you know about the reforms under the SCA 2007 or the old common law offence of incitement. This question requires a critical evaluation of the reforms, and as such, you need to address whether the reforms were necessary and/or over-complicated.

- Recite the statutory provisions of the SCA 2007 verbatim. It is much more important to demonstrate to the examiner that you understand the provisions of the Act, rather than showing that you are able to memorise them.

12

Accessorial liability

How this topic may come up in exams

Accessorial liability is commonly examined by problem questions. A problem question might test your knowledge of liability under the Accessories and Abettors Act 1861, the Serious Crime Act 2007 and the doctrine of joint enterprise. Problem questions lend themselves easily to simultaneous examination of inchoate liability; you may find questions involve a conspiracy as well. Problem questions will require you to have knowledge of other offences, such as burglary, theft and offences against the person. Essay questions might require you to critically evaluate the scope of the doctrine of joint enterprise or the overlap between accessorial liability and inchoate liability.

Attack the question

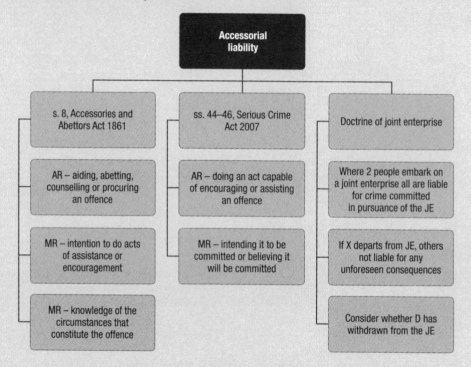

A printable version of this diagram is available from www.pearsoned.co.uk/lawexpressqa

❓ Question 1

Hugh is the leader of a radical political party which is calling for the restriction of immigration to the United Kingdom and the arrest of all asylum seekers. Tony, a civil rights activist, decides in the interest of safeguarding civil rights and the prevention of racism, to kill Hugh. Tony discusses his intentions with Valerie, a fellow civil rights activist, and she encourages Tony's decision, telling Tony that it is important to make a stand for civil liberties, even if that means sacrificing one's own liberty in the process.

Albert, Tony's brother, has connections with convicted criminals. Tony tells Albert that he needs a knife and asks Albert if he can get one for him. Albert suspects that Tony is up to something and that he might use the knife for 'something illegal'. Nevertheless, Albert manages to obtain a knife and gives it to Tony. Tony decides to carry out his attack at the next meeting of Hugh's political party. He turns up at the meeting in disguise and manages to get in. While Hugh is mingling with party members, Tony sneaks up behind him and stabs him in the back. Mark is a member of Hugh's political party, but has recently been having serious doubts about the party's policies. Upon seeing Tony stab Hugh, Mark is secretly pleased. Mark does not rush to Hugh's aid but instead in his mind he wills Tony to kill Hugh. Tony stabs Hugh again, killing him.

Discuss the criminal liability of the parties.

Answer plan

→ Consider Tony's liability as principal offender.

→ Examine secondary liability in respect of Valerie under section 8, Accessories and Abettors Act (AAA) 1861 and the Serious Crime Act (SCA) 2007.

→ Examine secondary liability in respect of Albert under section 8 of the AAA 1861 and the SCA 2007 and whether his suspicions constitute sufficient mens rea.

→ Consider whether Mark is liable as a secondary party for secret encouragement and failure to help Hugh.

Diagram plan

Liability of Tony	Liability of Valerie	Liability of Albert	Liability of Mark
• Principal offender • Common law offence of murder	• Secondary party • Counselling murder under s. 8, AAA 1861 • Intentionally encouraging murder under s. 44, SCA 2007	• Is Albert a secondary party? • Aiding murder? Sufficient MR? *Bainbridge* (1960) • Assisting crime under ss. 45–46, SCA 2007. Does he have sufficient MR?	• Not a secondary party • Present at the scene • But no encouragement so not abetting: *Allan and others* (1965)

A printable version of this diagram plan is available from www.pearsoned.co.uk/lawexpressqa

Answer

[1] Always begin by dealing with the liability of the principal offender before exploring the potential liability of secondary parties.

Tony will be criminally liable as a principal offender in respect of the death of Hugh.[1] As Tony has killed Hugh with the knife, he will be charged with the common law offence of murder. In order to secure a conviction, the prosecution will need to prove that Tony unlawfully caused the death of Hugh and that he intended to kill or cause grievous bodily harm (***Vickers***). Tony will be the principal offender here as he is the most direct cause of the actus reus with the appropriate mens rea.[2]

[2] This demonstrates your understanding of the terminology surrounding accessorial liability, in particular that of a principal offender.

Valerie might also be charged as a secondary party to the GBH. She could be charged with aiding, abetting, counselling or procuring the commission of the offence of GBH under section 8, Accessories and Abettors Act (AAA)1861. According to Lord Widgery CJ in ***Attorney General's Reference (No. 1 of 1975)*** [1975] QB 773, these words should be given their ordinary meaning. There is a great deal of overlap between these words and the prosecution will charge Albert with 'aiding, abetting, counselling or procuring' in accordance with the Court of Appeal decision in ***Bryce*** [2004] EWCA Crim 1231.[3]

[3] This shows that you are aware of procedural matters, such as matters relating to the drafting of the indictment.

The actus reus of this offence would be satisfied by proof that Valerie counselled, i.e., encouraged, the offence of murder. Counselling occurs before the commission of the offence (***Giannetto*** (1997) 1 Cr App R 1). She counsels the commission of the offence by encouraging Tony to kill Hugh before the offence.

The prosecution would also need to prove that the mens rea of the offence was satisfied. The first element of mens rea is intention to do the acts of assistance (this was confirmed in *National Coal Board v Gamble* [1959] 1 QB 11). This will clearly be established because Valerie did intend to encourage Tony to kill Hugh here. The second element of mens rea is that Valerie knew of the circumstances which constituted the offence (this element was confirmed in *Johnson v Youden* [1950] 1 KB 544). This is unlikely to be a problem here as Tony discussed his plan with Valerie, thus Valerie does know that Tony intends to kill Hugh.

⁴ The SCA 2007 obviously now overlaps heavily with the AAA 1861, thus you will need to discuss both pieces of legislation wherever a defendant has assisted (aided) or encouraged (abetted or counselled) an offence.

Valerie might alternatively be charged under the SCA 2007, with intentionally assisting the commission of an offence under section 44 of the Act.[4] The actus reus here is clearly made out as Valerie expressly encourages the offence. The mens rea requires that Valerie intends to assist the commission of an offence: section 44(1)(b) and section 47(2) – this is clearly present here. The requirement under section 47(5)(a) is also likely to be met because Valerie believes or is at least reckless as to whether Tony intends to kill or cause GBH. Similarly, under section 47(5)(b), Valerie believes or is at least reckless as to the consequences which result (i.e. that Tony will kill Hugh).[5]

⁵ Do not forget to deal with the complicated mens rea provisions under the SCA 2007.

Albert assists Tony by supplying him with a knife. As such, Albert could be liable as a secondary party. Albert could be charged with aiding, abetting, counselling or procuring the commission of GBH under section 8 of the AAA 1861. The actus reus of this offence would be satisfied by proof that Albert aided (i.e. assisted the offence of murder), namely by supplying the knife. Aiding occurs before or during the commission of the offence. The prosecution would need to prove that the mens rea of the offence was also satisfied. The first element of intention to do the acts of assistance will clearly be established because Albert did intend to supply Tony with the knife. The second element, namely that Albert knew of the circumstances which constituted the offence is more problematic because Albert might argue in his defence that he has no knowledge of the circumstances which constitute the offence. This element requires Albert to have knowledge of the elements which amount to the actus reus of the offence as well as the elements of the mens rea of the offence committed by Tony. Albert does not know specifically that Tony is going to the meeting to kill Hugh, but he is suspicious that Tony wants the knife for something illegal. According to Lord Parker CJ in *Bainbridge*

[6] Learn key judicial comments so that you are able to cite these in the exam.

[1960] 1 QB 129, 'there must not be merely suspicion but knowledge that a crime of the type in question was intended'.[6] If Albert knows that Tony intends to use the knife to kill or cause serious harm, then he will have the mens rea of a secondary party. He does not need to have knowledge of the precise details relating to the offence, such as who the intended victim is and where the offence will take place.

Alternatively, Albert might be charged with an offence under the SCA 2007. Albert is unlikely to be convicted of intentionally assisting the offence of GBH under section 44 because the prosecution would be unable to prove that he intended to assist in the commission of the offence. However, he may be charged with an offence under section 45 or section 46. He has the actus reus because he does an act which is capable of assisting the commission of one or more offences of violence by supplying Tony with the knife. The mens rea will be present if he believes that one or more offences will be committed and that his act will assist its commission. However, although belief does not equate to knowledge, it requires proof of more than

[7] Explain any unclear terms using case law and then be sure to apply the explanation to the facts of the question.

mere suspicion (see *Moys* (1984) 79 Cr App R 72).[7] Thus, it is not clear on the facts that this will be established.

Finally, Mark will not be liable for a criminal offence as a secondary party. He witnesses the attack by Tony and does nothing to prevent it. However, this does not equate to aiding, abetting, counselling or procuring the commission of an offence. He certainly does not assist any offence, neither does he encourage it. Abetting requires proof of encouragement as well as presence at the scene, and presence alone is not enough: see *Wilcox* v *Jeffery* [1951] 1 All ER 464. It has specifically been held that merely witnessing a fight and doing nothing to prevent it is insufficient for liability as a secondary party:

[8] Where there is a clear authority on the point of law in question, cite it and apply the principle without setting out the facts of the case in detail.

see *Allan and others* [1965] 1 QB 130. This is so even despite any secret intention that Mark might have had to join in and help.[8] No criminal liability is imposed for 'evil thoughts' alone – a defendant must perform some act of encouragement or assistance in order to be liable as a secondary party.

✓ **Make your answer stand out**

- Refer to judicial comment to support the arguments you put forward in your answer. You should learn several short key quotes from leading cases, along with the name of the relevant judge in order that you can use these to demonstrate an awareness of judicial opinion on this subject.
- When referring to secondary liability under section 8, AAA 1861, be sure to identify precisely which of the four actus reus elements the defendant has performed and explain why.
- You should refer to any new authorities on this developing area of common law.
- You could refer to the recommendations made by the Law Commission in 2007 in the Report, *Participating in Crime* (Law Commission No. 305, 2007). This area of law is likely to be subject to reform shortly and you should try to show an awareness of any prospective changes to the law.

! **Don't be tempted to . . .**

- Forget to address the offences under the SCA 2007. Remember that there is now a significant overlap between the offences under sections 44–46, SCA 2007 and section 8, AAA 1861, such that where a defendant is guilty of an offence under section 8, AAA 1861, he is also likely to be guilty of an offence under sections 44–46, SCA 2007.
- Fail to set out and apply both the actus reus and the mens rea of all the offences and in respect of each party. A common mistake made in exam answers to questions on secondary parties is to deal with whether the defendant has aided, abetted, counselled or procured the offence, but then to forget to cover the mens rea of this liability.

Question 2

Anne, Jane and Catherine decide to carry out a raid on Tudors Jewellers, an exclusive jewellery shop. Anne acts as a look-out from inside the shop and stays close to the door. Jane and Catherine both threaten the shop assistant and demand that he hand over various expensive items, which he does. They agree that Jane would carry an unloaded gun in order to scare the shop assistant. However, Jane actually carries with her a loaded gun, but she doesn't tell Anne or Catherine about this. Anne harbours a suspicion that Jane might go a step too far and kill a shop assistant as she knows that Jane has a violent past. During the raid, Jane produces the gun. Fearing that Jane is going to kill the shop assistant, Anne shouts, 'I can't do this!' and runs out of the shop. Jane shoots the shop assistant, killing him.

Discuss the criminal liability of Anne, Jane and Catherine.

Answer plan

→ Consider the conspiracy to commit a robbery.

→ Apply the doctrine of joint enterprise in respect of the robbery and the fact that Anne may be liable under the AAA 1861 and the SCA 2007.

→ Discuss the fact that Jane and Catherine are joint principals in the robbery.

→ Consider whether Jane departs from the common purpose and whether Anne and Catherine can escape liability for the murder under the doctrine of joint enterprise.

Examine whether Anne has withdrawn from the joint enterprise.

Diagram plan

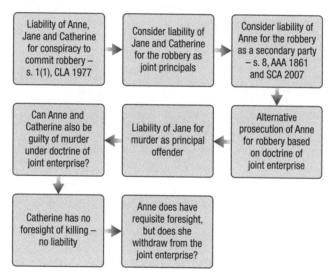

A printable version of this diagram plan is available from www.pearsoned.co.uk/lawexpressqa

Answer

[1] Generally speaking, when a question involves joint enterprise, it is usually preceded by a conspiracy between the parties. Be sure to deal with this in your answer.

The first offence committed in the problem scenario is a conspiracy to commit robbery.[1] Anne, Jane and Catherine could each be charged with statutory conspiracy to commit robbery under section 1(1) of the Criminal Law Act 1977. The actus reus of a conspiracy is present as two or more people do agree to pursue a course of conduct amounting to a criminal offence. They agree to carry out a raid on a jeweller, which amounts to robbery. The mens rea of conspiracy requires firstly that the parties intend to enter into the agreement; this is clear on the facts. The second requirement is that the defendants intend that the agreement be carried out and that the robbery be committed: see *McPhillips* [1989] NI 360 and *Yip Chiu-Cheung* v *R* [1995] 1 AC 111. Under section 1(2) of the Act it must also be proved that the defendants intended or knew that the circumstances constituting the actus reus of the offence exist. As the robbery does in fact take place, the mens rea elements of conspiracy are satisfied. Thus, Anne, Jane and Catherine are guilty of a conspiracy to commit robbery.

[2] Deal with the liability of the principal offenders before considering secondary liability.

Jane and Catherine both commit the robbery and are joint principals[2] in this regard as they are both the direct cause of the actus reus of robbery with the relevant mens rea. Thus, they will be charged as principals to robbery under section 8 of the Theft Act 1968. The actus reus of robbery is satisfied because they both steal jewellery and before doing so, and in order to do so, they put or seek to put the shop assistant in fear of force by threatening him.[3]

[3] So ensure that you establish the liability of the principal offenders by reference to the offence committed.

However, Anne is not a principal offender in respect of the robbery. Nevertheless, she may be convicted as a secondary party to the robbery. There are three offences she could be charged with in this regard. First, she could be charged with aiding, abetting, counselling or procuring the robbery, contrary to section 8, AAA 1861. By acting as look-out inside the shop, she does not carry out the actus reus of the robbery, but she does aid the offence, helping Jane and Catherine to commit the robbery. She also has the mens rea of a secondary party because she intends to do the act of assistance as she intends to keep look-out (*National Coal Board* v *Gamble* [1959] 1 QB 11). It is also clear that Anne knew of the circumstances which constituted the offence (*Johnson* v *Youden* [1950] 1 KB 544). Alternatively, Anne might be charged with intentionally assisting the robbery under section 44, SCA 2007.[4]

[4] Consider all available options that the prosecution have. The AAA 1861, SCA 2007 and doctrine of joint enterprise overlap heavily here and are all worthy of discussion.

The actus reus here is clearly made out as Anne does an act capable of assisting the offence by acting as look out. The mens rea requires that Anne intends to assist the commission of an offence: section 44(1)(b), which she does. Additionally, under section 47(5)(a), it is clear that Anne believes that Jane and Catherine intend to commit robbery. Similarly, under section 47(5)(b), Anne believes that the act would be done in the circumstances or with the consequences required of the anticipated offence (robbery). She knows the details relating to the robbery and would be convicted of either of these offences.

The third option available to the prosecution is to charge Anne with robbery under section 8 of the Theft Act 1968 on the basis of joint enterprise. The classic definition of joint enterprise was given by Lord Parker CJ in **Anderson and Morris** [1966] 2 QB 110, '. . . where two persons embark on a joint enterprise, each is liable for the acts done in pursuance of that joint enterprise, and that includes liability for unusual consequences if they arise from the execution of the agreed joint enterprise but . . . if one of the adventurers goes beyond what has been tacitly agreed as part of the common enterprise, his co-adventurer is not liable for the consequences of that unauthorised act'.[5] Under this doctrine, Anne would also be guilty of robbery even though she did not perform the actus reus of the robbery. Anne will be convicted on the basis that she embarked upon a joint venture with Jane and Catherine and they all acted in pursuance of a common purpose, namely robbery.

[5] Although this is a long quote, it is the classic definition of joint enterprise and well worth citing. There is no need to learn the quote verbatim, the examiners are looking for you to demonstrate your understanding of joint enterprise.

When Jane kills the shop assistant, she departs from the common purpose[6] and becomes the principal offender in respect of murder. She performs the actus reus of murder by unlawfully killing the shop assistant and she has the mens rea of murder because she intends to kill or cause GBH to the shop assistant (**Vickers** [1957] 2 QB 664). However, the question of whether Anne and Catherine can also be liable in respect of the murder as secondary parties requires further consideration. The key issue here is whether Anne and Catherine have the requisite degree of foresight in respect of the murder to be held liable for the murder under the doctrine of joint enterprise. In **Powell and Daniels; English** [1997] 4 All ER 545, Lord Hutton stated that: '. . . where two parties embark on a joint enterprise to commit a crime, and one party foresees that in the course of the enterprise the other party may carry out, with the requisite mens rea, an act constituting another crime, the former is liable for that crime if committed by the latter in the course of the enterprise'.[7] Thus, Anne and Catherine will also be guilty of murder if they foresaw that Jane might kill during the robbery with the intention to kill or cause GBH. There is no evidence that Catherine foresaw the killing as she believed that an unloaded gun would be carried, thus it is likely that she will be able to escape liability for the murder. However, Anne suspects that Jane might kill with the requisite mens rea for murder, thus Anne might be convicted of murder under the doctrine of joint enterprise.[8]

[6] Explore liability for the robbery before moving onto the murder.

[7] This is a key passage from the leading authority on joint enterprise and you must make reference to it in any answer to a question on joint enterprise.

[8] These sentences show that you have drawn conclusions based upon the facts of the problem scenario and you have applied the law to the relevant facts in the question.

The final issue to consider is whether Anne has withdrawn from the joint enterprise. A participant in a joint enterprise may withdraw from the joint enterprise. However, as Anne tries to withdraw from the robbery after it has begun, she is required to do more than merely communicate her intention to play no further part in the joint enterprise to Jane and Catherine. According to Roskill LJ in **Becerra and Cooper** (1976) 62 Cr App R 212, the defendant would have to 'countermand' or 'repent'. Thus, Anne would be required to do far more than merely communicate withdrawal; she would be expected to try to prevent the offence from occurring by physically intervening.[9] Consequently, Anne's withdrawal is not effective and she will be held criminally liable for the murder under the doctrine of joint enterprise.

[9] Do not just state that she has failed to withdraw, but also explain what Anne would have needed to do in order for the withdrawal to be effective.

✓ Make your answer stand out

- You must adopt a logical structure when dealing with questions involving joint enterprise.
- First you should deal with the principal offender and any secondary liability in respect of the offences committed in pursuance of the common purpose. Then you should consider the liability of the principal offender for any departure from the common purpose, before finally discussing any secondary liability in respect of the departure.
- You should consider and apply any relevant recent decisions of the Supreme Court and Court of Appeal, including *Gnango* [2011] UKSC 59, *Mendez and another* [2011] 3 WLR 1 and *A* [2011] QB 841.
- Ensure that you are able to explain the doctrine of joint enterprise clearly. This is a very complicated doctrine which requires careful explanation. You should make reference to the key authorities when defining joint enterprise.

! Don't be tempted to . . .

- Restrict your answer to a discussion of the doctrine of joint enterprise. Do not forget to explore liability for conspiracy, and secondary liability under the SCA 2007 and section 8, AAA 1861.
- Misstate the test for secondary liability in respect of a departure from the common purpose by the principal offender. The defendant must foresee that the principal would act as he/she did, and must foresee that the principal would do so with the requisite mens rea: see *Powell and Daniels; English*.
- Forget to distinguish between withdrawal from a joint enterprise before the offence has begun and withdrawal once the offence has started as different rules apply to each.

 **Question 3**

The law on accessorial liability is confusing, over-complicated and lacks any coherent rationale. Discuss.

Answer plan

→ Consider secondary liability under the AAA 1861.

→ Discuss prosecuting on the basis of the doctrine of joint enterprise.

→ Assess the theoretical justifications for imposing liability on accessories and the extent of that liability.

→ Evaluate the overlap with inchoate liability created by sections 44–46 of the SCA 2007.

Analyse the Law Commission's proposals for reform.

Diagram plan

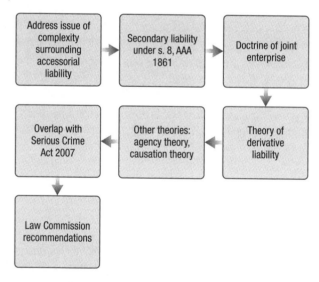

A printable version of this diagram plan is available from www.pearsoned.co.uk/lawexpressqa

Answer

Although there is usually a clear and identifiable theoretical basis for imposing criminal liability upon the acts of a principal offender, the justifications for the punishment of secondary parties is ill defined

[1] Address the question in your introduction.

and confusing.[1] The law relating to accessorial liability has always been plagued by complications and the recent reforms under sections 44–46 of the Serious Crime Act 2007 ('SCA 2007') in respect of inchoate liability have added further confusion by creating a significant overlap with the current law on accessorial liability. As a result, the law is over-complicated and confused.

Prior to the enactment of the SCA 2007, the traditional form of liability for a secondary party requires that the defendant aided, abetted, counselled or procured the commission of the substantive offence by the principal offender. The procedure and punishment for such liability is set down in section 8 of the Accessories and Abettors Act 1861 ('AAA 1861'). This provision provides for punishment of the secondary party as if he were a principal offender. This form of liability requires proof that the defendant did some act of assistance or encouraged the commission of the substantive offence by the principal. There must also be proof that the defendant intended to do the acts of assistance or encouragement (*National Coal Board* v *Gamble* [1959] 1 QB 11) and that he has knowledge of the circumstances that constitute the offence (*Johnson* v *Youden* [1950] 1 KB 544). Thus, although the secondary party may have done acts which were of a different and significantly lesser level of culpability than those performed by the principal, the secondary party is punished as if he were as culpable as the principal.[2] For instance, where the principal offender commits murder by shooting the victim, the secondary party who merely aided the murder by supplying the principal with the gun in the knowledge that the principal might use it to commit murder will be punished as if he had himself shot the victim. Under the AAA 1861 this is true even where the secondary party was not present at the scene of the shooting. Thus, the secondary party is punished for his involvement in the offence even though the elements of the substantive offence could not be established in respect of the secondary party. Wilson explains that the system 'operate[s] on the basis that those who help or encourage the commission of a criminal offence should be punished along with the perpetrator for that offence (which they have not committed) rather than for the wrong they have committed – helping or encouraging a person to commit a crime. Liability is derivative' (Wilson 2008). Thus, the liability of any party who 'associates' himself with the principal offender by providing assistance or encouragement intentionally is derived from that of the principal.[3]

[2] Be sure to explain how the principle of secondary liability works.

[3] Explain the meaning of derivative liability in your own words to show that you understand this.

This form of secondary liability overlaps significantly with the doctrine of joint enterprise. The Court of Appeal has stated that joint enterprise liability does not differ doctrinally from the ordinary principles of secondary liability, but that joint enterprise liability is instead an aspect of secondary liability (***Mendez and another*** [2011] 3 WLR 1). The doctrine of joint enterprise imposes liability upon any party who is part of the joint venture for the acts done by the principal offender in pursuance of the common purpose. This includes imposing liability upon a party for the foreseeable acts of the principal offender which were not part of the common purpose. Unusually, under this doctrine, a defendant may do no more than merely be present at the scene of the offence sharing the common purpose of the principal and he will be liable for the acts of the principal committed in pursuance of that joint enterprise: ***Anderson and Morris*** [1966] 2 QB 110.[4] His continued participation in the common purpose along with the requisite foresight that the principal might commit the offence with the necessary intention[5] is enough to impose liability upon the accessory for the offence committed by the principal: ***Powell and Daniels; English*** [1997] 4 All ER 545.

[4] This demonstrates your understanding of the doctrine of joint enterprise. Cite *Anderson and Morris* as a key authority for the application of the doctrine.

[5] Ensure that you correctly state the degree of foresight required to be liable under the doctrine of joint enterprise.

One rationale for imposing liability upon a defendant under this doctrine rests with his continued acquiescence with the common purpose and continued participation with the joint venture,[6] referred to by Wilson (2008) as 'co-operative association'. Simester and Sullivan explain that it is the defendant's 'commitment to a common unlawful purpose that adds the crucial extra normative ingredient' for liability (Simester and Sullivan (2010), p. 236). Another rationale is the agency theory. In ***Stewart and Schofield*** [1995] 1 Cr App R 441, Lord Hobhouse distinguished between secondary liability under the AAA 1861 and the doctrine of joint enterprise. His Lordship took the view that the doctrine of joint enterprise is based upon the civil concept of agency, such that the principal offender is the agent of the other members of the venture. Gardner takes a different approach to accessorial liability and argues that the secondary party should not be liable for the acts of others, but should only be liable for their contribution in causing the harm to the victim (Gardner (2007)).

[6] Address the issue raised in the question of whether there is a clear underlying theoretical basis for accessorial liability.

[7] This demonstrates that you are aware of the impact of the SCA 2007 on accessorial liability as well as inchoate liability.

There is currently a further overlap between accessorial liability and inchoate offences, caused by the enactment of the SCA 2007.[7] Sections 44–46 of the SCA 2007 created new offences of encouraging or assisting crime which replaced the old common law offence of incitement. However, these offences were not restricted to inchoate liability and thus also apply to secondary parties who have assisted or encouraged an offence which is actually committed by the principal. The consequential overlap has further complicated an already confusing area of law. These provisions have been subjected to criticism in respect of inchoate liability and it is questionable whether they were needed in the first place. In light of the overlap with accessorial liability, it is difficult to see why Parliament pursued these reforms without simultaneously leading a more significant

[8] Provide your own critique of the law and reforms under the SCA 2007.

overhaul of the law relating to accessorial liability.[8] This is even more puzzling in light of the fact that in the year that the SCA 2007 received Royal Assent, the Law Commission made further recommendations for reform of accessorial liability in their Report, *Participating in Crime* (Law Commission 2007b), in which the Commission proposed separating out liability for assisting or encour-

[9] Ensure that you refer to any proposals for reform put forward by the Law Commission.

aging crime from liability under a joint venture.[9]

The current law on accessorial liability is confusing and over-complicated. There is a significant overlap between the AAA 1861, the SCA 2007 and the doctrine of joint enterprise such that it is difficult for prosecutors to know upon which basis to conduct their prosecution. There are also competing theories justifying the imposition of accessorial liability. It is time for Parliament to overhaul the law to make it clearer and more accessible with a coherent underlying rationale for liability.

✓ Make your answer stand out

- Refer to further academic opinion, such as Wilson, Attributing liability to secondary parties, in *Central Issues in Criminal Theory* (2002), Oxford: Hart Publishing; Sullivan, G.R., Participating in Crime [2008] Crim LR 19 and Taylor, R., Procuring, causation, innocent agency and the Law Commission [2008] Crim LR 32.

- You could spend more time exploring the derivative theory and other theoretical justifications for imposing liability upon secondary parties.

- Provide a more detailed analysis of the reasoning in *Mendez and another* [2011] 3 WLR 1.

- You could provide further discussion of the Law Commission proposals and the reasons underlying these recommendations.

! Don't be tempted to . . .

- Provide a purely descriptive narrative of the case law on secondary liability and the doctrine of joint enterprise.
- Misstate the mens rea requirement under *Powell and Daniels; English* in respect of the doctrine of joint enterprise.
- Forget to discuss the new offences under the SCA 2007 whenever you are asked to critically evaluate accessorial liability.

www.pearsoned.co.uk/lawexpressqa

 Go online to access more revision support including additional essay and problem questions with diagram plans, You be the marker questions, and download all diagrams from the book.

Mixed questions

How this topic may come up in exams

This chapter provides examples of mixed problem questions. Although you could be examined on any mixture of offences and defences, there are certain topics which are inevitably examined together, largely due to the fact that they are inherently linked to one another. This chapter will provide examples of such questions, although you should be ready to deal with any mixture of offences and defences. While mixed problem questions may cover several topics, you are expected to deal with these in less detail than you would for a question which focuses on one or two key areas of criminal law.

Attack the question

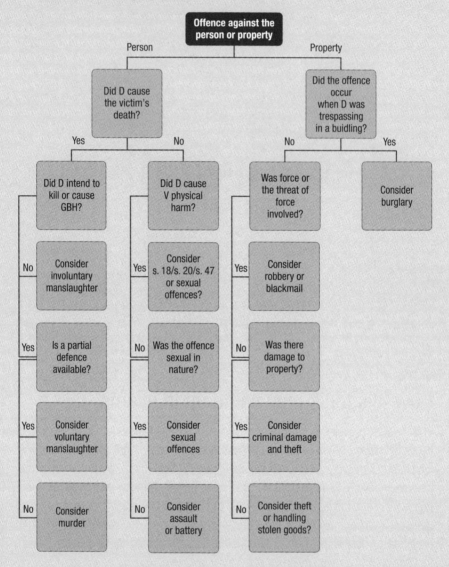

Offence against the person or property

Person

Property

Did D cause the victim's death?

Did the offence occur when D was trespassing in a buidling?

Yes — Did D intend to kill or cause GBH?

No — Did D cause V physical harm?

No — Was force or the threat of force involved?

Yes — Consider burglary

No — Consider involuntary manslaughter

Yes — Consider s. 18/s. 20/s. 47 or sexual offences?

Yes — Consider robbery or blackmail

Yes — Is a partial defence available?

No — Was the offence sexual in nature?

No — Was there damage to property?

Yes — Consider voluntary manslaughter

Yes — Consider sexual offences

Yes — Consider criminal damage and theft

No — Consider murder

No — Consider assault or battery

No — Consider theft or handling stolen goods?

A printable version of this diagram is available from www.pearsoned.co.uk/lawexpressqa

❓ Question 1

Claire and Dominic have been married for ten years. One day, while in a rage with Claire, Dominic throws a glass of wine over her. However, the glass leaves his hand and breaks, cutting Claire's face. When Claire goes to bed that evening, Dominic repeatedly asks Claire to perform oral sex on him. Claire does so reluctantly. Later that night, Dominic cuts off Claire's ponytail while she is asleep. In the morning, Claire wakes up to discover that Dominic has cut her hair. Horrified, she goes to the kitchen to get a knife and slashes his favourite Italian designer suits. Incensed, Dominic tells Claire that he is leaving her for their next door neighbour, Susan. Armed with the knife Claire knocks on Susan's door and stabs her in the chest when she answers the door.

Discuss the criminal liability of the parties.

Answer plan

→ Consider whether Dominic is guilty of a non-fatal offence against the person in respect of the wine glass.

→ Address Claire's consent to oral sex by submission such that Dominic is not guilty of rape.

→ Examine Dominic's liability for assault occasioning actual bodily harm in respect of Claire's hair.

→ Consider whether Claire is guilty of criminal damage and theft of Dominic's suits.

→ Evaluate Claire's liability in respect of killing Susan and whether she has a partial defence of loss of control.

Diagram plan

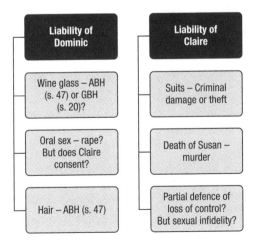

A printable version of this diagram plan is available from www.pearsoned.co.uk/lawexpressqa

Answer

In respect of Claire's injuries from the wine glass, Dominic will be liable for assault occasioning actual bodily harm under section 47 of the Offences Against the Person Act 1861 ('OAPA 1861') or wounding or inflicting grievous bodily harm under section 20, OAPA 1861. There is clearly a wound here because the glass cuts Claire's face and breaks the continuity of the skin: *Moriarty v Brooks* (1834) 6 C & P 684. The mens rea of section 20 requires proof that Dominic intended or was reckless as to whether some harm was caused: *Savage; Parmenter* [1992] 1 AC 699. Dominic intended to inflict force upon Claire by throwing wine over her but it is not clear that he intended to cause harm. If he foresaw the risk of causing some harm and took that risk (*Cunningham* [1957] 2 QB 396), then he will be reckless but this is not clear on the facts.[1] Dominic will be convicted of assault occasioning actual bodily harm under section 47, OAPA 1861. Proof of a battery is required and it is clear that Dominic intentionally inflicted unlawful force on Claire (*Fagan v MPC* [1969] 1 QB 439) when he tried to throw the wine over her. This battery caused a more severe injury which may constitute ABH because it is an injury calculated to interfere with the health or comfort of Claire: *Miller* [1954] 2 WLR 138. A small laceration is sufficient to constitute ABH under the CPS Charging Standards.[2] The mens rea under section 47 is that for the battery and there is no additional requirement of mens rea in respect of the degree of harm caused: *Savage; Parmenter*. Thus, Dominic will be guilty under section 47.

[1] You should correctly state the mens rea of section 20 and look for evidence of this in the facts. If there is no evidence, then say so and move on to the next offence down in the hierarchy.

[2] If you can refer to the CPS Charging Standards, then do so as these are what will be used in practice to determine the charge.

The next incident involves an act of oral sex to which Claire reluctantly consents. This will not constitute rape under section 1 of the Sexual Offences Act 2003 ('SOA 2003') unless it can be proved that Claire did not consent and that Dominic did not reasonably believe that she was consenting. She will be deemed to be consenting if she agreed by choice with the freedom and capacity to make that choice (s. 74, SOA 2003). If she feared that Dominic might use violence against her, it may be presumed that she did not consent[3] (s. 75(2)(a) and s. 75(1), SOA 2003) and there will be an evidential burden on Dominic to adduce evidence to the contrary. However, there appears to be no such evidence on the facts. Dominic will also be guilty of an offence under section 47, OAPA 1861 in respect of cutting Claire's hair. There is a clear battery here, as he intentionally

[3] Although this is slightly speculative, it is mentioned because there is evidence of violence by Dominic on Claire earlier in the question.

inflicts unlawful force on her and it has been held that cutting a person's hair is sufficient to constitute ABH (see **DPP v Smith** [2006] 1 WLR 1571).

Claire will be guilty of criminal damage and theft of Dominic's suits. She will more likely be charged with criminal damage under section 1(1) of the Criminal Damage Act 1971. She does intentionally damage property belonging to another (Dominic). This could also constitute theft under section 1 of the Theft Act 1968.[4] The actus reus of theft is widely construed and appropriation involves assuming the rights of the owner (s. 3). By damaging Dominic's suits, Claire assumes a right over them. It is also clear that only one single right of the owner need be assumed: **Morris** [1983] 3 All ER 288. Claire only assumes one right here – the right to destroy or damage the suits. The suits are tangible property under section 4 and belong to Dominic (s. 5). Thus, the actus reus elements of theft are satisfied. Claire would have the mens rea of theft if it can be proved that the honest and reasonable person would regard what she did as dishonest and that she realises this[5] (**Ghosh** [1982] 1 All ER 491). However, although the reasonable person might regard this as wrong, it might not be considered to be dishonest. There is no defence under section 2(1). It can also be argued that she intends to permanently deprive Dominic of the suits because she intends to dispose of the property by treating the suits as her own to deal with as she likes (see **DPP v Lavender** [1994] Crim LR 297). On a stricter interpretation of intention to permanently deprive, Claire would need an intention to return the suits in such a changed state that it could truly be said that all of their goodness and virtue has gone: **Lloyd** [1985] QB 829. This might depend upon the degree of damage caused. If the suits are shredded, then this would be satisfied.

Claire will also be charged with murder in respect of killing Susan. Murder is a common law offence defined as unlawfully causing the death of a person within the Queen's peace and with the intention to kill or cause GBH:[6] **Vickers** [1957] 2 QB 664. Claire is clearly the factual cause (applying the 'but for' test: **White** [1910] 2 KB 124) and the legal cause of Susan's death (applying the 'significant contribution' test: **Cheshire** [1991] 3 All ER 670).[7] The mens rea of murder is present as Claire does intend to kill Susan by stabbing her in the chest. Claire might have a partial defence to murder available to her which would reduce her liability to manslaughter.

[4] This demonstrates to the examiner that you have a good understanding of the law and are thinking widely. Do not forget that the actus reus of theft is so widely construed that damage to property could constitute appropriation.

[5] In order to save time, you should state and apply the *Ghosh* test in one sentence.

[6] As this question involves many different issues, you should state the definition simply. There is no need to make reference to Coke's classic definition here.

[7] As causation is clearly satisfied here, you should deal with causation in a sentence. There is no need to go into any more detail.

Claire might rely on loss of control under section 54(1) of the Coroners and Justice Act 2009. There are three main elements of the defence: (a) at the time of the killing, Claire must have suffered a loss of self-control; (b) there must have been a qualifying trigger under section 55; and (c) someone of the same age and sex as Claire, with a normal degree of tolerance and self-restraint and in the circumstances of Claire, might have reacted in the same or a similar way. Whether Claire suffered a loss of self-control is subjectively assessed. Under section 54(2), it does not matter whether the loss of control was sudden or not. On the facts, there is likely to be sufficient evidence to prove that Claire did suffer a loss of control. The next question is whether there is a qualifying trigger under section 55. Claire will not be able to rely on the anger trigger under section 55(4)[8] because Dominic's confession that he is having an affair with Susan constitutes sexual infidelity, which must be disregarded under section 55(6)(c), although it may be considered as part of the contextual background to a case where there is another potential qualifying trigger (**Clinton** [2012] EWCA Crim 2). There is no evidence that the fear trigger applies,[9] thus Claire may not rely on loss of control as a partial defence and will be guilty of murder.

[8] Be clear from the start that this will not constitute a qualifying trigger due to the exclusion of sexual infidelity under section 55(6)(c).

[9] Do not spend time explaining the fear trigger if there is no evidence of this trigger on the facts.

✓ Make your answer stand out

- As there are quite a few offences to deal with here, you will need to ensure that you adopt a clear and logical structure. Use separate paragraphs for each major issue or offence.

- You could also use headings to distinguish between each incident and ensure you remained focused.

- Where the defendant might be charged with a number of different offences, you should opt for the most appropriate ones as you will not have time to discuss them all. For instance, there is no real point discussing liability for assault or an offence under section 18 OAPA 1861 re the injury caused by the wine glass. Sections 47 and 20 are much more appropriate here.

- You might also choose to provide some academic opinion on controversial provisions or cases that you have relied upon. In particular, in this question you might refer to academic critique about the defence of loss of control and the case of *Clinton*.

! Don't be tempted to . . .

- Waste time unnecessarily explaining principles of law which are not contentious or which do not apply on the facts. For instance, there is no need to provide a detailed discussion of causation in respect of any of the offences here as causation is not likely to be disputed.

- Spend a disproportionate amount of time discussing one issue. This question covers a number of different offences and you should not spend all your time discussing non-fatal offences against the person to the detriment of the other issues in the question. You will lose valuable marks if you do not address all the key issues in the scenario.

? Question 2

Matt and Dan are career criminals who have made their living through deceiving and threatening people. Matt meets Deborah through an internet chat room. Deborah is married to a very wealthy and famous businessman, Simon, but they have been going through marital difficulties. Matt spends hours in an internet chat room consoling Deborah about her problems. He then suggests that they meet and while she is feeling vulnerable, Deborah embarks upon an extra-marital affair with Matt. Three months after the affair begins, Matt sends Deborah an email telling her that unless she gives him £20,000 he will expose their affair. Deborah is terrified and sends Matt the money.

When he thinks that both Deborah and Simon are away on a business trips, Matt decides to break into their house in order to steal valuable items of property. However, Simon is in the house at the time and he hears Matt break in. Concerned that his property is being stolen, Simon arms himself with a saucepan and strikes Matt round the head with it, causing serious harm. Matt escapes.

In revenge for the attack by Simon, Matt telephones a national newspaper and falsely informs the reporter that Simon's business is facing massive financial difficulties and is likely to go into administration. The reporter doesn't believe Matt and so does not print the story. Still intent on revenge, Matt tells Dan that he will break his legs unless Dan carries out a robbery on Simon. One evening, Dan waits for Simon after work and follows him home. He pushes Simon violently to the ground and steals his Rolex watch.

Discuss the criminal liability of the parties.

Answer plan

→ Examine Matt's liability for blackmail and burglary.

→ Address Simon's liability for GBH and the defence of prevention of crime.

→ Discuss Matt's liability for fraud by false representation.

→ Consider Dan's liability for robbery and/or theft and any potential defence of duress.

Diagram plan

Liability of Matt

Blackmail

Burglary s. 9(1)(a)

Fraud by false representation

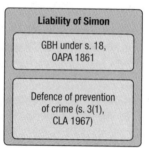

Liability of Simon

GBH under s. 18, OAPA 1861

Defence of prevention of crime (s. 3(1), CLA 1967)

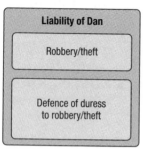

Liability of Dan

Robbery/theft

Defence of duress to robbery/theft

A printable version of this diagram plan is available from www.pearsoned.co.uk/lawexpressqa

Answer

Matt may be liable for blackmail and burglary, and Simon may be charged with GBH in respect of striking Matt with the saucepan, but he might plead the prevention of crime as a defence. Matt might also be liable for fraud; while Dan might be liable for robbery and theft, but he may plead duress.[1]

[1] Use the introduction to make brief reference to the offences and defences you will be discussing in your answer to show the examiner what you plan to explore.

Matt might first be guilty of blackmail under section 21 of the Theft Act 1968. This offence is satisfied because Matt makes an unwarranted demand for £20,000 towards Deborah with menaces, namely that he will expose their affair if she does not give him the money. He intends to make the demand and he does so with a view to gain £20,000 from her. Thus, the offence is made out.

Matt could also be charged with burglary in respect of his entry into Deborah and Simon's home. Under section 9(1)(a) of the Theft Act 1968, a defendant commits burglary if he enters a building or part of a building as a trespasser with the intention to steal, inflict GBH or do unlawful damage (s. 9(2)). It is clear that Matt enters a building when he gains entry to the house and he does so without permission, and thus as a trespasser. Matt has the requisite mens rea in respect of the trespass because he knows that he is trespassing. He will have the mens rea of burglary under section 9(1)(a) if he enters the house with the intention to steal something. There is evidence on the facts that he has such an intention upon entry. There appears to be no offence of burglary under section 9(1)(b), because Matt does not actually steal anything or inflict GBH on Dan and nor does he attempt to do so.[2]

[2] You should rule out section 9(1)(b) in a short sentence in order to show the examiner that you have considered both offences of burglary.

Simon might be charged with wounding or causing GBH under section 18 of the Offences Against the Person Act 1861. He clearly causes GBH to Matt and has the intention to do so. However, he may rely on the defence of the prevention of crime under section 3(1) of the Criminal Law Act 1967. This defence permits the use of reasonable force in the prevention of crime.[3] This defence is wider than the common law defence of self-defence, and section 76 of the Criminal Justice and Immigration Act 2008 now applies to both defences. The question here will be whether Simon was acting in the prevention of crime rather than out of revenge, and whether the degree of force he used was reasonable in the circumstances. If pleaded successfully, the prevention of crime will provide a complete defence to any charge of GBH and Simon will be acquitted.

[3] Be sure to show your awareness of the difference between the common law defence of self-defence and the statutory defence of the prevention of crime.

Matt might be convicted of fraud in respect of the telephone call to the national newspaper. Fraud is an offence under section 1 of the Fraud Act 2006, which may be committed in one of three ways. Matt might be guilty of fraud by false representation under section 2.[4] The actus reus of this offence requires that Matt makes a false representation, which he does when he informs the reporter that Simon's business is in financial difficulties. Under section 2(3), a representation includes a representation as to fact, which this is. This is a false representation under section 2(2)(a) because Matt does not have any information as to the financial state of Simon's business and certainly has no information that it is in financial difficulties. The mens rea requires that Matt knows that the representation is or might be untrue or misleading under section 2(2)(b). Matt clearly knows that the representation is untrue because he has made it up and is making the call out of revenge. The offence of fraud also requires proof of dishonesty. The **Ghosh** test must be applied here. Applying the first objective limb of **Ghosh** [1982] 2 All ER 689, the honest and reasonable person would regard making such a false statement as dishonest. The second limb is subjective and requires consideration of whether Matt realised that the honest and reasonable person would regard this as dishonest. If he did, then he will be dishonest. The final mens rea element which needs to be established is that Matt intended to make a gain for himself or another or cause loss to another or to expose another to a risk of loss (s. 2(1)(b)).[5] Under section 5(2)(a), gain and loss extend only to gain or loss of money or other property. Property includes real or personal property, things in

[4] Identify the most relevant of the three ways in which fraud can be committed.

[5] Do not forget to set out and apply this final element of mens rea.

action and other intangible property (s. 5(2)(b)). Matt intends to expose Simon's business to a risk of loss in the sense of a loss in confidence in his business by shareholders which might result in the company share price decreasing.[6] Thus, Matt will be guilty of fraud.

[6] This sentence demonstrates your application of the law to the facts of the question.

Dan may be convicted of robbery in respect of the Rolex watch. This is charged under section 8 of the Theft Act 1968 and requires proof that immediately before or at the time of stealing, and in order to steal, Dan used force on Simon or put or sought to put Simon in fear of being then and there subjected to force. There is evidence here that Dan did actually use force as he pushed Simon violently to the ground.[7] All the elements of robbery (and incidentally, theft under section 1 of the Theft Act 1968) are satisfied. Dan will raise the defence of duress by threats, which is a complete defence to robbery and theft if pleaded successfully. The test for duress is set out in the Court of Appeal decision in *Graham* (1982) 74 Cr App R 235 and the House of Lords authority of *Hasan* [2005] UKHL 22.[8] The test requires consideration of two questions: the first asks whether the defendant was impelled to act as he did because he reasonably feared that if he didn't, he would be subjected to death or serious personal injury? This is the subjective limb (looking at the actual defendant's belief) which contains an objective element (whether the fear felt by the defendant was reasonable). The second question asks whether a sober person of reasonable firmness, sharing the defendant's characteristics, would have responded to the defendant's belief in the same way. This is the objective limb (comparing the response of a reasonable man) which contains a subjective element (the reasonable man may share certain characteristics of the defendant: *Bowen* [1996] 2 Cr App R 157). The threat here was one of serious injury to Dan himself and the threat is immediate. Only Dan's age and sex will be taken into account in determining whether a sober person of reasonable firmness would have responded to the defendant's belief in the same way. There is no evidence of any other characteristics of the defendant which might be relevant here.[9] There is a sufficient nexus between the threat and the offence: *Cole* [1994] Crim LR 582. Thus, the defence of duress is likely to be successful here.

[7] Be sure to identify whether force has actually been used or whether it has been threatened as either is sufficient for the offence of robbery.

[8] You should really cite both of these cases in respect of the test for duress in order to show the examiner that you are aware of the importance of each one.

[9] Ensure you only apply relevant facts. Do not speculate about the existence of facts you are not given any evidence of.

✓ **Make your answer stand out**

- Ensure that you adopt a logical structure and deal with each offence chronologically. You might wish to use headings to divide up your answer and ensure that you remain focused.
- You should also consider the offence of blackmail in more detail, making reference to case law where appropriate.
- You should explore the defence of the prevention of crime under section 3(1), CLA 1967 in more detail. Your discussion should encompass the principles under section 76, CJIA 2008.
- You should also explore and apply the principles of duress by threats in more detail.

! **Don't be tempted to . . .**

- Consider the possibility of fraud having been committed by a failure to disclose information or fraud by abuse of position if they are not relevant to the facts in the problem question.
- Spend too much time discussing each issue, as there are so many of them in this question. Ensure that you identify all of the relevant offences and defences and apply the main principles of law with appropriate supporting authorities.
- Misstate the *Ghosh* test in respect of fraud and theft.

Question 3

Imran and Gareth are discussing ways in which to spice up their respective sex lives. Imran suggests to Gareth that the element of surprise might be a turn-on for Gareth's long-suffering girlfriend. Gareth suggests to Imran that a nice meal and several bottles of wine will guarantee Imran sex with his girlfriend. Later that evening, Imran and his girlfriend enjoy a lovely meal and four bottles of red wine at an exclusive restaurant. Imran's girlfriend drinks most of the wine. They return home and Imran carries his sleepy girlfriend into the bedroom. He begins to have sex with her and she doesn't resist.

Knowing that his girlfriend gets off the bus at a certain bus stop and has to walk home through a secluded park, Gareth decides to jump out and surprise her. Gareth's girlfriend suffers from a heart condition. When he jumps out to surprise her in the park, his girlfriend is so shocked that she suffers a heart attack. Gareth telephones for an ambulance and his girlfriend is taken to hospital and placed on a life support machine. Whilst sleepwalking, another patient on the ward switches off the life support machine and Gareth's girlfriend dies.

Consider the criminal liability of Imran and Gareth.

Answer plan

→ Evaluate Imran's liability for rape.

→ Discuss the issues of consent and intoxication.

→ Consider Gareth's liability for unlawful act manslaughter.

→ Does the conduct of the patient break the chain of causation?

Diagram plan

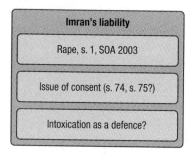

Imran's liability

Rape, s. 1, SOA 2003

Issue of consent (s. 74, s. 75?)

Intoxication as a defence?

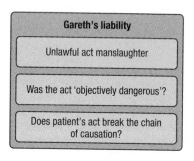

Gareth's liability

Unlawful act manslaughter

Was the act 'objectively dangerous'?

Does patient's act break the chain of causation?

A printable version of this diagram plan is available from www.pearsoned.co.uk/lawexpressqa

Answer

[1] Identify the key issues (as well as the offences) that you will need to discuss in your opening paragraph.

Imran might be liable for rape in respect of his girlfriend, but there are issues relating to consent and intoxication which need discussion here. Gareth might be liable for unlawful act manslaughter in respect of the death of his girlfriend, although he may argue that the chain of causation was broken by the patient in the hospital.[1]

[2] Do not forget to state and apply the mens rea in respect of consent. This is often forgotten by students and your answer will be incomplete without it.

Rape is defined under section 1(1) of the Sexual Offences Act 2003 ('SOA 2003'). The actus reus requires the penetration of the vagina, anus or mouth, with the defendant's penis, where the complainant does not consent. The mens rea is intentional penetration, where the defendant had no reasonable belief in consent. Imran has sexual intercourse with his girlfriend and there is nothing to doubt the fact that the intercourse involved the penetration of the vagina or anus of his girlfriend with Imran's penis. It is also clear that the penetration is intentional; thus, the issue here is really one of consent. In order to secure a conviction, the prosecution must establish that Imran's girlfriend was not consenting and that Imran did not reasonably believe that she was consenting.[2]

Consideration must be given to the evidential presumptions under section 75(1), SOA 2003. Section 75(1) sets out two evidential presumptions: that the complainant did not consent and that the defendant did not reasonably believe that she consented. These are relevant where one of the circumstances under section 75(2) is applicable and the defendant knew this.[3] These presumptions may apply if his girlfriend is asleep when Imran begins to have intercourse with her (s. 75(2)(d)). Although we are told that she is 'sleepy', it is unclear on the facts whether she is actually asleep or otherwise unconscious or not at this stage.[4] If she is, and if Imran is aware that his girlfriend is asleep, the evidential presumptions under section 75(1) are triggered, which means that she is presumed not to have consented and it is presumed that Imran did not reasonably believe that she was consenting. These presumptions are rebuttable and Imran may adduce evidence to the contrary; however, he is unlikely to be able to in this scenario. However, if she is not asleep or unconscious, the prosecution will seek to rely on section 74[5] to argue that she did not consent because due to her intoxication she did not agree by choice, with the capacity and freedom to make that choice. According to **Bree** [2007] EWCA Crim 804, the complainant will not consent to sexual intercourse if he/she loses his/her capacity to consent through the consumption of alcohol. However, if the complainant still has the capacity to choose to consent to sexual intercourse despite his/her intoxication, he/she may still consent to sex. It will be for the jury to determine whether the girlfriend had the capacity to consent in this scenario.

Finally, Imran may himself attempt to plead intoxication as a defence of sorts. He may seek to claim that he was intoxicated and that his intoxicated state negates his mens rea for rape. After the Court of Appeal decision in **Heard** [2007] EWCA Crim 125 (a sexual assault case), it is likely that rape is a basic intent offence to which voluntary intoxication is no defence. Thus, any plea on the basis of voluntary intoxication is likely to be unsuccessful.

Gareth might be charged with unlawful act manslaughter in respect of the death of his girlfriend. It is clear that he does not have the mens rea for murder as he has no intention to kill or cause GBH[6] (**Vickers** [1957] 2 QB 664). Gareth might be guilty of unlawful act manslaughter. This offence was defined in **Larkin** (1944) 29 Cr App R 18: there must be an intentional act, which is unlawful, objectively

[3] Do not forget that there are two presumptions which are made under section 75(1) and one relates to the mens rea of the defendant.

[4] You should not assume that she is asleep, but you need to deal with the facts exactly as given to you. Do not invent or twist the facts to suit an answer which is more convenient.

[5] Remember to provide an alternative argument which may be used by the prosecution.

[6] Rule out murder from the start where there is clearly no mens rea for murder. This demonstrates a logical thought process in arriving at the decision to discuss involuntary manslaughter.

dangerous and which causes death (Lord Salmon, **DPP v Newbury & Jones** [1977] AC 50).

The prosecution must prove that Gareth intentionally did an act. This must be a positive act: **Lowe** [1976] QB 702. His act is intentionally jumping out on his girlfriend. The act must be unlawful in the sense that it must constitute a criminal offence: **Franklin** (1883) 15 Cox CC 163. The criminal act here is assault. Both the actus reus and mens rea elements of the assault must be established: **Lamb** [1967] 2 QB 981. The elements of assault are satisfied. Gareth causes his girlfriend to apprehend immediate and unlawful violence and he may be reckless about doing so (**Fagan v Metropolitan Police Commissioner** [1969] 1 QB 439).[7]

[7] Once you have identified the unlawful act, you must also show that both the actus reus and mens rea elements of that offence are satisfied.

It must also be proved that the act was objectively dangerous. The test was laid down in **Church** [1966] 1 QB 59, in which it was stated that 'the unlawful act must be such as all sober and reasonable people would inevitably recognise must subject the other person to, at least, the risk of some harm . . . albeit not serious harm'. The reasonable man is deemed to have the knowledge that the defendant had or ought to have had at the time of the offence: **Dawson** (1985) 81 Cr App R 150. If the risk of harm becomes obvious during the commission of the offence, the reasonable man is attributed with that knowledge: **Watson** [1989] 1 WLR 684. If Gareth was not aware of his girlfriend's heart condition and he ought not to have been aware of it, the dangerous element of the offence is not satisfied and Gareth will not be liable for unlawful act manslaughter. If he was aware, then the act was dangerous.[8]

[8] This fact is crucial to the determination of liability, but it is not clear on the facts. Thus, you should set out both possible outcomes.

Finally, the usual rules of causation apply. Applying the test for factual causation: but for Gareth's act, his girlfriend would not have died: **White** [1910] 2 KB 124. His act was also a more than minimal cause of death: **Cato** [1976] 1 WLR 110. However, there may be an intervening event as another patient turns off the life support machine. This may be treated as an act of a third party. An act of a third party will break the chain of causation if it is a voluntary act, i.e. 'free, deliberate and informed' (**Pagett** (1983) 76 Cr App R 279). This is a difficult issue to address and there may be different interpretations available.[9] Arguably, this is an involuntary act because the patient was sleepwalking. On this interpretation it would not break the chain of causation and Gareth could be guilty of unlawful act

[9] Remember that there is no one 'right answer'. So, where there are different possible interpretations of a situation, you should state this and then explore these.

manslaughter. However, as it was not reasonably foreseeable, it could be deemed to break the chain of causation (see **Roberts** (1971) 56 Cr App R 95). On this interpretation, Gareth would only be guilty of an assault.

✓ Make your answer stand out

- You should explore further the issue of the complainant's intoxicated consent, referring to case law and academic critique.
- You should also expand upon the issue of voluntary intoxication and sexual offences. You could discuss the criticisms levelled at the decision in *Heard* and consider the *Majewski* rules [1977] AC 443.
- You might also elaborate on the issue of causation and refer to other cases as well as academic opinion.
- Where there are alternative arguments or interpretations to a particular issue, you should ensure that you explore all possible arguments along with any supporting authorities. In addition, you should incorporate any relevant academic opinion, if relevant, including any preferences that academics have expressed over any particular arguments.

! Don't be tempted to . . .

- Invent facts or assume that certain facts are present. For instance, the question states that the complainant was 'sleepy' but does not specifically state that she was 'asleep'.
- You are also not told whether Gareth knew of his girlfriend's heart condition or not. Do not assume that he did know about this on the basis that he is her boyfriend. Similarly, do not assume that he did not know. You must work with the facts that you have and provide an analysis based on each possibility.

❓ Question 4

Martin and Debbie are animal rights activists. They have heard that Hertsco, a local company, have been testing their products on animals. Martin and Debbie decide to break into the laboratories at Hertsco in order to free the animals there. Martin and Debbie go straight to the laboratories. They decide which window they are going to break in through, but as they approach the window, a light goes on inside the building. Afraid of being noticed, Martin and Debbie make a quick get-away. They decide to try again later that evening.

Later that evening, Debbie acts as look-out while Martin breaks open a window. Both of them then climb in through the window. They find a number of animals locked up and use the jemmy to free them. Debbie sees a puppy which she likes and decides to take him home with her. As she picks the puppy up, they are confronted by an employee of Hertsco who had been working late. Martin pulls out a gun and points it at the employee. Debbie shouts, 'You never mentioned guns! Don't shoot!' and escapes from the building. Martin shoots and kills the employee.

Advise Martin and Debbie as to their criminal liability, if any.

Answer plan

→ Discuss the conspiracies to commit criminal damage and burglary.

→ Assess whether Martin and Debbie are liable for attempted burglary.

→ Consider Martin's liability for burglary and criminal damage and Debbie's corresponding liability as a secondary party.

→ Evaluate Debbie's liability for theft and burglary.

→ Apply the doctrine of joint enterprise and whether Debbie is liable for the murder of the employee as a secondary party.

Diagram plan

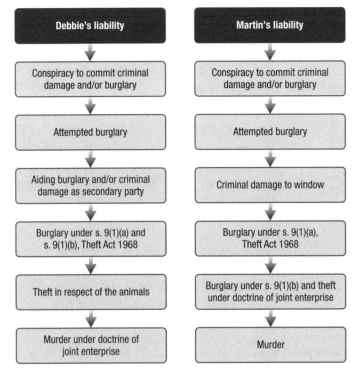

A printable version of this diagram plan is available from www.pearsoned.co.uk/lawexpressqa

Answer

[1] Whenever you see a question on accessorial liability there will usually be an agreement to commit an offence at the start of the question, requiring consideration of conspiracy.

The first offences to arise in the scenario are the conspiracies to commit criminal damage and/or burglary.[1] Conspiracy is charged contrary to section 1(1) of the Criminal Law Act 1977. There may be an agreement here between two people (Martin and Debbie) to pursue a course of conduct which amounts to an offence. It must be asked whether Martin and Debbie agree to commit criminal damage in the process of breaking into the property or once inside the building. If they do, the actus reus of a conspiracy to commit criminal damage is certainly present. If they agree to enter in order to commit criminal damage, they may be guilty of a conspiracy to commit burglary. The requisite mens rea of conspiracy is an intention to carry out the agreement. According to **Siracusa** (1990) 90 Cr App R 340, to 'play some part' in the offence means no more than that the defendant must continue to concur with the activity of another or to fail to stop the offence from being committed. This means that participation can be passive. This can be contrasted against the decision of the House of Lords in Anderson [1986] AC 27, which appears to require active participation. Either way, the mens rea of a conspiracy is satisfied here.[2]

[2] Where there are conflicting authorities, be sure to mention both.

Martin and Debbie may also be convicted of attempted burglary when they first approach the building with a view to breaking into it. Attempted burglary would be charged contrary to section 1(1) of the Criminal Attempts Act 1981. An attempt involves taking steps which are more than merely preparatory towards the commission of an offence. Martin and Debbie both approach a window to the building, with a view to breaking in. If Martin and Debbie merely approach the window without touching it, this is unlikely to be considered enough for an attempted burglary and is more likely to amount to mere preparation. In Campbell (1991) 93 Cr App R 350, the defendant was not convicted of attempted robbery of a post office because although he was loitering outside the building, he never actually entered the post office.[3] However, in the case of *Tosti* [1997] Crim LR 746, examining a padlock on a door was enough to constitute an attempt to commit burglary. The necessary mens rea of an attempt is the intention to commit the full offence, so Martin and Debbie must intend to commit burglary, which on the facts they may do. It would be necessary to ascertain their intention once inside the building. Although the facts state that they intend to free the animals, it is less clear whether they will commit criminal damage in order to do so, or even whether they will take the animals away with them.

[3] Cite an authority to support the conclusion that you draw and justify that conclusion with a brief explanation.

Later that evening when they return to the building, Debbie may be convicted of aiding, abetting, counselling or procuring the burglary and criminal damage by keeping look-out under section 8 of the Accessories and Abettors Act 1861. Aiding merely means assisting which Debbie is certainly doing by keeping look-out. The mens rea for aiding an offence is: (i) an intention to do the acts of assistance (Debbie clearly intends to aid Martin here by keeping look-out); and (ii) knowledge of the circumstances which constitute the offence: *Bryce* [2004] EWCA Crim 1231 (Debbie is clearly aware of the circumstances which constitute the offence as she has been involved in the planning of the offence throughout).[4]

[4] These sentences are what the examiner is looking for to demonstrate your application of the law to the question.

Martin will be liable for criminal damage to the window under section 1(1) of the Criminal Damage Act 1971. He clearly destroys or damages property belonging to another here. He also has the requisite mens rea because he intends to break the window, or is at the very least subjectively reckless as to whether the window would be broken. Martin and Debbie will also be convicted of burglary under section 9(1)(a) of the Theft Act 1968. Martin and Debbie both enter the building as trespassers as they have no permission to be there: **Collins** [1973] QB 100. They intend to enter the building and know that they are trespassing. Their intention on entry must be explored: if they intend to commit criminal damage or steal or inflict GBH inside, they will be guilty of burglary under section 9(1)(a). They probably at least enter with intent to commit criminal damage or to steal the animals (even merely setting the animals free could constitute theft as it amounts to appropriation, provided of course that the necessary intention to permanently deprive can be proved).[5]

[5] This sentence also demonstrates application of the law to the specific facts of the question.

Debbie will also be guilty of burglary under section 9(1)(b) of the Theft Act 1968 because having entered the building as a trespasser, knowing that she was trespassing, Debbie does steal the puppy. The elements of theft need to be established here. Under section 1(1) of the Theft Act 1968, theft is defined as the dishonest appropriation of property belonging to another with intent to permanently deprive. Debbie appropriates the dog as she assumes a single right of the owner over the dog (under s. 3 and Morris [1984] AC 320), that of possession.[6] The dog is certainly property under section 4 and it belongs to another (presumably Hertsco). Thus, the actus reus elements of theft are satisfied. Section 2(1) does not apply here, and **Ghosh** [1982] QB 1053 only need be applied where dishonesty needs further explanation to the jury. This is unlikely to be the case here as it would be difficult to argue that she lacked dishonesty. Debbie will intend to permanently deprive the owner of the dog if she intends to treat the thing as her own to dispose of regardless of the other's rights. It must be asked what she plans to do with the dog.

[6] You should be able to set out the principles of law on appropriation and apply them in one sentence.

Under the doctrine of joint enterprise, Martin will also be guilty of burglary under section 9(1)(b) if Debbie is, because this burglary was committed in pursuance of the common purpose. However, when Martin pulls out a gun and kills the employee, he deliberately departs from the common purpose. Martin will be guilty of murder as the principal offender because he unlawfully causes the death of the

[7] Be sure to establish the liability of the principal before looking at that of the accessory as the accessory's liability is derived from that of the principal.

[8] This sentence succinctly highlights the main issue here and states the key principle with the appropriate leading authority.

employee with the intention to kill or cause GBH (Vickers [1957] 2 QB 664).[7] The next key issue is then whether Debbie may be convicted of murder under the doctrine of joint enterprise. This will depend upon her state of mind in respect of the killing. Applying Powell and Daniels; English [1997] 4 All ER 545, Debbie will also be guilty of murder if she foresaw that Martin might kill with an intention to kill or cause GBH.[8] Debbie only needs to foresee the murder as a possibility. The final issue to consider is whether, if she did have the necessary foresight, Debbie successfully withdraws from the joint enterprise and evades liability for the murder. Once the offence is being committed, nothing less than physical intervention will do in order to withdraw: ***Becerra and Cooper*** (1976) 62 Cr App R 212. On the facts, Debbie merely shouts out then runs away, and this would not be enough for a withdrawal.

✓ Make your answer stand out

- Although this is obviously a question involving inchoate and accessorial liability, you should not cover the inchoate offences, Accessories and Abetters Act ('AAA') 1861 and doctrine of joint enterprise in great detail to the exclusion of other key offences.

- This question requires some exploration of various property offences, such as criminal damage, burglary and theft, which play a significant part in the question.

- You must demonstrate that you are able to distinguish accurately between the offences of burglary under sections 9(1)(a) and (b) of the Theft Act 1968.

- Ensure that you provide a balanced answer that gives appropriate attention to the important issues in the question.

! Don't be tempted to . . .

- Spend too much time exploring one issue or offence to the detriment of others.

- Misstate the tests for the mens rea of a secondary party either under section 8, AAA 1861 or under the doctrine of joint enterprise.

- Misstate the test for withdrawal from a joint enterprise at the scene of the crime once the offence has begun.

Bibliography

Allen, M. J. (2009) *Textbook on Criminal Law*, 10th edn. Oxford: Oxford University Press.

Allgrove, B. and Sellers, S. (2009) The Fraud Act 2006: is breach of confidence now a crime? 4 JIPLP 278.

Ashworth, A. (1989) The scope of criminal liability for omissions. LQR 424.

Ashworth, A. (1993) Taking the consequences. In S. Shute (ed.), *Action and Value in Criminal Law*. Oxford: Clarendon Press.

Ashworth, A. (2007) Principles, pragmatism and the Law Commission's recommendations on homicide law reform. Crim LR 333.

Ashworth, A. (2009) *Principles of Criminal Law*, 6th edn. Oxford: Oxford University Press.

Bamforth, N. (1994) Sado-masochism and consent. Crim LR 661.

Bantekas, I. (2008) Can touching always be sexual when there is no sexual intent? 73 *Journal of Criminal Law* 251.

Bingham, Lord (2007) The Rule of Law. CLJ 67.

Bohlander, M. (2010) The conflict between the Serious Crime Act 2007 and section 1(4)(b) Criminal Attempts Act 1981 – a missed repeal? Crim LR 483.

Campbell, K. (1994) The test of dishonesty in *Ghosh*. 43 CLJ 349.

Clarkson, C. M. V. (2000) Context and culpability in involuntary manslaughter. In A. Ashworth (ed.), *Rethinking English Homicide Law*. Oxford: Oxford University Press.

Coke, Sir E. 3 Inst. 47 *Institutes of the Lawes of England* 47.

Criminal Law Revision Committee (1980) 14th Report, *Offences Against the Person*. London: The Stationery Office.

Crosby, C. (2008) Recklessness – the continuing search for a definition. 72 JCL 313.

Crown Prosecution Service, Offences Against the Person Charging Standards, http://www.cps.gov.uk/legal/l_to_o/offences_against_the_person/#a24.

Dennis, I. H. (1982) The Criminal Attempts Act 1981. Crim LR 5.

Dennis, I. (2006) Reviewing the law of homicide. Crim LR 187.

Dennis, I. (2008) A pointless exercise. Crim LR 507.

Elliott, D. W. (1982) Dishonesty in theft: a dispensable concept. Crim LR 395.

Farrell, S., Yeo, N. and Landenberg, G. (2007) *Blackstone's Guide to the Fraud Act 2006*. Oxford: Oxford University Press.

Forston, R. (2008) *Blackstone's Guide to the Serious Crime Act 2007*, Oxford: Oxford University Press.

Gardner, J. (1994) Rationality and the rule of law in offences against the person. 53 CLJ 502.

Gardner, J. (2007) Complicity and causality. 1 *Criminal Law and Philosophy* 127.

Gardner, S. (1996) Appreciating Olugboja. 16 Legal Studies 275.

Gobert, J. (2008) The Corporate Manslaughter and Corporate Homicide Act. 71(3) MLR 413.

Gough, S. (2000) Surviving without *Majewski*. Crim LR 719.

Greaves, C. (1862) *The Criminal Law Consolidation and Amendment Acts*, 2nd edn. London: Stevens, Sons and Haynes, Sweet and Maxwell.

Griew, E. J. (1985) Dishonesty: the objections to Feely and Ghosh. Crim LR 341.

Griew, E. (1986) *The Theft Acts 1968 and 1978*. London: Sweet & Maxwell.

Griffin, S. and Moran, J. (2010) Accountability for deaths attributable to the gross negligent act or omission of a police force: the impact of the Corporate Manslaughter and Corporate Homicide Act 2007. 74 JCL 358.

Gunn, M. and Ormerod, D. (1995) The legality of boxing. 15 Legal Studies 181.

Halpin, A. (2004) *Definition in the Criminal Law*. Oxford: Hart Publishing.

Hart, H. L. A. and Honoré, A. M. (1985) *Causation in the Law*, 2nd edn. Oxford: Oxford University Press.

Heaton, R. (2003) Dealing in death. Crim LR 497.

Hogan, B. (1987) Omissions and the duty myth. In P. Smith (ed.), *Criminal Law: Essays in Honour of J C Smith*. London: Butterworths.

Home Office (2002) Protecting the Public, Cm 5668, p. 9.

Home Office (2003) Government Reply to the Fifth Report from the Home Affairs Committee Session 2002–2003, Cm 5986, pp. 1–2.

Home Office/DHSS (1975) Report of the Committee on Mentally Abnormal Offenders (The Butler Report), Cmnd. 6244, London: HMSO.

Horder, J. (2002) Strict liability, statutory construction and the spirit of liberty. LQR 458.

Hyman Gross, A. (1979) *A Theory of Criminal Justice*. Oxford: Oxford University Press.

Jefferson, M. (2011) *Criminal Law*. London: Pearson Longman.

Law Commission (1980) Report, *Attempt: The Impossibility in Relation to Attempt, Conspiracy and Incitement* (No. 102).

Law Commission (1989) Report, *Draft Criminal Code* (No. 177).

Law Commission (1994a) Consultation Paper, *Consent and Offences Against the Person* (No. 134).

Law Commission (1994b) Consultation Paper, *Criminal Law: Involuntary Manslaughter* (No. 135).

Law Commission (1996) Report, *Legislating the Criminal Code: Involuntary Manslaughter* (No. 237).

Law Commission (1999) Consultation Paper, *Legislating the Criminal Code: Fraud and Deception* (No. 155).

Law Commission (2002) Report, *Fraud* (No. 276).

Law Commission (2005) Consultation Paper, *A New Homicide Act for England and Wales?* (No. 177).

Law Commission (2006) Report, *Inchoate Liability for Assisting and Encouraging Crime* (No. 300).

Law Commission (2007a) Consultation Paper, *Conspiracy and Attempts* (No. 183).

Law Commission (2007b) Report, *Participating in Crime* (No. 305) line 6333.

Law Commission (2009) Report, *Intoxication and Criminal Liability* (No. 314).

Law Commission (2010) Consultation Paper, *Unfitness to Plead and the Insanity Defence*. www.lawcom.gov.uk/insanity.htm.

Law Commission (2012) Scoping Paper, *Insanity and Automatism* http://lawcommission.justice.gov.uk/docs/insanity_scoping.pdf.

Leigh, L. (2009) Duty of care and manslaughter. 173 JPN 296.

Leigh, L. (2010) Two new partial defences to murder. 174 JPN 53.

Mackay, R. D. (1990) Fact and fiction about the insanity defence. Crim LR 247.

Mackay, R. D. (1998) *Mental Condition Defences in Criminal Law*. Oxford: Oxford University Press.

Mackay, R. D. and Kearns, G. (1999) More fact(s) about the insanity defence. Crim LR 714.

Mackay, R. D., Mitchell, B. and Howe, L. (2006) Yet more facts about the insanity defence. Crim LR 399.

Mackay, R. D. and Reuber, M. (2007) Epilepsy and the defence of insanity – time for a change. Crim LR 782.

Malcolm, T. (2012) How far is too far? The extent to which consent is a defence to non-fatal offences against the person. In N. Geach and C. Monaghan, *Dissenting Judgments in the Law*. London: Wildy, Simmonds and Hill.

Marston, G. (1970) Contemporaneity of act and intention in crimes. 86 LQR 208.

Mitchell, B. (2008) Minding the gap in unlawful and dangerous act manslaughter: a moral defence of one-punch killers. 72 JCL 537.

Monaghan, C. (2010) To prosecute or not to prosecute? A reconsideration of the overzealous prosecution of parents under the Fraud Act 2006. 74 *Journal of Criminal Law* 259.

Monaghan, N. (2012) *Criminal Law Directions*, 2nd edn. Oxford: Oxford University Press.

Norrie, A. (1999) After *Woollin*. Crim LR 532.

Norrie, A. (2010) The Coroners and Justice Act – partial defences to murder (1) loss of control. Crim LR 275.

O'Doherty, S. (2008) The Corporate Manslaughter and Corporate Homicide Act 2007. 172 JPN 244.

Ormerod, D. (2007) The Fraud Act 2006 – criminalising lying?. Crim LR 193.

Ormerod, D. (2008) *Smith and Hogan Criminal Law*, 12th edn. Oxford: Oxford University Press.

Ormerod, D. (2009) Cheating the public revenue. Crim LR 202.

Ormerod, D. (2011) *Smith and Hogan Criminal Law*, 13th edn. Oxford: Oxford University Press.

Ormerod, D. and Forston, R. (2009) Serious Crime Act 2007: the Part 2 offences. Crim LR 389.

Ormerod, D. and Taylor, R. (2008) The Corporate Manslaughter and Corporate Homicide Act 1007. Crim LR 589.

Ormerod, D. and Williams, D. (2007) *Smith's Law of Theft*, 9th edn. Oxford: Oxford University Press.

Padfield, N. (2008) The Criminal Justice and Immigration Act 2008. Archbold News 5.

Raz, J. (1977) The Rule of Law and its virtue. 93 LQR 195.

Rogers, J. (2006) The Law Commission's proposed restructuring of homicide. 70(3) JCL 223.

Rogers, J. (2008) The codification of attempts and the case of 'preparation'. Crim LR 937.

Ryan, S. (2006) Reckless transmission of HIV: knowledge and culpability. Crim LR 981.

Shute, S. (2002) Appropriation and the law of theft. Crim LR 445.

Simester, A. (2006) *Appraising Strict Liability*. Oxford: Oxford University Press.

Simester, A. (2009) Intoxication is never a defence. Crim LR 3.

Simester, A. and Sullivan, R. (2007) *Criminal Law: Theory and Doctrine*. Oxford: Hart Publishing.

Simester, A. and Sullivan, R. (2010) *Criminal Law: Theory and Doctrine*. Oxford: Hart Publishing.

Smith, A. T. H. (2001) Theft and sharp practice: who cares now?. CLJ 21.

Smith, J. C. (1982) Commentary, *R v Ghosh*. Crim LR 608.

Smith, J. C. (1991) Proximity in attempt. Crim LR 576.

Smith, J. C. (1993) Case Commentary, *R v Gomez*. Crim LR 304.

Spencer, J. R. (1982) Dishonesty: what the jury thinks the defendant thought the jury would have though. CLJ 222.

Stephen, J. F. (1883) *A History of the Criminal Law of England*. London: Macmillan.

Stephen, J. F. (1887) *A Digest of the Criminal Law*. London: Macmillan.

Sullivan, G. R. (1993) Cause and contemporaneity of actus reus and mens rea. CLJ 487.

Sullivan, G. R. (2008) Participation in crime. Crim LR 19.

Tadros, V. (2002) Recklessness and the duty to take care. In S. Shute and A. Simester (eds.), *Criminal Law Theory*. Oxford: Oxford University Press.

Taylor, R. (2008) Procuring, causation, innocent agency and the Law Commission. Crim LR 32.

Temkin, J. (2002) *Rape and the Legal Process*. Oxford: Oxford University Press.

Temkin, J. and Ashworth, A. (2004) Rape, sexual assaults and the problem of consent. Crim LR 328.

Weait, M. (2005) Knowledge, autonomy and consent: R v Konsani. Crim LR 763.

Wells, C. (1982) Swatting the subjectivist bug. Crim LR 209.

Wells, C. (1996) The Law Commission Report on Involuntary Manslaughter. Crim LR 545.

Williams, B. (1991) Criminal omissions: the conventional view. LQR 86.

Williams, G. (1976) Case commentary. CJL 15.

Williams, G. (1983) *Textbook of Criminal Law*. London: Stevens & Sons.

Williams, G. (1987) Oblique intention. CLJ 417.

Williams, G. (1989) The mens rea for murder: leave it alone. 105 LQR 387.

Williams, G. (1991) Wrong turning on the law of attempt. Crim LR 416.

Wilson, W. (2002) *Central Issues in Criminal Theory*. Oxford: Hart Publishing.

Wilson, W. (2006) The structure of criminal homicide. Crim LR 471.

Wilson, W. (2008a) *Criminal Law: Doctrine and Theory*, 3rd edn. London: Longman.

Wilson, W. (2008b) A rational scheme of liability for participating in crime. Crim LR 3.

Wilson, W. (2011) *Criminal Law: Doctrine and Theory*, 4th edn. London: Longman.

Withey, C. (2007) The Fraud Act 2006 – some early observations and comparisons with the former law. 71 JCL 220.

Index